Fort Niobrara

National Wildlife Refuge

Comprehensive Conservation Plan

Fort Niobrara
National Wildlife Refuge

Comprehensive Conservation Plan

September 1999

Prepared by
U.S. Fish and Wildlife Service
Ft. Niobrara/Valentine NWR Complex
HC14, Box 67
Valentine, NE 69201

and

U.S. Fish and Wildlife Service
Land Acquisition and Refuge Planning
P.O. Box 25406, DFC
Denver, CO 80225

Approved: _Ralph O. Morgenweck_   Date: _9/30/99_
Regional Director, Region 6, Denver, Colorado

Submitted By:

(signature) 9/30/99
Royce Huber Date
Refuge Manager
Fort Niobrara/Valentine NWR Complex

Concur:

(signature) 9/30/99
Larry Shanks Date
Associate Manager
Southern GARD

(signature) 9/30/99
Joseph Webster Date
Geographic Assistant Regional Director
Southern Ecosystems

(signature) 9/20/99
Ken McDermond Date
Programmatic Assistant Regional Director
Refuges and Wildlife

Table of Contents

Summary 7
Introduction / Background 11
Refuge Overview: History of Establishment, Acquisition & Management 11
    Fort Niobrara National Wildlife Refuge History 11
    Habitat Management History 12
    Water Rights/Management History 12
    Wildlife Management History 12
        Bison 12
        Elk 13
        Pronghorn Antelope 13
        Bighorn Sheep 13
        Native Birds and Other Wildlife 13
        Texas Longhorn Cattle History 14
    Public Use History 14
Figure 1. Canoeing - Tubing Visitation 1993-1997 14
    Current Refuge Resources Management 15
        Grassland/Fenced Animal Management 15
        Riparian and Woodland Management 16
        Threatened and Endangered Species 16
        Native Birds and Other Wildlife 16
        Exotic and Invading Species 16
        Public Use 17
        Cultural and Paleontological Resources 18
Purpose of and Need for Comprehensive Conservation Plan 18
Figure 2. Vicinity Map 19
National Wildlife Refuge System Mission, Goals and Guiding Principles 21
U.S. Fish and Wildlife Service Mission 22
Fort Niobrara National Wildlife Refuge Vision Statement 23
Legal and Policy Guidance 23
Existing Partnerships 24

Planning Process 25
Description of Planning Process 25
Planning Issues 26
    Texas Longhorn Cattle 26
    Recreational Use and Resources of the Niobrara River 27
    Habitat and Wildlife Management 29
    Funding and Staffing to Manage the Refuge 30
    Other Public Uses and Recreation 30
    Public Involvement Methodology 31

Summary of Refuge and Resource Descriptions 33
Geographic/Ecosystem Setting 33
    Climate 34
    Air Quality 34
    Topography 34
    Geology 34
    Soils 34
Refuge Resources, Cultural Values and Uses 35
    Water Resources and Associated Wetlands 35
    Vegetation 35
        Grasslands 35
        Woodlands 36
Figure 3. Wetland Map 37
Figure 4. Vegetation Map 39
    Wildlife 41
        Birds 41
        Mammals 41
        Amphibians and Reptiles 41
        Fishes 42
        Threatened and Endangered Species 42
    Cultural and Paleontological Resources 43
    Socio-Economic and Political Environment 43
    Public Uses 43
Special Management Areas 44
    Special Legislated Designations 44
        Wilderness Area 44
            Definition of Wilderness 44
            Principles Governing the Management of Wilderness Areas 44
        Wild and Scenic River 45
            Congressional Declaration of Policy 45
            Designation of Sections of the Niobrara River as Wild and Scenic 45
            Review Requirements for Early Designations and Management Plans 45
        Research Natural Area 45
            National Recreational Trail System 45
            National Historic Building 45
            National Register of Historic Places 45

Management Direction 47
Refuge Management Direction: Goals, Objectives, and Strategies/Projects 47
    Refuge Goals and Objectives 47
        Habitat Management 48
        Wildlife 49
        Threatened and Endangered Species 51
        Interpretation and Recreation 51
        Ecosystem (Partners) 52

Implementation and Monitoring 53
Funding and Personnel 53
    Staffing Needed to Implement This Plan 53
    Funding Needed to Implement This Plan 53
CCP Implementation and Step-down Management Plans 54
    Habitat Management and Monitoring 54
    Wildlife Management and Monitoring 55
    Threatened and Endangered Species Management and Monitoring 55
    Interpretation and Recreation Resources Management and Monitoring 56
        Niobrara River Use Management and Monitoring 56
        Public Use Management and Monitoring 56
    Ecosystem (Partners) Management and Monitoring 57
    Cultural and Paleontological Resources Management and Monitoring 57
Partnership Opportunities 58
Monitoring and Evaluation 58
Plan Amendment and Revision 59

Appendix A. Glossary 61
Appendix B. Bibliography 65
Appendix C. Refuge Operating Needs System (RONS) List 67
Appendix D. Maintenance Management System (MMS) List 79
Appendix E. Compatibility Determinations 93
Appendix F. List of Animal and Plant Species at Fort Niobrara NWR 103
Appendix G. Compliance Requirements 115
Appendix H. NEPA Documentation 119
Appendix I. Summary of Public Involvement/Comments and Consultation/Coordination 129
Appendix J. Mailing List 131
Appendix K. List of Preparers 133
Appendix L. Intra-Service Section 7 Consultation 135

Summary

Fort Niobrara National Wildlife Refuge (NWR) is 19,131 acres in size and located along the Niobrara River in north-central Nebraska. The Refuge is a unique and ecologically important component of the National Wildlife Refuge System (System) which includes over 500 refuges totaling approximately 93 million acres across the United States. Fort Niobrara NWR was established by Executive Order in January, 1912 as a "preserve and breeding ground for native birds." Its purpose was expanded later that same year to include the preservation of bison and elk herds representative of those that once roamed the Great Plains. Furthermore, the unusual, and unique assemblage of plant communities currently present at the Refuge (Sandhills Prairie, Mixed Prairie, Rocky Mountain Coniferous Forest, Eastern Deciduous Forest, and Northern Boreal Forest) support a rich diversity of wildlife generally unchanged from historic times. Under the Wilderness Act of 1964, a 4,635-acre portion of Fort Niobrara was designated a Wilderness Area in 1976; a portion of the Niobrara River through the Refuge was designated a National Canoe Trail by Congress in 1982; and, in 1991, a 76 mile stretch of the Niobrara River including the River through this Refuge was designated Scenic under the National Wild and Scenic Rivers Act.

This Comprehensive Conservation Plan (Plan) for the Fort Niobrara National Wildlife Refuge (Refuge) in Cherry County in north-central Nebraska is an updated and revised version of the Draft Comprehensive Conservation Plan and Environmental Assessment completed earlier this year. It has been written to provide continuity of management of Refuge lands for the benefit of wildlife and people.

All efforts leading to the preparation of this Plan were undertaken to provide the Refuge with a vision for the future, guidelines for wildlife and habitat management over the next 15 years to ensure progress is made toward attaining the mission and goals of Fort Niobrara and the Refuge System, and to comply with Congressional mandates stated in the National Wildlife Refuge System Improvement Act of 1997. The planning effort provided opportunities for interested people, Federal and State agencies, State and local governments, and private organizations to give input on future management of the Refuge. This Plan provides clear goals and objectives for management of Refuge habitats, wildlife, threatened and endangered species, cultural and paleontological resources, compatible public uses, and partnerships, along with implementation strategies, and recommended staffing and funding. This Plan meets the planning requirements of the National Wildlife Refuge Improvement Act enacted by Congress in 1997.

The draft Environmental Assessment considered four alternatives for management of Fort Niobrara NWR. Each of the alternatives was evaluated for environmental consequences in accordance with the National Environmental Policy Act (NEPA). This Plan, in its present form, contains the goals, objectives, and strategies found by the Service to best support purpose of the Refuge and the mission of the Refuge System.

For a summary of the alternatives considered during the planning process, see Appendix H. Further information on alternatives considered can be found in the Fort Niobrara National Wildlife Refuge Draft Comprehensive Conservation Plan and Environmental Assessment (U.S. Fish and Wildlife Service, 1999).

Clockwise from upper left: Bison have been managed on Fort Niobrara National Wildlife Refuge since 1913 to preserve a population representative of the large herds that once roamed the Great Plains; Fort Niobrara National Wildlife Refuge and the surrounding area is the only place in North America where Rocky Mountain coniferous forest, northern boreal forest, eastern deciduous forest, mixed-prairie and sandhill prairie vegetation communities meet and intermingle; Longhorn cattle will no longer be managed by this Refuge; river floating is a popular recreational activity on Fort Niobrara; the Fort Falls Nature Trail allows visitors to experience the habitats and wildlife along the Falls and the Niobrara River; elk, especially bulls with growing antlers, can be found near or in Refuge ponds and streams during the hot days of summer; the loud rolling "pulip pulip" call of upland sandpipers signal that spring has come to the prairie; in April, prairie chicken males display on traditional breeding grounds on the Refuge; habitat created by prairie dogs attract a variety of wildlife including burrowing owls which use the underground burrows for nesting.

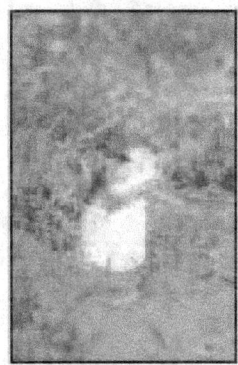

Introduction / Background

Refuge Overview: History of Establishment, Acquisition & Management

Fort Niobrara National Wildlife Refuge History

Fort Niobrara NWR was established by Executive Order 1461 on January 11, 1912, which reserved 13,279 acres from the public domain as a "preserve and breeding ground for native birds." The reserve was established at a time when tremendous concern existed over the exploitation of birds and near extinction of bison.

Two environmental groups, National Association of Audubon Societies and American Bison Society, were very influential in the establishment and determination of purpose of several Federal parks and refuges including Fort Niobrara during the first two decades of the 20th century. The National Association of Audubon Societies was formed in 1905 and its first president, William Dutcher, was a friend of U.S. President Theodore Roosevelt. Numerous correspondence was exchanged between them regarding over-harvest of birds, funding for the Bureau of Biological Survey, and protection of bird sites (refuges), and included a letter dated January 1, 1908, which discussed protection of birds and game on the Fort Niobrara Military Reservation. The American Bison Society, headed by Dr. William Hornaday, was directly responsible for establishing Wichita Mountains NWR in Oklahoma, National Bison Range in Montana, and Wind Cave National Park in South Dakota for the preservation of bison in the early 1900's and was also instrumental in bringing bison to Fort Niobrara. Dr. Palmer, a member of the American Bison Society and 2nd Vice President of the Audubon Society, states in the 1912 Annual Report of the American Bison Society that "on January 12, 1912, the Niobrara Bird Reservation was created by Executive Order. This reservation comprises some 10,000 or 12,000 acres of land along the Niobrara River, near Valentine, including some grazing land, and only needs a fence to make it an ideal reservation for buffalo and other big game of the Great Plains."

A 1913 report from the Chief of the Bureau of Biological Survey to the Secretary of Agriculture summarizes the events leading up to the addition of the big game purpose to Fort Niobrara. The following is an excerpt from that report: "In the early part of the year 1912, Mr. J.W. Gilbert, owner of a small big-game park at Friend, Nebraska, generously offered his herd of buffalo, elk, and deer to the Government for preservation on national territory within the State of Nebraska. The lack of suitable quarters caused some delay in accepting the offer, but on November 14, 1912, an Executive Order was issued setting aside as a game preserve a tract of land additional to the Niobrara bird reservation near Valentine, Nebraska. The herd was then officially accepted by the Secretary of Agriculture and preparations began for establishing it on this very favorable location. Through the cooperation of the National Association of Audubon Societies and the citizens of Valentine, an enclosure was provided at an expense of $1,700. Some of the buildings remaining on the old Fort Niobrara Military Reservation were utilized as headquarters, and a warden was appointed on December 16, 1912."

The Refuge was expanded again by Executive Orders in 1920 and 1936, the Resettlement Administration, subsequent purchases from private individuals, and a donation from the Nebraska Public Power District bringing the Refuge's total acreage to 19,131. Refuge reports state that the 1920 expansion was for protecting/providing winter roost sites for sharp-tailed grouse and prairie chickens, and tracts of land acquired in 1936 were for various purposes including planting of grain crops for migratory birds, pronghorn antelope management, and administrative efficiency (in holdings, straighten boundaries).

In 1960, a 200 acre stand of Ponderosa pine in the northern portion of the Refuge was designated as a Research Natural Area; in 1976, approximately 4,635 acres in the northern portion of the Refuge, including the Niobrara River corridor, was designated as Nebraska's first Wilderness Area.

In 1982, five miles of the Niobrara River on the Refuge was designated as a National Canoe Trail, and in 1991, a total of 76 miles of the Niobrara River including the entire stretch of River through the Refuge was designated by Congress as a Scenic River.

Habitat Management History

Management efforts from the Refuge's establishment through the early 1940's considered the needs of both birds and big game. Initial work involved a general reconnaissance of the area and its bird life, and a survey of the boundary and big game enclosure. Construction of boundary fences of Refuge lands north of the Niobrara River for use by expanding bison and elk herds was planned in 1915 with the project completed in the early 1920's. Earthen dams were built across various tributary streams beginning in 1922 to improve conditions for waterfowl. In the 1930's, the Civilian Conservation Corps and Work Projects Administration staff rebuilt several original earthen dams, constructed new dams, planted various wetland plants, constructed predator fencing around ponds to improve nesting conditions, and planted shelterbelts for birds. Corrals, additional fence, and watering facilities south of the Niobrara River were also constructed during this time. Approximately 150 acres of Refuge lands were planted to various grain crops for grouse and waterfowl in the late 1930's.

Refuge reports and other correspondence suggest a shift in management from a dual purpose (birds, big game) to more of a single purpose (big game) beginning in the early 1940's, although emphasis varied depending upon the viewpoint of management. Numbers of bison, elk, and longhorns maintained on the Refuge fluctuated according to forage availability and genetic management needs. For example, during the 1940's and 1950's, up to 10,000 acres of Refuge grasslands were annually hayed or grazed by permittees and not available for use by big game herds. Approved winter herd levels during this time period were 175 bison and 150 longhorns. Following a review of management programs in the mid-1950's, permittee haying and grazing was terminated and more fence and water facilities were constructed to allow areas to be rested, encourage recovery of grasses, better distribute grazing by the bison and longhorns, and enable management to consider the needs of prairie grouse. Herd levels following the review in 1956 and until the mid-1980's varied with approximately 225 bison, 40 elk, and 200-300 longhorns maintained under a deferred grazing rotation. Bison and longhorn herds were allowed to increase in the late-1980's to implement high intensity, short duration grazing, and meet suggested genetic management recommendations. Longhorn numbers peaked in 1991 at 370, and the bison herd reached its Refuge high of 400 animals in 1992-1996. Maintenance of bison and longhorns at high herd levels limited habitat management options and raised concern that native bird populations, especially prairie grouse, were not receiving adequate management consideration. A review of the habitat and fenced animal management programs was initiated and included consultation with the U.S. Department of Agriculture (USDA) Natural Resources Conservation Service (NRCS) on grassland condition assessment and grazing program recommendations, consultation with geneticists and review of literature regarding bison and longhorn management, and review of scientific literature as it relates to native bird management.

Water Rights/Management History

Fort Niobrara NWR holds no water rights permits with the State of Nebraska; however, lands reserved from the public domain for creation of the Fort Niobrara NWR carry with them a Federal Reserved Water Right that the United States has not asserted at this time.

The Refuge has 25 windmill driven stock water wells and six domestic wells which do not require groundwater permits. Also, the 12 low level spring-fed impoundments are exempt from special dam construction or water storage permits because of their size and because diversion or withdrawal of water from the reservoirs is nonexistent.

A portion of the Niobrara River was designated as Wild and Scenic in 1991. The National Park Service has asserted, as yet unquantified, a Federal Reserve Water Right to maintain instream flow.

In 1986, the Nebraska Public Power District quitclaimed land to the United States that included the Cornell Dam and Power House.

Wildlife Management History

Bison

An estimated 30 million bison once roamed the Great Plains; however, by the late 1880's, fewer than 1,000 animals were alive due to loss of habitat and hunting. Free-ranging bison are believed to have been extirpated from Nebraska in 1878 (Jones *et al.* 1983). Bison were reintroduced to Fort Niobrara in January 1913 as part of the national effort to preserve this native herbivore with the donation of six bison (sex unknown) from J.W. Gilbert of Friend, Nebraska and the transfer of two bulls from Yellowstone National Park. Additional introductions were made in 1935 (4 males, Custer State Park), 1937 (4 males, Custer State Park), and 1952 (5 males, National Bison Range) to minimize inbreeding and maintain the species as closely genetically as possible to those surviving the bottleneck of near extinction.

Policy/philosophy implemented over the years has been to preserve and maintain a representative herd under reasonably natural conditions in numbers sufficient to ensure their continued existence. Management actions have included culling, controlled herd movements, branding, brucellosis vaccination, disease testing, and limited genetic monitoring.

Elk

Elk were once abundant in the northern Great Plains, including the area of Fort Niobrara. Aughey (1880:118) described the elk herds along the Niobrara River in the late 1860's as magnificent; however, by the early 1880's, elk were extirpated from Nebraska due to hunting and loss of habitat (Jones 1964). Elk were reintroduced to Fort Niobrara in January 1913 with the donation of 17 elk by J.W. Gilbert of Friend, Nebraska. Management policy/philosophy implemented over the years has been to maintain a representative herd under reasonably natural conditions in numbers sufficient to ensure their continued existence. Periodic introductions of elk to the Refuge herd have occurred over the years in an effort to minimize the negative effects of inbreeding. Elk numbers have varied with winter population levels exceeding 100 in the early 1930's and recent population levels averaging 50 to 60.

Pronghorn Antelope

Pronghorn antelope were historically common on the open prairies of the Sandhills through the late 1800's; however, by 1908, they were on the decline and observed only in the western and northern portions of Nebraska. Efforts to reintroduce pronghorn antelope to Fort Niobrara NWR began in 1924 with the transfer of 10 animals from Nevada. The herd gradually increased to 17 animals in 1932, but then steadily decreased in numbers. Attempts to establish a second herd of antelope with the transfer of 34 animals in 1936 also failed. Coyote predation is the primary factor influencing the survival of pronghorn on Fort Niobrara. Pronghorn have not been actively managed for in recent years.

Bighorn Sheep

Bighorn sheep formerly occurred in Nebraska on the Pine Ridge and adjacent badlands in the northwest part of the State in breaks along the Niobrara River east to near Long Pine, Wildcat and Bighorn Ridges, and among the rough buttes and canyons along the North Platte River (Jones 1964). The species was extirpated on the northern Great Plains in the 1920's (Jones *et al.* 1983).

A feasibility study of reintroducing bighorn sheep to the Refuge was completed in 1979; however, no action was taken.

Native Birds and Other Wildlife

Management of native birds and other wildlife has varied in intensity over the years with the greatest impact indirectly or directly due to habitat management practices. Prairie grouse, a term used to describe sharp-tailed grouse and prairie chicken, were once plentiful on the Great Plains, but by the late 1800's, demand for birds in eastern markets, development of efficient railway shipping, and willingness of individuals to exploit a seemingly unlimited resource, combined to dramatically reduce prairie grouse populations. Extirpated in many parts of their ranges, remnant populations of sharp-tailed grouse and prairie chicken populations survived in the Sandhills of Nebraska due to lack of intensive agriculture altered habitat (Mitchell and Wolfe 1984). Prairie grouse were identified in one of the first quarterly reports of the Refuge as native birds for management consideration and emphasis. Over the years, management decisions and actions have addressed prairie grouse needs to varying degrees and included enlargement of the Refuge, feeding stations, farming/food plot program, revision of grassland haying and grazing programs in 1956, and population monitoring. Prairie grouse surveys were initiated in 1956 as part of a multiple Refuge research project that studied prairie grouse populations in relation to land use. This study conducted from 1956 to 1965 in grasslands south and east of the Niobrara River suggested that the combination of rapidly increasing amounts of idle grassland (one phase of revised Refuge haying and grazing program) and favorable conditions for reproduction resulted in a rapid increase in grouse numbers on Fort Niobrara between 1956 and 1959. The substitution of bison grazing for rest in approximately 4,200 acres beginning in 1963 did not depress the grouse population; however, researchers questioned what levels grouse populations would have reached if this grassland block had been left idle. They believed that habitat conditions (structure, species composition) which is correlated to use (grazing, haying) determined the average population size, but other factors (i.e., weather) operated equally in good and poor habitat to cause similar rates of annual population change. Annual counts of displaying sharp-tailed grouse and prairie chicken males conducted since the completion of this research project support that relationship or effect. Prairie grouse numbers have cycled with higher average population levels occurring on the Refuge when forage utilization [represented by Animal Use Months (AUM)] by bison, longhorns, and elk was lower.

Other wildlife management activities completed over the years include reintroduction of Canada geese (1914), turkey (1925), and bobwhite quail (1956) and predator control (coyote, raccoon, skunk, mink, bobcat, badger) in the early years to enhance bird production. Also, periodic control of prairie dogs was conducted. Descriptions in Refuge reports suggest prairie dogs were found in the headquarters area (current location), "east" habitat unit, the tableland north of the Niobrara River, and south of the Refuge. Presence/absence and statements of relative abundance have been made for various groups of wildlife species beginning with birds in 1913 and species lists have been compiled and updated as needed.

Texas Longhorn Cattle History

Longhorns have been managed at Fort Niobrara since 1936 to assure perpetuation of a historically significant animal. The following information, taken from Dobie (1994) and Halloran (1964), provides insight as to the historical significance of the longhorn and how the government became involved in the preservation effort.

Longhorn cattle originate from Spanish cattle that were brought to the New World in about 1521 by Gregorio Villalobos. Early explorers, including Coronado, brought these cattle from Mexico into what is now Arizona, New Mexico, and Texas. The herds eventually spread from Louisiana to California. Although utilized by Native Americans and settlers, the Spanish cattle roamed more or less uncontrolled for over 300 years gradually evolving into the "longhorn." Longhorns were the first major beef supply in the United States and were the cattle that made famous the Chisolm, Dodge, and Boseman Trails. Beginning in the mid-1860's and ending by 1895, an estimated five million head of longhorns were trailed from Texas to Kansas, Nebraska, the Dakotas, Wyoming, Montana, and Colorado, some walking approximately 2,000 miles. The attributes which helped the longhorn to survive heat, drought, flies, predators, limited forage, and travel great distances were a liability in the late 1800's, and by the early 1920's, the longhorn was threatened with extinction. Through a special Congressional appropriation, funds were made available to locate and manage representative, true-to-type longhorns at Wichita Mountains National Wildlife Refuge. Over 30,000 head of cattle were inspected, and in 1927, a herd of 20 cows, 3 bulls, 3 steers, and 4 calves were shipped to Wichita Mountains. A second gene pool of this founding herd was established at Fort Niobrara with the transfer of 4 cows, 1 bull, and 1 steer in May of 1936.

The decision to establish a second gene pool of this founding herd at Fort Niobrara is considered departmental or internal as no record of an Executive Order, Congressional legislation, or Congressional intent exists. Longhorn management over the years has attempted to allow natural factors to influence and maintain historic herd traits such as foraging ability, milk production, calving ease, hardiness and protection of young from predators. In addition, animals selected/perpetuated by management have exhibited representative conformation, horn structure, color variability, and genetic diversity.

Public Use History

Since the Refuge's establishment, recreational opportunities on the Refuge have centered around wildlife/wildlands observation and education. Early management emphasized development of a foot trail and motorized tour route to allow Refuge visitors the opportunity to observe bison, elk, and Texas longhorns in a wild setting. A museum constructed in the 1930's was a popular attraction for school groups and Refuge visitors over the years. It contained information and interesting photographs about the old military Fort Niobrara, a collection and explanation of paleontological finds, a collection of mounted birds and museum skins of mammals, and a native grass display. The current visitor center was constructed in the mid-1970's and contains various photographs, text, items, and computer/ interactive program interpreting Refuge history, wildlife, wildlands, management and the military fort. The Fort Niobrara Natural History Association has various books, postcards, posters, and miscellaneous wildlife related items for sale in the center.

Canoeing the Niobrara River was referred to as "increasing in popularity" in 1972. However, the estimated 2,960 activity hours reported in 1972 in the Fort Niobrara Wilderness Study was not considered excessive to prevent inclusion of the River corridor in the area to be designated as wilderness pursuant to criteria under the Wilderness Act. Since then, the number of people canoeing and tubing down the Niobrara River within Fort Niobrara NWR has steadily increased. Beginning in 1993, outfitters and the Service recorded the number of people canoeing and tubing the River through the Refuge. This information showing the increase in floating use is found in Figure 1. Increased River use has raised concerns about disturbance to wildlife, impacts on vegetation, the quality of experience for Refuge visitors, and compatibility with the Wilderness Act and the Wild and Scenic River Act. Management began to address River recreation concerns through the Environmental Assessment process in 1994 and efforts are ongoing.

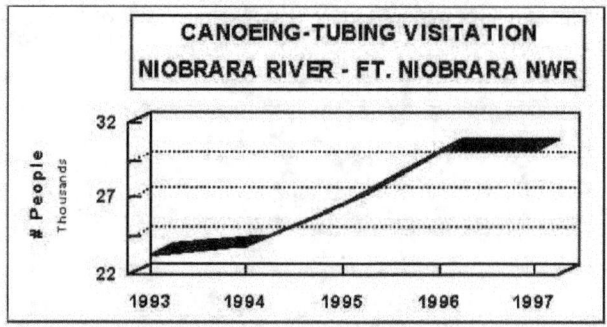

Figure 1. Canoeing - Tubing Visitation 1993-1997

Current Refuge Resources Management
Grassland/Fenced Animal Management

Approximately 350 bison, 70 elk, and 250 Texas longhorns are managed under reasonably natural conditions to assure a genetically sound breeding population, provide appropriate viewing opportunities for public enjoyment, and support scientific studies that are feasible within the management of representative herds. Bison and elk herd structures (sex and age ratios) approximate free ranging herds. In accordance with Service policy, bison, elk, and longhorn numbers above sustainable winter population levels are sold or donated annually. Refuge receipts from 1997 excess bison and longhorn auctions totaled $179,510. Introductions to the elk and Texas longhorn herds are accomplished periodically to maintain or improve genetic diversity.

Maintaining long-term population genetic variability of the bison, elk, and longhorn herds, which affects population fitness or health, is addressed through population size, sex and age ratio, and addition of animals from other populations. Elk and longhorn herds are maintained below minimum population levels, therefore, periodic introductions of animals from other populations are accomplished to minimize inbreeding. The bison herd at its current level and sex ratio provides the effective population size required for maintaining levels of genetic variability, without induced immigration, that commensurate with accepted standards of conservation biology (Berger 1996, Berger and Cunningham 1994).

Biological monitoring of the grasslands and herds is the minimum required to document current habitat condition and guide management. Range condition surveys and suggested initial stocking rates of the Refuge are completed by the USDA Natural Resources Conservation Service every 5 to 10 years. Visual obstruction reading transects are accomplished periodically to document vegetation structure. Fenced animal monitoring includes monthly population surveys, annual disease testing of excess animals, and infrequent (7 to 10 years) genetic testing. Detailed breeding records of longhorns are also maintained for genetic management purposes.

Grassland habitat management strategies are implemented that maintain or improve grassland health and provide forage for bison, elk, and Texas longhorns. Approximately 50 miles of interior fence and 50 miles of boundary fence (perimeter, River corridor, road right-of-way) are used to control timing of grazing and access/movement of the fenced animals. Grazing strategies (time of year, intensity, length) implemented in the estimated 40 habitat units vary according to species management needs and behavior, natural use patterns/seasonal movements of animals in pre-settlement times, staffing, water, climatic conditions, available Animal Use Months (AUM), range site and condition. Large ungulate herds consume and/or remove by trampling an estimated 8,400 AUMs of forage a year which is approximately 40 percent of the total plant production, leaving approximately 60 percent of the vegetation for plant vigor and use by other wildlife (Waller *et al.* 1986, USDA Natural Resources Conservation Service 1996). Texas longhorns, exhibition herds, and government horses are supplemented during the winter as conditions warrant with approximately 600 tons of prairie hay harvested from Valentine NWR. Other annual management actions include one or more years of rest on approximately 4 percent of the acreage, no planned grazing or burning on approximately 30 percent of the acreage during the native bird breeding season, prescribed burning of approximately 100 acres to invigorate native plants or control cedar invasion, and suppression of all wildfires.

Riparian and Woodland Management

Management of the Niobrara River, numerous streams, and their associated riparian habitat is minimal and emphasizes maintenance of current conditions. Nearly all of the Niobrara River and its associated riparian habitats are fenced to control access of bison, elk, and Texas longhorns except the tributary streams in the wilderness area.

The Cornell Dam is maintained to provide shallow-braided river and sandbar habitat upstream.

Twelve ponds formed by damming tributary streams are held at full capacity throughout most of the year for use by waterfowl and other birds, fenced animals, and fish rearing under cooperative agreement with the Nebraska Game and Parks Commission. Periodic drawdowns of these impoundments are accomplished for aquatic vegetation control and structure repair. Breached impoundments in the wilderness area are being allowed to return to a natural state. Several natural impoundments have been created by beavers.

Research of historic water rights is ongoing.

Limited monitoring of stream flow and contaminants is accomplished periodically.

Woodland management is minimal and includes control of cedars, exclusion of fenced animals, and removal of dead or downed timber presenting a safety or fire hazard or threatening facilities. Less than 3 percent of the Refuge is managed through prescribed burning each year to control cedars. Other invading and exotic plant species are controlled with beneficial insects, grazing, and herbicides.

Threatened and Endangered Species

Use by bald eagles, whooping cranes, and other federally listed species on the Refuge is documented through periodic surveys. Required habitat conditions are maintained. Protective actions are implemented as needed.

Native Birds and Other Wildlife

Current management strives to maintain the existing diversity and abundance of various native birds and other wildlife by providing a mosaic of habitat conditions. Biological monitoring of native birds and other wildlife is carried out to the greatest extent possible with current staffing and management priorities. Native bird management actions are accomplished to the extent possible given the primary consideration currently afforded to large ungulates in the Refuge. Limited flexibility exits in habitat management programs with approximately 96 percent of the Refuge being grazed annually.

A 20-acre black-tailed prairie dog colony is maintained and not allowed to expand in the exhibition habitat unit.

A maternity colony of big brown bats (estimated 200 individuals) inhabits the historic north barn during the late spring and summer with no management efforts made to alter their occupancy.

Prairie grouse lek counts are conducted each spring with data available for comparison dating back to 1956. A breeding bird survey route established in 1992 is conducted by staff or volunteers. Refuge staff cooperate with the Nebraska Game and Parks Commission by completing the annual Spring Coordinated Sandhill Crane Survey, Mid-December Goose Survey, Mid-winter Waterfowl Survey, Winter Turkey Survey, and Summer Turkey Brood Survey. A general wildlife observation log is maintained to document presence/absence and relative numbers of various species.

Exotic and Invading Species

Exotic and invading vegetation species are controlled through an integrated pest management approach. Various biological control agents are being used in the ongoing effort to reduce the occurrence of purple loosestrife along the Niobrara River. Four small patches (less than one-eighth acre each) of leafy spurge and two larger patches (one acre each) are controlled through mechanical and limited chemical applications. Small areas of exotic cool season grasses exist at disturbed sites (i.e., road ditch, old farm ground, cattle feed areas) and are being controlled with grazing and prescribed burning. Limited mechanical control and prescribed burning of eastern red cedar is being implemented. Reed canary grass is common along the River; however, no control measures are in place at this time.

Public Use

Visitation: Based on general observations and data collected in the visitor center and on the River, an estimated 100,000 people visit the Refuge annually for wildlife/ wildland observation, photography, interpretation/ education, picnicking, hiking, fishing, and floating on the Niobrara River. Recreational use of the Niobrara River for canoe and tube floating has steadily increased as more visitors travel to the Refuge to enjoy the riparian-dependent wildlife as well as the wilderness area of the Refuge.

Facilities: The visitor center, with a variety of over 20-year-old displays interpreting the history of the military fort, area wildlife and habitat, and Refuge management, is open Monday through Friday year-round and weekends Memorial Day to Labor Day with actual annual use recorded at approximately 6,000 visits.

Other interpretive facilities under some phase of development include a kiosk at the canoe launch with education panels entitled "Niobrara Valley," "Welcome to Fort Niobrara," "Canoeing the Niobrara River"; the observation deck above Fort Falls includes education panels titled "Prairie Oasis," "Fort Falls," "Sand, Rock & Water"; and an interpretive panel to be located in the exhibition habitat unit providing information on elk and prairie dogs.

The Bur Oak Picnic area is located along the Niobrara River at the Refuge entrance. Tables and rest rooms are used mainly by people visiting the Refuge for River floating or wildlife observation.

Trails & Tour Routes: The Fort Falls nature trail is approximately one mile long and educates the hiker through a brochure describing the different vegetation communities and associated wildlife found in this unique, biologically diverse area.

The 15-stop self-guiding auto tour route is located in the exhibition habitat unit and provides information on the prairie dog town, bison, elk, Texas longhorns, and other prairie inhabitants.

Environmental Education: Interpretation and environmental education services are provided when staff are available and include talks or guided tours for school groups (elementary through college level), scouts, 4-H and special projects (i.e., Old West Days Trail Ride). The public is invited to observe fall roundups and auctions of bison and longhorns, participate in Migratory Bird day activities, and other Refuge programs.

River Use: Floating the Niobrara River with canoes or tubes is a popular recreational activity on the Refuge. Over 18,000 vessels carrying more than 30,000 people were put in the Niobrara River from the Refuge launch facility in 1997. Most of the canoeing and tubing takes place during June (18 percent), July (37 percent), and August (40 percent), with Saturday morning being the most congested period. During an average Saturday in July 1997, approximately 1,200 people launched 684 vessels into the River from 8-11 a.m. which is one vessel launch every 16 seconds. Due to the alarming increase of River use documented in outfitter reports from 1993-1997, crowding and compatibility with wilderness designation and wildlife needs, Refuge management has in place a moratorium on new outfitters. Also, the existing 11 outfitters have been informed that any expansion of their business on the Refuge is at their own risk, and River use on the Refuge should be redistributed to week days.

The Refuge has been selected by the Service as a User Fee Demonstration Area due to the volume of River use, increasing cost of maintaining the launch area and public rest rooms, and the need for additional law enforcement. After receiving input from canoe and tube outfitters, National Park Service, Nebraska Game and Parks Commission, Natural Resources District, and other interested parties, the Refuge staff set up a fee and collection system which is thought to be fair and simple. The first year of the user fee program was 1998. Review of monitoring protocol for public use levels on the Niobrara River, effects of use on Refuge wildlife/wildlands and wilderness, and determination of acceptable use/levels began in 1998. A social carrying capacity study was conducted the summer of 1998.

Hunting, Fishing and Trapping: The Refuge is currently closed to hunting.

The Niobrara River is open to fishing with a Fishing Plan expected to be completed in the near future. Angler opportunities are limited with most fishing occurring immediately below Cornell Dam. Kid's Fishing Day is held annually in September and includes trout, catfish, and bluegill fishing in the corral pond, fish identification and casting contests, cleaning, and cooking. The event is a cooperative effort between the Nebraska Game and Parks Commission (NG&PC), Niobrara Natural History Association, volunteers, and the Refuge staff.

The Refuge is closed to recreational trapping. Trapping for depredation or damage control purposes is accomplished as necessary through force account or a special use permit in accordance with State and Service regulations.

Cultural and Paleontological Resources

Limited cultural resource studies have been conducted by the U.S. Fish and Wildlife Service (Service), National Park Service, and various research institutions to locate and describe and evaluate cultural and paleontological resources (Burgett and Nickel 1999). Less than 1 percent of the Refuge has been inventoried for these resources. The remains of old Fort Niobrara, including the north barn, have been determined eligible for Nomination to the National Register of Historic Places. Twelve of the 21 Refuge buildings are over 50 years old and need to be evaluated for historic significance. Minimal interpretation and protection of the various cultural resources is available. The remainder of the main military complex surrounds the present Refuge headquarters. Virtually all the buildings were sold and removed between 1906 - 1912; however, foundations, roads and minor surface features remain.

Purpose of and Need for Comprehensive Conservation Plan

The Service has recognized the need for strategic planning for all the components of its System. The System now has more than 513 refuges totaling approximately 93 million acres. Fort Niobrara NWR, located in north-central Nebraska (see Figure 2), is a unique and ecologically important component of the System. In September 1996, Executive Order 12996 was enacted which gave the System guidance on issues of compatibility and public uses of its land. Congress passed the National Wildlife Refuge System Improvement Act in October 1997. This "organic act," for the first time in the System's history, required that comprehensive conservation plans be prepared for all refuges within 15 years.

The Service was an active participant in this historic legislation and supported the planning requirement. The planning effort helped this Refuge (and thus the entire System) to aid in meeting the changing needs of wildlife species and the public. The planning effort provided the opportunity to meet with Refuge neighbors, and customers, and other agencies to ensure that this Plan was relevant and truly addressed natural resource issues and public interests. It is our goal to have the System be an active and vital part of the United States' conservation efforts. This Plan explains the planning process, the Refuge's characteristics, and the direction management will take in the next 15 years. It is provided to give the reader a clear understanding of the purposes of the Refuge and how the Service will manage it over the next 15 years to attain the stated purpose of the Refuge.

Vicinity Map of North Central Nebraska

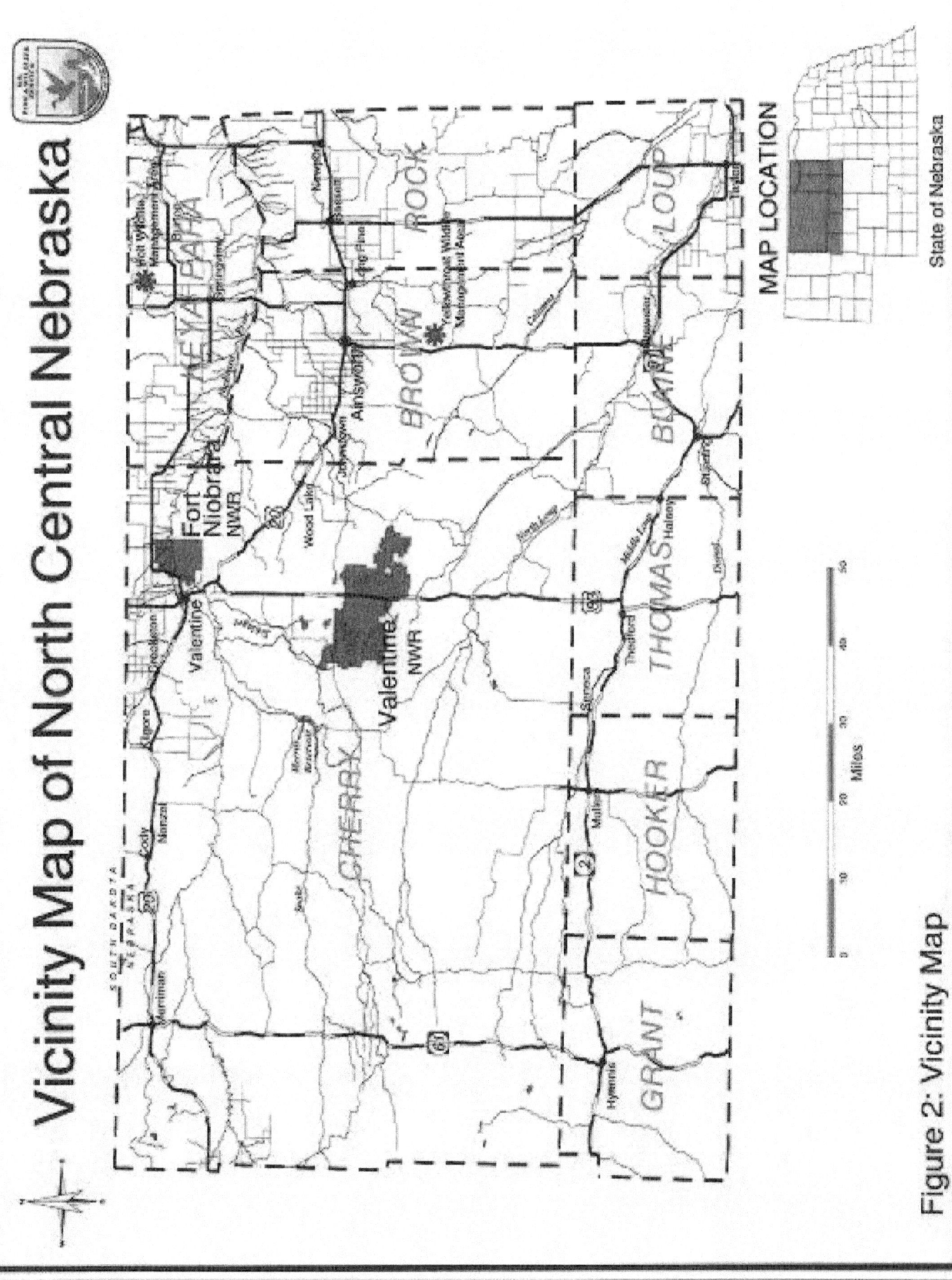

Figure 2: Vicinity Map

National Wildlife Refuge System Mission, Goals and Guiding Principles

The National Wildlife Refuge System is the world's largest collection of lands set aside specifically for the protection of fish, wildlife and plant populations and their habitats. The first unit of the System was created in 1903, when President Theodore Roosevelt designated 3-acre Pelican Island, a pelican and heron rookery in Florida, as a bird sanctuary. Today, more than 500 national wildlife refuges located in the 50 States and a number of U.S. Territories exists. Today, the System encompasses more than 93 million acres.

This System provides important habitat for many native mammals, birds, reptiles, amphibians, fish, invertebrates, and plants. The System plays a vital role in preserving endangered and threatened species, and offers a wide variety of wildlife-dependent public uses; annually, national wildlife refuges receive 34 million visitors.

However, the System's importance goes far beyond these services. It contributes directly and indirectly to human welfare through a number of ecosystem services and functions. The section on "Management Direction" contains a detailed discussion of ecosystem services. For the entire biosphere, the estimated annual economic value of all the world's ecosystem services and functions is about $33 trillion (Constanza, *et al.* 1997).

The Mission of this System is "to administer a network of lands and waters for the conservation, management, and where appropriate, restoration of the fish, wildlife, and plant resources and their habitats within the United States for the benefit of present and future generations of Americans" (National Wildlife Refuge System Improvement Act of 1997, Public Law 105-57). The goals of the System are aimed at fulfilling this mission and are the following:

Goal 1: *To preserve, restore, and enhance in their natural ecosystems all species of animals and plants that are endangered or threatened with becoming endangered;*

Goal 2: *To perpetuate the migratory bird resource;*

Goal 3: *To preserve a natural diversity and abundance of fauna and flora on refuge lands; and*

Goal 4: *To provide an understanding and appreciation of fish and wildlife ecology and man's role in his environment and provide visitors with high quality, safe, wholesome, and enjoyable recreation experiences oriented toward wildlife to the extent these activities are compatible with the purposes for which the refuge was established.*

National wildlife refuges are acquired under a variety of legislative acts and administrative orders and authorities. These orders and authorities usually have one or more purposes for which land can be transferred or acquired. Most refuges within the System provide breeding, migration, or wintering habitat for Federal Trust Species. Nearly all refuges also supply habitats for big game species and resident or nonmigratory wildlife as well.

Individual refuges provide specific requirements for the preservation of trust resources. For example, waterfowl breeding refuges in South and North Dakota provide important wetland and grassland habitat to support populations of waterfowl as required by the Migratory Bird Treaty Act and the North American Waterfowl Management Plan. Valentine NWR supports breeding populations of migratory birds as well as provides migration habitat during spring and fall migration periods for these birds. Sabine NWR and other refuges in Louisiana and Texas provide wintering habitat for these populations. The network of lands is critical to these birds survival. Any deficiency in one location will affect the species and the entire networks ability to maintain adequate populations.

Other refuges may provide habitat for threatened and endangered plants or animals that exist in unique habitats which occur in only very few locations. Refuges in these situations ensure that populations are protected and habitat is suitable for their use. Refuges, by providing a broad network of lands throughout the United States, help to prevent species from being listed by providing secure habitat for their use and provide recovery habitats in portions or all of a species range.

The National Wildlife Refuge System Improvement Act of 1997 amends the Refuge Administration Act's Section 4(A) with the following additions:

P   *"each refuge shall be managed to fulfill the mission of the System, as well as the specific purposes for which that refuge was established;*

P   *compatible wildlife-dependent recreation is a legitimate and appropriate general public use of the System, directly related to the mission of the System and the purposes of many refuges, and which generally fosters refuge management and through which the American public can develop an appreciation for fish and wildlife;*

P   *compatible wildlife-dependent recreational uses are the priority general public uses of the System and shall receive priority consideration in refuge planning and management; and*

P   *when the Secretary determines that a proposed wildlife-dependent recreational use is a compatible use within a refuge, that activity should be facilitated, subject to such restrictions or regulations as may be necessary, reasonable, and appropriate.*

(4) In administering the System, the Secretary shall—

P   *provide for the conservation of fish, wildlife, and plants, and their habitats within the System;*

P   *ensure that the biological integrity, diversity, and environmental health of the System are maintained for the benefit of present and future generations of Americans;*

P   *plan and direct the continued growth of the System in a manner that is best designed to accomplish the mission of the System, to contribute to the conservation of the ecosystems of the United States, to complement efforts of States and other Federal agencies to conserve fish and wildlife and their habitats, and to increase support for the System and participation from conservation partners and the public;*

P   *ensure that the mission of the System described in paragraph (2) and the purposes of each refuge are carried out, except that if a conflict exists between the purposes of a refuge and the mission of the System, the conflict shall be resolved in a manner that first protects the purposes of the refuge, and, to the extent practicable, that also achieves the mission of the System;*

P   *ensure effective coordination, interaction, and cooperation with owners of land adjoining refuges and the fish and wildlife agency of the States in which the units of the System are located;*

P   *assist in the maintenance of adequate water quantity and water quality to fulfill the mission of the System and the purposes of each refuge;*

P   *acquire, under State law, water rights that are needed for refuge purposes;*

P   *recognize compatible wildlife-dependent recreational uses as the priority general public uses of the System through which the American public can develop an appreciation for fish and wildlife;*

P   *ensure that opportunities are provided within the System for compatible wildlife-dependent recreational uses;*

P   *ensure that priority general public uses of the System receive enhanced consideration over other general public uses in planning and management within the System;*

P   *provide increased opportunities for families to experience compatible wildlife-dependent recreation, particularly opportunities for parents and their children to safely engage in traditional outdoor activities, such as fishing and hunting;*

P   *continue, consistent with existing laws and interagency agreements, authorized or permitted uses of units of the System by other Federal agencies, including those necessary to facilitate military preparedness;"*

The National Wildlife Refuge System Improvement Act of 1997 further defines the wildlife-dependent recreational uses as: wildlife observation and photography, environmental education and interpretation, and fishing and hunting.

U.S. Fish and Wildlife Service Mission

The mission of the Service is to work with others to conserve, protect, and enhance fish, wildlife, and plants, and their habitats for the continuing benefit of the American people. To fulfill this mission, Congress has charged the Service with conserving and managing migratory birds, endangered species, anadromous and inter-jurisdictional fish, and certain marine mammals. The Service carries out these responsibilities through several functional entities. The National Wildlife Refuge System is one of those entities.

Fort Niobrara National Wildlife Refuge Purpose(s)

The Fort Niobrara NWR was created by Executive Order 1461, January 11, 1912, (with a designated acreage of 13,279 acres) "...reserved and set apart for the use of the Department of Agriculture as a preserve and breeding ground for native birds." Shortly after the Refuge's establishment, J.W. Gilbert, owner of a private game park at Friend, Nebraska, "offered his buffalo, elk, and deer to the Federal Government for preservation on a national reservation, with the understanding that they would remain in Nebraska. The acceptance of this offer was delayed through lack of a suitable range in the State. On November 14, 1912, however, an Executive Order was issued enlarging the Fort Niobrara Game Preserve (then known as the Niobrara Reservation) by adding thereto the area formerly used as the parade grounds and headquarters for the old military post. This made the total area of the preserve about 14,200 acres. Mr. Gilbert's offer was then formally accepted by the Secretary of Agriculture, and arrangements were made to transfer the animals to Fort Niobrara." (Ruth 1938) As a result, the Refuge is to be managed (1) as a preserve and breeding ground for native birds, and (2) for the preservation of bison and elk herds representative of those that once roamed the Great Plains.

Furthermore, the Wilderness Act of 1964 calls for designated wilderness areas within a National Wildlife Refuge to receive equal consideration in management decisions and become a supplemental purpose of the Refuge. Section 4. (a) of this Act reads: *"The purposes of this Act are hereby declared to be within and supplemental to the purposes for which national forests and units of the national park and national wildlife refuge systems are established and administered."* Thus, the purpose of the designated wilderness area within this Refuge is to be supplemental and not subservient to the other purposes of the Refuge.

Fort Niobrara National Wildlife Refuge Vision Statement

Fort Niobrara NWR will strive to preserve, restore, and enhance the exceptional diversity of native flora and fauna and significant historic resources of the Niobrara River Valley and Sandhills of Nebraska for the benefit of present and future generations of Americans.

Fort Niobrara NWR habitat management goals will seek to maintain a healthy Refuge environment that will provide opportunities for visitors to enjoy wildlife-dependent uses of the Refuge in a natural setting. Interpreting a unique assemblage of habitats, wildlife and the Refuge's historical heritage, as well as improving facilities will enhance the visitor's experience while protecting the cultural integrity of the area. To meet these challenges, the Service will seek partnerships with other agencies, interest groups, landowners, and local communities. These efforts will result in greater protection of wildlife, fish, and plant resources throughout north-central Nebraska.

Legal and Policy Guidance

National Wildlife Refuges are guided by the mission and goals of the National Wildlife Refuge System (System), the designated purpose of the Refuge unit as described in the establishing legislation and/or executive orders, Service laws and policy, and international treaties (for a complete list see Appendix G).

Key concepts included in laws, regulations, and policies that guide management of the System include primary versus multiple-use public lands, compatibility, and priority wildlife-dependent recreational activities. Examples of relevant guidance include the National Wildlife Refuge System Administration Act of 1966, as amended by the National Wildlife Refuge System Improvement Act of 1997, the Refuge Recreation Act of 1962 (50 CFR), Executive Order 12996 (Management and General Public Use of the National Wildlife Refuge System), and selected portions of the Code of Federal Regulations, the Refuge Manual, and the Fish and Wildlife Service Manual.

The National Wildlife Refuge System Administration Act of 1966, as amended, provided guidelines and directives for administration and management of all areas in the System, including wildlife refuges, areas for the protection and conservation of fish and wildlife threatened with extinction, wildlife ranges, game ranges, wildlife management areas, or waterfowl production areas. Use of any area within the System was permitted, provided that such uses were compatible with the major purposes for which such areas were established.

The National Wildlife Refuge System Improvement Act of 1997 amends the Refuge System Administration Act by including a unifying mission for the System, a new formal process for determining compatible uses on refuges, and a requirement that each refuge will be managed under a Comprehensive Conservation Plan (CCP or Plan). This Act states that wildlife conservation is the priority of the System lands and that the Secretary of the Interior (Secretary) shall ensure that the biological integrity, diversity, and environmental health of refuge lands are maintained. Each refuge must be managed to fulfill the mission of the System and the specific purposes for which it was established. Additionally, this Act identifies and establishes the legitimacy and appropriateness of the six wildlife-dependent recreational uses. These are hunting, fishing, wildlife observation and photography, and environmental education and interpretation. As priority public uses of the System, these uses will receive enhanced consideration over other uses in planning and management. Furthermore, this Act requires that a CCP be in place for each refuge by the year 2012 and that the public have an opportunity for active involvement in Plan development and revision. It is Service policy that CCPs are developed in an open public process and that the agency is committed to securing public input throughout the process. This Act amended portions of the Refuge Recreation Act and National Wildlife Refuge System Administration Act of 1966.

Lands within the System are different from other, multiple-use public lands in that they are closed to all public uses unless specifically and legally opened. Unlike other Federal lands that are managed under a multiple-use mandate (i.e., national forests administered by the U.S. Forest Service and public lands administered by the U.S. Bureau of Land Management), the System is managed specifically for the benefit of fish, wildlife, and plant resources and their habitats. Compatible wildlife-dependent recreation is a legitimate and appropriate general public use of the System.

Compatible wildlife-dependent recreational uses involving hunting, fishing, wildlife observation and photography, and environmental education and interpretation are priority public uses of the System. These uses must receive enhanced consideration over other public uses in refuge planning and management.

Before any uses, including wildlife-dependent recreational activities, are allowed on national wildlife refuges, Federal law requires that they be formally determined to be "compatible."

A compatible use is defined as a use that, in the sound professional judgement of the refuge manager, will not materially interfere with or detract from the fulfillment of the mission of the System or the purposes of the Refuge. Sound professional judgement is further defined as a finding, determination, or decision that is consistent with the principles of sound fish and wildlife management and administration, available science and resources (funding, personnel, facilities, and other infrastructure), and adherence with applicable laws. If financial resources are not available to design, operate, and maintain an activity, the refuge manager will take reasonable steps to obtain outside assistance from the State and other conservation interests. No refuge use may be allowed unless it is determined to be compatible.

The Service has completed compatibility determinations for Fort Niobrara NWR (see Appendix E). All six priority wildlife-dependent recreational activities—wildlife observation, wildlife photography, environmental interpretation, environmental education, hunting and fishing—were determined to be compatible. Hunting currently is not permitted, but the Refuge may allow future occasional hunts for the purpose of managing elk and, if reintroduced, bighorn sheep populations to achieve habitat management goals.

The Refuge Recreation Act, as amended, authorized the Secretary to administer refuges, hatcheries, and other conservation areas for recreational use when such uses did not interfere with the area's primary purpose.

Executive Order 12996 (March 23, 1996) identified a new mission statement for the System; established six priority public uses (hunting, fishing, wildlife observation and photography, environmental education and interpretation); emphasized conservation and enhancement of the quality and diversity of fish and wildlife habitat; stressed the importance of partnerships with Federal and State agencies, Tribes, organizations, industry, and the general public; mandated public involvement in decisions on the acquisition and management of refuges; and required identification, prior to acquisition of new refuge lands, of existing compatible wildlife-dependent uses that would be permitted to continue on an interim basis pending completion of comprehensive planning.

Existing Partnerships

The Refuge works with a variety of organizations and individuals on natural resource projects including private landowners (Partners For Wildlife program); Natural Resources Conservation Service (Refuge grazing program, Wetland Reserve Program); Farm Service Agency (easement program); Nebraska Game and Parks Commission (wildlife surveys, fish rearing in Refuge ponds); Cherry County Extension Service (youth programs, research); local law enforcement agencies (enforcement, youth rehabilitation); Inter Tribal Bison Cooperative (bison donations and management); zoos, conservation districts and other non-profit qualifying entities (bison, elk, and longhorn donations); veterinarians for the State of Nebraska, other lower 48 states, and U.S. Department of Agriculture (disease and health issues, tests, research); Rocky Mountain Elk Foundation (interpretative panels, animal transfers); Fort Niobrara Natural History Association (Refuge projects, sale of books, postcards, posters, etc.); Valentine Chamber of Commerce (community projects); Niobrara Council (River management); Texas Longhorn Breeders Association of America and International Texas Longhorn Association (longhorn pedigree, registration); The Nature Conservancy (fire management, research); Rural Fire Protection Districts (wildfire suppression on-and off-Refuge); and various universities (research).

Planning Process

Description of Planning Process

The development of this CCP was guided, in the beginning, by the Refuge Planning Chapter of the Fish and Wildlife Service Manual (Part 602 FW2.1, November 1996) and later also by the Service's Draft Comprehensive Conservation Planning Policy. Key steps included: (1) preplanning; (2) identifying issues and developing a vision; (3) gathering information; (4) analyzing resource relationships; (5) developing alternatives and assessing environmental effects; (6) identifying a preferred alternative; (7) publishing the Draft Plan and soliciting public comments on the Draft Plan (the comment period for input from the public spanned a total of 105 days); (8) review of comments and effecting necessary and appropriate changes to the draft CCP; and, (9) preparation of the final Plan for approval by the Region 6 Regional Director, and finally (10) implementation of the Plan.

Comprehensive conservation planning efforts for Fort Niobrara NWR began in January 1997 with a meeting of regional management and planning staff and field station employees at Fort Niobrara NWR. At that meeting a core planning team was designated with the major responsibilities of gathering information and writing the plan. A review team was set up to provide guidance and direction to the core planning team. A working group was also organized to provide interchange of information between Service personnel, outside agencies, and interested stakeholders of the Refuge.

On March 20, 1997, an open house scoping session was held in the Cherry County Hall meeting room, Valentine, Nebraska. The open house provided participants an opportunity to learn about the Refuge's purposes, mission and goals, and issues currently facing management. People attending were provided the chance to speak with Service representatives and to share their comments.

A two-day Refuge tour was held with the working group and Service management and planning staffs in April 1997. The tour gave participants a chance to view fenced animal management and prominent wildlife species of the Refuge, discuss management aspects of the Refuge, and give planning staff ideas for consideration in the planning process.

On October 28, 1997, a meeting was held with Refuge permittees that are actively involved with canoeing and tubing on the Niobrara River through the Fort Niobrara NWR. The CCP addresses this issue, and the meeting provided an opportunity for Refuge staff and permittees to share information concerning this use. This and other meetings were scheduled to let people know what the Service was doing to manage the wildlife and habitats of the Fort Niobrara NWR and to elicit their input on topics of interest to them.

During the planning process, the review and working groups had access to information on objectives and alternatives being considered. Written comments were exchanged and verbal conversations were held. The Draft CCP/EA was the first opportunity that these groups and the public had to review the entire planning effort and the Draft Plan. The Draft Plan was released on the last week of April 1999 and distributed in the first week of May 1999. A 60-day comment period was provided in which the Service requested information, comments, concerns, suggestions, and complaints from the public regarding the Draft CCP/EA. Because of the tremendous amount of public interest in this Plan, the Service extended the comment period for an additional 45 days, for a total of 105 days of public comment. With this extension, the public comment period did not close until August 19, 1999.

The voluminous amount of comment letters and electronic mail communications were reviewed and summarized by category and subject. After reading and compiling all the comments received, the review team had a briefing meeting with the Regional Director and Assistant Regional Director of the Service's Region 6, the Programmatic and Southern Ecosystems Assistant Regional Directors, the Refuge Supervisor for Fort Niobrara NWR, the Chief of the Branch of Land Acquisition and Refuge Planning, and the Regional Wildlife Biologist. The summary of the comments received was reviewed at this meeting and appropriate modifications were made to the Draft CCP/EA in accordance with scientifically based new information provided during the comment period and the goals and objectives of the Refuge. The present Plan contains the changes made by the Service in accordance to the recommendations of the directorate and Service biologists and managers. All the actions undertaken in the preparation of this Plan satisfy the requirements under the National Environmental Policy Act of 1969.

This Plan will guide the management on the Refuge for the next 15 years. Plans are ultimately signed by the Regional Director, Region 6, thus providing regional direction to the station project leader. A copy of this Plan will be provided to all those interested. The project leader of the station will review the Plan every five years to decide if it needs revision.

Planning Issues

Issues, concerns, and opportunities were identified through discussions with planning team members, key contacts, and through the public scoping process, which began with an Open House in March 1997. Comments were received orally at the meetings, via e-mail messages and in writing, both before and during the scoping and the public comment period phases of the comprehensive conservation planning process. The following issues, concerns, and comments are a compilation and summary of those expressed by the public, other Federal and State agencies, local and county governments, private organizations and individuals, environmental groups and persons concerned for the natural resources of the Fort Niobrara NWR. This section also contains information developed by the Service throughout the planning process on the same issues.

Texas Longhorn Cattle

Many people were concerned, for various reasons, about the Service's proposal to remove this historic herd from the Refuge. Some other commentators met this proposal with approval.

Loss of Revenue to the County: It was speculated that Cherry County would experience a drastic reduction in revenue from the loss of monies provided by the receipts of the sales of Texas longhorn cattle from Fort Niobrara NWR should this herd be removed from the Refuge.

The Service believes that Cherry County should not see any drastic reduction of revenue from the relocation of this herd outside of the Refuge for the following reason: The annual average of the Refuge Revenue Sharing receipts, collected, deposited and credited towards the reserve acres for Fort Niobrara NWR for the past three years was $43,090 for longhorn cattle and $170,567 for bison. The average of the percent of these receipts credited to longhorn cattle for the same years was 20.26 percent. Therefore, if the longhorn cattle sales were no longer held at Fort Niobrara NWR and no receipts were collected, Cherry County would lose approximately 20.2 percent in revenue each year from the Refuge Revenue Share Program (RRSP).

This loss of revenue from the RRSP would generally be compensated by the Payment-in-Lieu-of-Taxes payment (PILT Law, Act of October 20, 1973, PL-94-5a65; 90 Stat 2662; 31 USC-1601) made by the Bureau of Land Management (BLM) each year. In the last three years, Cherry County has received a PILT payment from BLM for the same reserved acres based on the PILT formula minus the amounts paid by the U.S. Fish and Wildlife Service.

Therefore, if the Service were to make a payment under the RRSP which was less than the average in the last years because of the lack of revenue from the sale of longhorn cattle, then the BLM payment would make up the difference.

Loss of Historically Important Herd: The Service understands the historical significance and the importance to local tourism that this herd has for Cherry County and the City of Valentine. Nevertheless, the Service believes that given the need to achieve the habitat management goals of the Refuge to comply with the stated purpose of Fort Niobrara NWR, the herd must be removed from the Refuge. However, the Service has stated, to the City of Valentine, Cherry County officials, and other groups and individuals concerned about the removal of this herd from the Refuge, its willingness to participate in the creation of a non-profit organization that would receive this herd and manage it, in accordance with the same practices and standards used by the Service, within Cherry County, and if at all possible, within the limits of the City of Valentine. Thus, this herd could continue to exist within Cherry County and possibly in the vicinity of the City of Valentine where tourists could have access to it. Furthermore, the management entity could directly benefit from 100 percent of the proceeds of the excess animals from the herd rather than just 25 percent as it does under present conditions.

Recreational Use and Resources of the Niobrara River

Many people, groups, and agencies were concerned, for various reasons, about the Service's current and proposed policy on access to and management of the Niobrara River resources for recreational use.

Limiting Access to the Niobrara River: The Service has grown increasingly concerned over the possible environmental effects that the current burgeoning use of the Niobrara River resources by River floaters may be having on riparian and upland Refuge resources, as well as on wilderness values.

Recreational canoeing and tubing use of the stretch of the Niobrara River designated as scenic by Congress has increased dramatically in the past few years. In response to this, the Service has attempted to alleviate effects on Refuge resources (riparian habitats and the wildlife that depends upon it, wilderness values, etc.) by placing a temporary limit on the number of outfitter Special Use Permits issued by the Refuge and a cap on use while the environmental effects of this use are assessed. Furthermore, this temporary limit in use is expected to contain the overcrowding situation that has developed on this stretch of the Niobrara River and degraded the quality of wilderness experience. This temporary measure has been criticized as unfair, inadequate, and without basis on hard evidence and science. However, the Service believes that this interim management policy is better than complete shutdown of River use on this stretch of the Niobrara River (worst case scenario) as discontinuing all use would be no more justifiable than allowing uncontrolled growth of use. At this time, there is no logic in depriving all visitors of the wilderness experience.

Management Plan: The Service will prepare a Management Plan in the next two years dealing exclusively with the recreational use of the scenic Niobrara River as it flows through the Refuge. This Plan will be prepared by the Service with the participation of all interested parties, such as the National Park Service, the Niobrara Council, all River outfitters interested in participating, and any city and county officials interested in being part of this effort. The Plan will define acceptable use levels for weekdays and weekends that meet legal mandates. Also, actions to be taken when uses exceed threshold levels or negatively impact resources, and wilderness values will be clearly defined.

In the interim, River use will be capped at the 1998 levels and the moratorium on new outfitters will continue. Weekend and weekday use will be monitored along with habitat, wildlife, erosion, and social parameters to determine threshold levels.

It is not the intention of the Service to obstruct the development of a recreational and revenue-producing enterprise such as River use outfitting, but rather to ensure that this use continues to be compatible with Refuge goals and objectives and with the requirements of the Wild and Scenic River Act and the Wilderness Act promulgated by Congress for the benefit of the American people. The Service believes that the wise use of the River for recreational purposes will, in the end, be beneficial, not only to wildlife, but to the community as well. It is our belief that any decrease in use by River floaters is caused more by a degrading "wilderness" and "wild and scenic" experience caused by too many visitors at certain times of the year, rather than by the Service's limits on Special Use Permits. Ensuring visitors a wildlife-oriented as well as a wilderness experience when using the River would also ensure a healthy tourist industry for the City of Valentine and Cherry County.

While not presently documented on Fort Niobrara NWR riparian habitats along the wild and scenic Niobrara River, a large body of research exists (mostly from studies conducted in California, Colorado and in eastern states) on the issue of effects on migratory birds as public use of rivers increases. Heavy recreation use of riparian areas during the summer (bird breeding season) can have devastating effects on the avifauna, during all portions of their natural history cycle. Riparian habitats are one of the most important wildlife habitats occurring in the Service's Region 6. Seventy-five percent of the terrestrial species occurring in this Region are dependent on riparian and adjacent aquatic zones during some portion of their life cycle. The effects of heavy recreation on the riparian habitats and its associated wildlife species is two-fold: disturbance to the individuals, and disturbance to the vegetation used by wildlife. These effects have not been fully assessed for the riparian habitats of Fort Niobrara NWR. The Service, as a precautionary measure, decided to place limits on recreational use of the segment of the wild and scenic Niobrara River that flows through the Refuge until these effects can be qualified and quantified. The Service's mission is the preservation of wildlife and the habitats on which they depend. Recreational use of Refuge lands must come second to wildlife and be carried out in a compatible way with the purposes of the Refuge. Thus, the necessary use limits at this time until a River Management Plan is developed and implemented.

Restricted Access and User Fees: Fort Niobrara NWR, through its land management authority, has restricted access and use of certain roads and bridges and has instituted fees for use of public facilities as the need for these provisions has grown. Changes in the operation of the Refuge canoe launch have been implemented over the years as the number of visitors to the area has increased. Furthermore, Congress directed refuges to implement fees in areas where collection could be made and used to pay for the costs of operating the activities for which a fee is collected. This fee amount was based on fees charged at other Federal areas. Monies collected from the fee program have been used to pump rest rooms, for signs, for costs related to collections, but primarily to pay the salary of a law enforcement officer to patrol the River in an attempt to stop certain inappropriate uses of the River (alcohol consumption, disorderly conduct, littering, no life jackets, etc.). Access to the River from a County road had to be stopped for safety reasons because people were unloading gear and canoes on the road, on the road shoulder, and crossing the road on foot to get to the parking area, thus creating a safety hazard. Cherry County has a right-of-way across the Refuge for a road. The right-of-way is not for public recreation such as launching of canoes or tubes.

Authority to Control River Activities: The Department of Interior Solicitor's Office provided the Service with an opinion regarding the Refuge's authority to control activities on the surface of the wild and scenic section of the Niobrara River flowing through the Refuge. However, some visitors to the Refuge and residents of Cherry County disagree with the Solicitor's opinion, and this continues to be a point of contention. Nevertheless, the nine miles of the Niobrara River that span the Refuge are part of the segment designated by Congress as part of the Wild and Scenic River System in 1991. The Service was thus accorded exclusive management authority on this portion and National Park Service on the remainder of the wild and scenic Niobrara River. The entire segment is considered a component of the National Park Service system, and Congress holds the Service and the National Park Service accountable for the preservation and management of this National resource, not subordinate partners that may or may not exist.

Bridge and Launch Area: Some people launching at the Refuge are not aware that they are within the boundary of a National Wildlife Refuge. The Service must educate the public to the fact that (1) the Niobrara River flowing through the Refuge is a designated scenic River, (2) five miles of the Niobrara River is designated as a Wilderness Area, and (3) the Service must manage these resources in accordance with these Congressional designations and the management that they imply. The Service will require that all future outfitter literature and public contact refer to the launch site as "Fort Niobrara National Wildlife Refuge Canoe Launch Site."

Cornell Dam: Some commented that the Cornell Dam has outlived its usefulness; that a study weighing its environmental and cultural values, as well as safety, should be undertaken directly to determine whether the Dam should survive. A few commentators recommended breaching the dam as restoration of natural stream flow is entirely consistent with Congressional intent of the Wild and Scenic Rivers Act. Furthermore, they added that the current Nation's sentiment is for removal of outmoded, functionless dams, specially if they block otherwise pristine, natural flowing rivers. They pointed to the need for an environmental consequences analysis for retaining this dam.

The Service's decision to leave Cornell Dam untouched at this time stems from the Service's concern and responsibility towards federally listed species that have been known to benefit from the habitats created by this structure. However, the Service is open to further study this situation, and if warranted in the future, to eliminate this structure if it is shown to be no longer necessary to maintain habitats for threatened and endangered species.

Habitat and Wildlife Management

Many people, agencies, and environmental groups were concerned about the loss of bird habitat due to the priority given to large ungulate management. They also felt that protecting and enhancing bird habitats should be a priority over other wildlife issues. Some felt that other wildlife species, including butterflies and other insects, should be considered, and that enhancement of wildlife off the Refuge should be discussed as well. Concern was expressed about the design of the perimeter fence, vegetation management, and any additional structures and how they would affect the movements of wildlife to and from the Refuge, as well as the appearance of the area. A comment was made that current wildlife management practices should be evaluated before any changes are made.

Legislation (National Wildlife Refuge System Administration Act, as amended) mandates wildlife conservation as the overriding mission of the National Wildlife Refuge System and, as such, it is the most important issue at Fort Niobrara NWR. Protection of wildlife habitat, especially for feeding, resting, and nesting birds and their young, would define the types of visitor activities and access allowed at the Refuge. Another responsibility of this and other national wildlife refuges will be to preserve, restore, and enhance threatened and endangered species and migratory birds. To carry out this responsibility, the Refuge's flora and fauna must be protected from human adverse impacts (i.e., pollution, and disruptive or incompatible activities). Public use of the scenic section of the Niobrara River, the Refuge's Wilderness Area, and the rest of the Refuge lands must be managed to be compatible with avian and other wildlife objectives. Nonnative plant species must be controlled and/or eradicated to restore native plant communities in upland and wetland areas, thereby enhancing habitat for migratory birds. How to provide wildlife-dependent recreation and opportunities for environmental education, while at the same time ensuring habitat and wildlife protection, is an issue to be resolved through the CCP process.

Bison: Some commentators expressed opposition to the Service's proposed new strategy to manage bison by elimination of some interior fencing.

The Service is confident bison, as the major grassland management tool at the Refuge, can be managed to attain the proposed habitat goals for avian populations. The Service will only remove that portion of interior fence that is not necessary for habitat management and handling of big game animals. Interior wire will be removed incrementally (over-time) to ensure appropriate resource management. Bison can also be managed, as stated throughout this Plan, through methods other than fencing, such as prescribed fire, water manipulation and salt supplements. Also the winter population herd levels of bison will remain at 350 animals, unless research regarding habitat, native birds, and bison herd genetics objectives reveals a need to reduce the bison herd population levels to a number between 350 and 200 animals.

Bighorn Sheep: Some commentators expressed opposition to the Service's proposal to introduce bighorn sheep to the Refuge (i.e., the species never occurred at the Refuge; would give Refuge a zoo atmosphere; fenced herd would not be capable of migrating and this practice contradicts contemporary wildlife management principles; could lead to an epizootic disease, etc.). While many expressed support for this proposal, some opposed the proposed limited hunt to reduce herd size. The opposition to this proposed hunt presented more than one facet, but with most opposition hinging on the premise that the area of the Refuge where bighorn sheep could be introduced is not large enough to allow for a "sportsman's" opportunity to hunt sheep.

The Service believes that the remains of bighorn sheep in the general vicinity of the Refuge, in areas with similar habitats as those presently found in parts of this Refuge, point to the likely prior existence of bighorn sheep in parts of what is today Fort Niobrara NWR.

After reviewing public comments, and during internal meetings, the Service has decided to postpone the possible introduction of this species into the Refuge.

The Service has been invited and will participate in the preparation of the State of Nebraska's Bighorn Sheep Management Plan. This participation will proceed any introduction attempts of this species at this Refuge. This Management Plan should address habitat needs that will be used by the Service to assess the possibility or lack thereof of any introduction effort. Only after the State's Bighorn Sheep Management Plan has been finalized and the Service has consulted with the State on this issue will the Service make a determination whether to introduce this species onto the Refuge. Additionally, should the proposed introduction take place, no hunting of bighorn sheep would be allowed if the Service determines that a fair chase, sporting-type hunt cannot be obtained.

Elk: Some concern has been expressed that Chronic Wasting Disease (CWD) will become a serious disease in elk within Nebraska and will contaminate the Refuge elk herd. Disease is a constant threat to the wildlife populations within the State and Nation. Elk and elk management has been a goal and objective of the Refuge since 1912. During this time the Service has managed the elk herd without any significant disease related problems. However, the Service will remain vigilant in its effort to combat new diseases like CWD. The Service will participate in the development of an Elk Management Plan for the State of Nebraska which will address disease concerns about the State's population of elk and methods (i.e. modified fencing, etc.) to reduce the possibility of the spread of diseases.

Some opposition to the hunting of elk was received because the Refuge is fenced and only 19,131 acres in size which would not allow for sufficient space to have a sporting opportunity to hunt elk. The Service has decided to delay the hunting of elk until the Nebraska Elk Management Plan has been completed and the Service has consulted the State on this issue. The hunting of elk on the Refuge will only be allowed if the Service has determined that a fair chase, sporting type hunt can be obtained.

Black-tailed Prairie Dogs: Many commentators expressed, with different degrees of intensity, opposition to the Service's proposal to allow for the expansion of black-tailed prairie dogs at the Refuge citing many reasons: inability of the Service to contain them within the Refuge; damage to habitats; possibility of prairie dogs spreading diseases to human beings; too many prairie dogs already exist, etc. Comments were also received in support of this proposal.

Black-tailed prairie dogs are an integral part of many grassland ecosystems in the western states of our Nation. Many other animal species, some listed as endangered, other deemed species of special concern (i.e., black-footed ferrets, bald eagles, burrowing owls, mountain plovers, swift foxes), and migratory birds (raptors) are either inextricably dependent on or make common use of prairie dog colonies to obtain basic food, shelter and/or habitat for nesting and rearing of their young. Fort Niobrara NWR is located well within the historical range of this species and has benefitted from the presence of black-tailed prairie dogs as an integral part of a healthy ecosystem and as a tourist attraction.

In this Plan, the Service is proposing to allow for the expansion of the black-tailed prairie dog colony that presently exists in the Refuge. This proposed expansion is in line with the Service's efforts to protect the ever decreasing numbers in the number and size of black-tailed prairie dog colonies nationwide. The Service has estimated that this species' range has decreased by an alarming 95 percent from the time of the European settlement of the west. The Service has been petitioned to list this species under the Endangered Species Act given the precipitous decline in the species populations and the Service is currently reviewing this listing petition.

The Service will allow black-tailed prairie dogs to expand to a manageable population size and control them within the boundaries of the Refuge.

Funding and Staffing to Manage the Refuge

Managing this Refuge requires adequate funding and staffing to effectively carry out habitat and population management activities, as well as to ensure public uses that are compatible with the System mission. Some people expressed concern that the Service might not be allocated sufficient funding to implement all the goals and objectives stated in this Plan. Some commentators felt that building partnerships with public agencies, private organizations, and volunteers would increase the Refuge's management ability.

The Service is aware that adequate funding to carry out all ongoing and proposed management activities may not be readily available to the Refuge. Nevertheless, this Plan outlines the recommended course of action for the Refuge and this Plan may be the best vehicle to obtain the necessary funding to accomplish the mission for which Congress designated this area a National Wildlife Refuge.

Other Public Uses and Recreation

Some commentators expressed opposition to captive wildlife hunting while requesting the expansion of turkey, deer, prairie grouse and pronghorn hunting opportunities, if not with rifles, maybe with archery, shotguns and muzzle-loading. These commentators argued that the Refuge can accommodate hunting.

The Refuge is currently closed to hunting. The original purpose of Fort Niobrara NWR was "a preserve and breeding ground for native birds." Later, this purpose was enlarged and, as a result, the Refuge is to be managed (1) as a preserve and breeding ground for native birds and (2) for the preservation of bison and elk herds representative of those that once roamed the Great Plains. Hunting for elk and, if reintroduced, bighorn sheep will to permit the taking of surplus animals (maybe one or two animals) under a limited, strictly controlled hunting environment. Unrestricted hunting for other species of wildlife on the Refuge would be a disturbance detrimental to bison and elk management.

Public Involvement Methodology

The Service, through this and other planning processes involving NEPA, finds itself involved in the complex and essential task of involving the public in the planning process. The public involvement process is often a difficult enterprise given the specific time-frames and schedules that accompany most Service actions, this Plan not being the exception.

Throughout the process that led to the preparation of this Plan, the Service complied with NEPA requirements to involve the public through meetings of different kinds (i.e., public scoping meetings, open house meetings, meetings with specific groups), personal communications, and the disbursement of the Draft CCP/EA that preceded this final Plan and other kinds of information, and finally, through a period of time in which all interested parties had 105 days in which to provide written comments on the proposed future Refuge goals, objectives, strategies and actions. The Service effected changes to the Draft CCP/EA as a consequence of comments and information received prior and during the public comment period.

The Service, throughout the preparation of the Draft CCP/EA, attempted to consult with and involve all the groups, entities, and individuals that expressed interest in participating. The refuge manager, his staff, and Region 6 Regional Office personnel conducted various meetings to disseminate information, address most, if not all possible issues, and collect all possible relevant data and comments for the preparation of these Draft Plans.

After these Draft Plans had been prepared, all those involved had an opportunity to provide written comments on the Draft CCP/EA. The original public comment period was open for 60 days, but due to the high volume of comments, the Service agreed to reopen the comment period for an additional 45 days. A typical public comment period is open for 30 days. Thus, the Service gave commentators a total of 105 days in which to provide written comments, by letter or electronic mail, to the Service.

An Open House was held on June 10, 1999, in Valentine, Nebraska. It was scheduled to take place from 3 to 8 PM; instead it ran from 2:45 until 9:30 PM due to the interest shown. The purpose of the Open House was to inform the public as to the major aspects of these Plans. The public was encouraged to provide their written comments to the Service. An Open House meeting format affords the event organizers the opportunity to reach out to a greater segment of the public and each individual person from the public to voice their comments and concerns.

Summary of Refuge and Resource Descriptions

Geographic/Ecosystem Setting

Fort Niobrara NWR is 19,131 acres in size and located in north-central Nebraska along the Niobrara River. The Refuge and surrounding area is recognized by ecologists for its biogeographic significance due to the co-occurrence of five distinctly different, major vegetation communities within and adjacent to the Niobrara River corridor. The region is the only place in North America where Rocky Mountain Coniferous Forest (eastern limit), Northern Boreal Forest (southern limit), Eastern Deciduous Forest (western limit), Mixed Prairie and Sandhill Prairie meet and intermingle (Kaul and Rolfsmeier 1993). The unusually diverse plant and animal assemblages found in this area are due to unique surface and subsurface geologic formations, water and soil conditions, current and past climates, and differential sun exposure (Churchill *et al.* 1988). Additional ecological factors that had significant affect on the biological diversity that evolved in this region prior to Euro-American settlement includes wildfire and the use of fire by aboriginal men (Higgins *et al.* 1986, Steuter 1991), and the unrestricted grazing and impacts associated with grazing of bison, elk, pronghorn antelope, and prairie dogs (Knopf 1994, Bragg and Steuter 1996). Though changes in composition and density of native flora and fauna have occurred since settlement, Bogan (1995) reported that Fort Niobrara is one of the few areas where the basic components of the 1850 landscape are still present and viable.

The Service has adopted an ecosystem approach to national natural resource management and has identified 52 ecosystems within the United States (USFWS, 1994). The Service has formed teams to address the most important conservation and restoration issues that each one of these identified ecosystems faces. Each one of these teams has advanced, depending on the complexity of issues within a determined area, at different paces in the identification and categorization of all of the conservation issues (Service's Resource Priorities) and goals for each of these ecosystems. The area where this Refuge lies has been difficult to characterize and include into one single ecosystem given the diversity of habitats and other natural resources found there.

Fort Niobrara NWR is bisected by the Niobrara River (which according to early Service watershed-based ecosystem maps separates two distinct ecosystems) and thus, theoretically, lies within two different ecosystems which are the Main Stem Missouri River Ecosystem (basically the northernmost area of the Refuge constituted mostly by the designated Wilderness Area on the northern banks of the Niobrara River) and the Platte/Kansas Rivers Ecosystem (the largest portion of the Refuge on the southern banks of the Niobrara River).

The Platte/Kansas Rivers Ecosystem team has been given the responsibility to address ecosystem issues on Fort Niobrara NWR. This team has identified the five main areas of concern that need to be addressed for this ecosystem.

The Service resource priorities for the Platte/Kansas Rivers Ecosystem are:

P Prairie Grassland (including the Sandhills region) restoration and preservation
P Species of Concern (rare species)
P Water quality
P Native fishes, small fishes and mussels
P Water Quantity

The Service believes that the Refuge's goals and objectives delineated in this Plan will help the Service attain the goals and objectives for these resource priorities for the Platte/Kansas Rivers Ecosystem.

Climate

The climate of the region is highly variable and characterized by cold winters and hot summers. Total annual precipitation averages 18 inches with approximately 65 percent occurring during the May-to-September growing season (NOAA National Climatic Data Center 1996). Winter precipitation is usually in the form of snow with the annual accumulation averaging 37 inches. Temperatures range from -39° F to 114° F with July and August being the warmest months (average high temperature 85-87° F) and January and February the coldest months (average low temperature 8-12° F). The average frost free period is approximately 150 days. Winds ranging from 5-15 mph are common throughout the year and are generally out of the north, west, or northwest direction in the winter and out of the south, west, or southwest direction during the summer. Low humidity, high temperatures and moderate to strong winds cause a rapid loss of soil moisture by evapo-transpiration during the summer.

Air Quality

Air quality is good due to the absence of significant air pollution sources. The Fort Niobrara Wilderness is a Class 2 Status Area under the Clean Air Act.

Topography

The Refuge topography is varied and well-defined. The Niobrara River valley extends from east to west across the Refuge and is entrenched 150 to 350 feet below the general upland level. High terraces, or benches, lie at different levels from 175 to 275 feet above the present River channel and from 30 to 250 feet below the general level of the uplands (Layton 1956). Most benches are discontinuous strips 1/4 to 3/4 of a mile wide with level to rolling or hummocky relief. Steep valley sides, or breaks, are on both sides of the River and along lower courses of its major tributaries. Table land north of the River valley is nearly level to gently rolling with several surface areas modified by narrow, steep-sided and shallow drainage ways, by small areas of typical sandhills, numerous hummocks, and low, elongated sandy ridges. Sandhill terrain south of the River is undulating to hilly with dune tops 10 to 100 feet higher than the surrounding area. The range of hills, with alternating pockets or narrow valleys, usually run parallel in an irregular northwest-southeast direction. Generally, the southerly (leeward) sides of the hills are steeper than the northerly (windward) sides. Elevations on the Refuge range from 2,000 feet above sea level to 2,800 feet.

Geology

The geologic framework of the Refuge, as summarized by Osborn 1979, consists of six formations and are as follows (from oldest to youngest): Rosebud Formation "bedrock" makes up the Niobrara River valley walls and lower courses of the major tributaries within the Refuge; Valentine Formation is a sandy, stream-deposited unit unconformably overlying the Rosebud and forming gentle slopes; Ash Hollow Formation is a hard, sandy unit with many ledges and layers of volcanic ash which forms a "caprock" on the north rim of the Refuge; High Terrace Deposits are sand and gravel deposits high above the present Niobrara River that were deposited during the later part of the Pleistocene Ice Age when the River was flowing at a higher elevation and forms the flats upon which the Refuge headquarters is built; Sandhills are stabilized dune sand of the late Pleistocene and Holocene age; Low Terrace and Floodplain Deposits are adjacent to the modern Niobrara River and contain rocks derived from older formations but are not of significant age geologically.

Soils

Soil groups and series found on the Refuge are mapped and described in detail in the 1956 Soil Survey of Cherry County (Layton 1956). Dominant soils south of the Niobrara River in the Sandhills portion of the Refuge are Valentine (fine sand, undulating), Valentine-Rosebud (loamy fine sands, undulating) and Dune Sand (stabilized, rolling). Within the Niobrara River valley, Tripp (fine sandy loam) soils are generally found on terraces above streams, Sarpy (loamy fine sand) soils occur on bottom land along the River and streams, and little soil development exists on rough broken land and steep bluffs. Benchland north of the Niobrara River and small areas near River "breaks" consist of mostly Holt (fine sandy loam, gently undulating) and Rosebud (loamy fine sand, gently undulating) soils.

Refuge Resources, Cultural Values and Uses
Water Resources and Associated Wetlands

The Niobrara River flows from west to east across the Refuge for approximately nine miles with the channel above Cornell Dam braided and shallow with the downstream portion of the River confined to a single, narrow channel. The River is laden with sand and silt and flows swiftly at about 6-8 miles per hour. River flow is fairly stable throughout the year, averaging close to 1,000 cubic feet per second (Bentall 1990). Numerous streams and seeps along the Niobrara River valley flow intermittently or perennially. Several waterfalls exist on the Refuge where spring creeks flow over hard rock layers. River and stream flows derive almost entirely from steady groundwater seepage from the Ogallala or High Plains aquifer. Floods along the Niobrara River mostly result from winter ice jams with spring and summer floods rare. Tributary creeks, especially on the north bank, flash flood occasionally during severe summer thunderstorms.

Small areas of palustrine wooded wetlands are situated alongside the River channel and consist of various tree species including cottonwood, green ash, peachleaf willow with an understory of shrubs (sandbar willow, western snowberry), grasses, grass-like plants and forbs. Palustrine emergent wetlands vegetated with cattail, bulrush, phragmites, sandbar willow, prairie cord grass and various sedges are present on River and tributary floodplains and channels, isolated catchments and slopes, and at 12 man-made impoundments near the mouth of some feeder streams. Total water/wetland acres on the Refuge are approximately 375. Refuge wetlands are shown on Figure 3.

Ground and surface water quality are generally good. The Nebraska Department of Water Quality rated the Niobrara River as Class A for which quality will be maintained and protected. Fecal coliform counts are generally within standards for water contact recreation; however, samples exceeding health standard levels were obtained at the confluence of a River tributary on the Refuge several years ago. A new wastewater treatment plant for the city of Valentine has improved the quality of water discharged into a Niobrara River tributary.

Vegetation

Churchill *et al.* (1988) recorded 581 species of vascular plants in this area which represents 1/3 of the total known for Nebraska. Native species equal 519 while 62 are introduced. Preliminary mapping of principal plant communities of the Refuge is found in Figure 4 with general descriptions (Churchill 1988, Kaul 1990, Kantak 1995) summarized below.

Grasslands

Sandhills prairie is found atop sand dunes south and west of the River and is dominated by a mixture of tall-, mid- and short-grasses with their relative abundance differing according to variation in water holding capacity of the sandy soil as influenced by topography. Common grass species include sand and little bluestems, sand lovegrass, prairie sandreed, switchgrass, blue and hairy grama, sand dropseed, sandhill muhly, needle-and-thread, prairie junegrass and western wheatgrass. Shrubs include leadplant, prairie rose, sand cherry, poison ivy, buckbrush, and yucca. Typical forbs are hoary vetchling, purple and silky prairie clovers, sand milkweed, spiderwort, bush morning glory, prairie coneflower, lemon scurfpea and several penstemon species.

Mixed prairie is located most extensively on the flat tableland above the pine-covered slopes north of the Niobrara River where drier, sandy loam soils support shallow-rooted, drought-tolerant species. This vegetation type also occurs south of the River where appropriate soil moisture characteristics exist. Dominant grass species include little bluestem, blue grama, side oats grama, needle and thread grass, and threadleaf sedge. Silver-leaf scurf pea, prickly-pear cactus, yucca, leadplant, prairie rose, and several other forbs and shrubs are present.

Total grassland acreage on the Refuge is approximately 14,264 acres. Included in this total is an estimated 148 acres of restored native prairie.

Woodlands

Ponderosa pine savanna and forest, the eastern extension of **Rocky Mountain Coniferous Forest**, is located on rocky soils and steep eroding cliffs of the north wall of the River valley and upper slopes of canyons on the south side where there is no shading by deciduous trees. Other native woody species found on these xeric sites include choke cherry, fragrant sumac, prairie rose, sand cherry, and yucca. Herbaceous understory species are typical of adjacent prairie. Total acreage on the Refuge is approximately 3,022 acres.

Eastern Deciduous Forest covers much of the River floodplain, south wall of the River valley, and canyons of larger tributaries where a permanent water supply is accessible via the shallow floodplain water table or from permanent spring seeps. This woodland type is also found in moist slopes and draws. Bur oak are common with ironwood, American elm, green ash, basswood, and hackberry present. The understory is varied and comprised of typical mesic, shade-tolerant species. Paper birch, a characteristic species of the **Northern Boreal Forest** community, is restricted and clustered around cold springs in sheltered spring branch canyons, or near spring-fed seeps along the steep canyon walls of the south side of the River valley. Understory consists of boreal-type (cold water marsh or bog habitats) grasses, sedges and mosses. Eastern red cedar has invaded these woodland communities and is dominant in some areas. Total Refuge acreage is approximately 1,296 acres.

Tree Plantations established in the 1930's by the Civilian Conservation Corps and later by Refuge staff are located mostly in administrative areas and consist of Eastern red cedar, black and honey locusts, American elm, green and white ash, and/or ponderosa pine totaling approximately 59 acres.

Exotic and Invading vegetation found on or near the Refuge includes leafy spurge, purple loosestrife, Canada thistle, Kentucky bluegrass, smooth brome, downy brome, sweet clover, reed canary grass, phragmites, Eastern red cedar, Russian olive, black and honey locusts.

Fort Niobrara
National Wildlife Refuge
Cherry County, Nebraska

R. 27 W. R. 26 W.

Research Natural Area

River

Refuge Headquarters

Valentine

Niobrara

T. 34 N.
T. 33 N.

Refuge Boundary

Wilderness Area

Open Water

Temporarily Flooded Wetland

Seasonally Flooded Wetland

Semipermanently Flooded Wetland

Miles

0   1   2   3

MAP LOCATION

State of Nebraska

Figure 3: Wetland Map

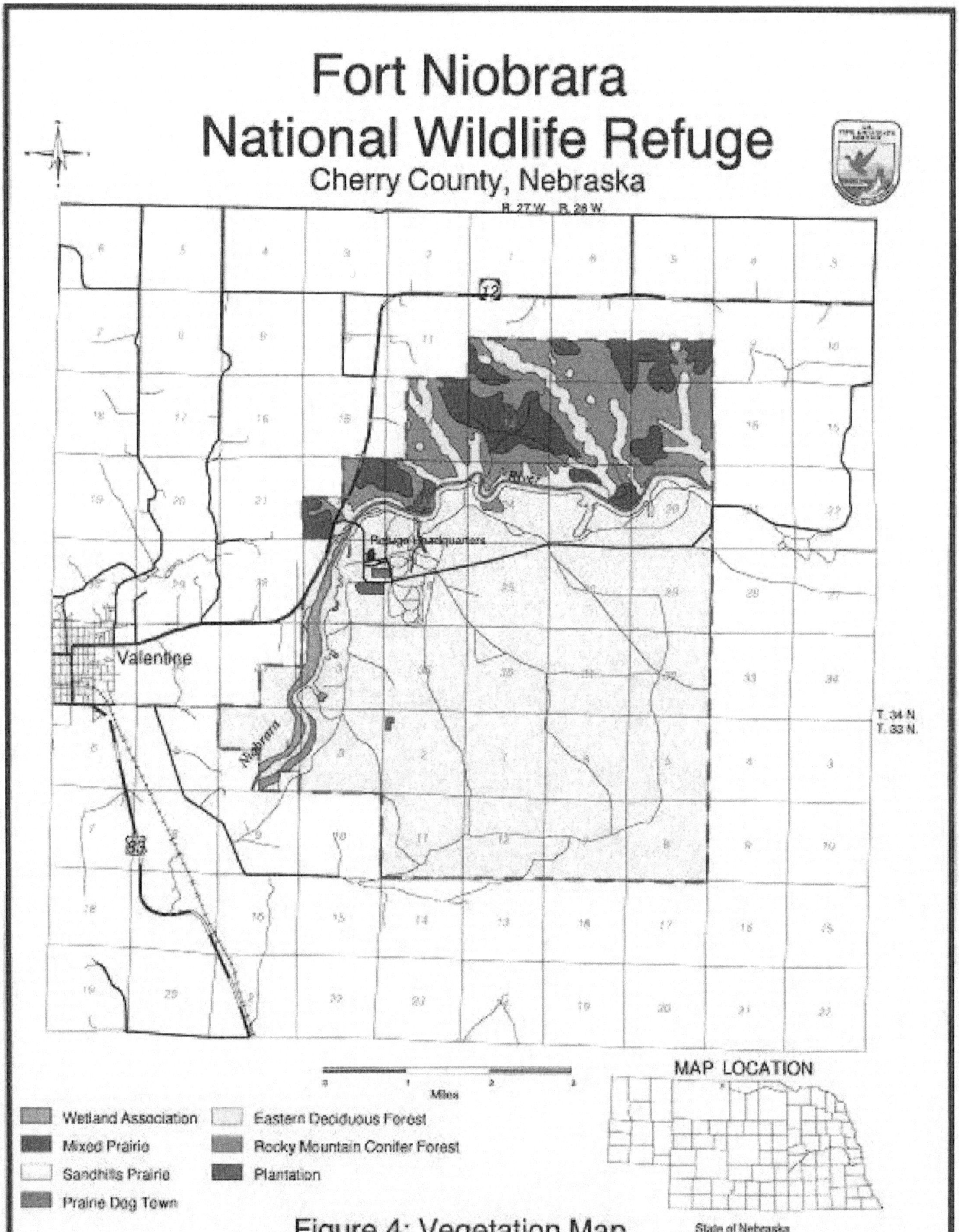

Fort Niobrara
National Wildlife Refuge
Cherry County, Nebraska

R. 27 W. R. 26 W.

Niobrara

Refuge Headquarters

Valentine

Niobrara

T. 34 N.
T. 33 N.

MAP LOCATION

0   1   2   3
Miles

Wetland Association
Mixed Prairie
Sandhills Prairie
Prairie Dog Town

Eastern Deciduous Forest
Rocky Mountain Conifer Forest
Plantation

State of Nebraska

Figure 4: Vegetation Map

Wildlife

A rich and significant diversity of wildlife species with eastern, western, northern and southern affinities as well as niches specific to the northern Great Plains inhabit the Refuge and surrounding area (Armstrong *et al. 1986,* Labedz 1990, Freeman 1990, Hrabik 1990). Population numbers vary according to amount of suitable habitat and other factors. Species lists for birds, mammals, amphibians, and reptiles are found in Appendix F.

Birds

A tremendous diversity of native birds inhabit Fort Niobrara NWR seasonally or year-round with a total of 227 species recorded since the Refuge's establishment. Approximately 48 percent of avian species have ecological affinities with the woodlands in and adjacent to the Niobrara River valley due to complex and varied habitat stratification. Dominant breeding species in the woody habitats include ovenbird, great crested flycatcher, black-and-white warbler, American redstart, black-capped chickadee, red-eyed vireo, house wren, eastern kingbird, orchard oriole, common yellowthroat, brown thrasher, and rufous-sided towhee (Sedgwick 1995). Wild turkey are common year-round residents of the woodlands while bobwhite quail are rare. Raptors likely to be seen in suitable woody habitat include Cooper's hawk, red-tailed hawk, merlin, kestrel, and rough-legged hawk. Bird species that evolved with ecological niches in grasslands comprise 11 percent of total Refuge species which is typical of the Great Plains. Species that are relatively abundant on Fort Niobrara NWR include grasshopper sparrow, western meadowlark, sharp-tailed grouse, greater prairie chicken, and upland sandpiper. Swainson's hawk, northern harrier, prairie falcon, and ferruginous hawk have grassland affinities and are present periodically in low numbers. Approximately four pair of burrowing owls inhabit the 20 acre prairie dog town and raise young each year. Thirty-two percent of Refuge bird species inhabit the Niobrara River, streams, ponds, and various wetlands. Canada goose, mallard, and wood duck are common breeders and several additional species of waterfowl, shorebirds, gulls, terns, marsh and waterbirds are present for several days or months but not often seen. Species encountered in multiple habitats and common on the Refuge include turkey vulture, mourning dove, belted kingfisher, and cliff swallow with golden eagle and osprey seen occasionally.

Peregrine falcons migrate through the area in late April and early May and in September and October. Sightings by Refuge staff are rare.

Species of management concern by the Service that have been recorded on the Refuge include burrowing owl, ferruginous hawk, northern harrier, long-billed curlew, upland sandpiper, short-eared owl, sedge wren, eastern meadowlark, dickcissel, grasshopper sparrow, Baird's sparrow, McCown's longspur, chestnut-collared longspur, red-headed woodpecker, olive-sided flycatcher, and loggerhead shrike.

Mammals

The mosaic of habitats found in this area of the northern Great Plains support an abundant diversity of native mammals. Approximately 44 of the original 52 native mammalian fauna currently inhabit the Refuge and surrounding area with seven additional species introduced or their ranges extended (Bogan and Ramotnik 1995). Bison and elk, extirpated in Nebraska in the late 1800's, were reintroduced to the Refuge in 1913. Other large native ungulates that are common include white-tailed deer and mule deer with pronghorn antelope being scarce. Black-tailed prairie dogs are found both on and off the Refuge in areas of "harder" ground but their numbers are limited. Smaller native mammals that are abundant include Ord's kangaroo rat, white-footed mouse, deer mouse, prairie vole, and western harvest mouse (Bogan 1995). Less numerous species include northern short-tailed shrew and masked shrew which are found in mesic sites. A maternity colony of big brown bats, estimated 200 individuals, inhabits the historic hay barn during the summer. Coyote are a common, widespread predator with bobcat less numerous and observed periodically in and adjacent to the River corridor. Beaver are widespread and found on the Niobrara River and numerous streams. River otter were historically common along the River but today are rarely sighted and are listed as endangered by the State of Nebraska. Species that extended their range into this area include raccoon, eastern fox squirrel, and black-tailed jackrabbit. Texas longhorn cattle, a nonnative species, was introduced to the Refuge in 1936 but had historically been trailed to Fort Niobrara Military Reservation during the late 1800's as a source of meat for Native Americans.

Amphibians and Reptiles

At least 24 species of reptiles and amphibians occur on the Refuge and/or surrounding area which is a significant proportion of the herptofauna of the northern Great Plains. Corn *et al.,* (1995) documented 16 of these species during surveys conducted 1991-1992. Species recorded in the Niobrara River, streams, and associated wetland habitat included Blanchard's cricket frog, western chorus frog, bull frog, northern leopard frog, common snapping turtle, and painted turtle. Species found in association with drier habitats include plains spadefoot, ornate box turtle, pale milk snake, bull snake, rattle snake and prairie racerunner. Woodhouse's toad, eastern yellow-bellied racer, and red-sided garter snake are widespread in distribution and common on the Refuge. A spiny softshell turtle was documented for the first time in Cherry County just off the Refuge in the Minnichaduza Creek in 1992. Yellow mud turtle, identified by the Service as a species of management concern, probably inhabits the Refuge; however, no recent sightings have been made.

Fishes

Fish communities found in the Niobrara River and its tributaries are unique to Nebraska. According to Hrabik (1990), relict populations of more typical northern, southern, eastern, and western species, as well as fishes common to the northern Great Plains, are found on the Refuge and surrounding area due to repeated glaciation and tectonic activity. The presence and distribution of these has not changed much since historic time due to the stable flows, consistent temperatures, reduced sedimentation, low dissolved solids of the Niobrara River drainage (Bentall 1990; Farrar 1983) and lack of degradation from agriculture (Case 1986). Numerous species of cyprinids, ictalurids, and percids are common. Species of concern (Nebraska List) that may inhabit waters on Fort Niobrara NWR include northern redbellied dace, earl dace, finescale dace, and blacknose shiner.

Twelve man-made ponds maintained by the Nebraska Game and Parks Commission periodically contain various species of game fish.

Threatened and Endangered Species

Several plant and animal species listed under provisions of the Endangered Species Act have been documented on the Refuge and/or in the surrounding area.

Bald eagles migrate through the area during the spring and fall and also spend the winter (late October-early April) along the Niobrara River. Winter populations average 5-7 with as many as 15 eagles recorded on the Refuge in some years. Wintering eagles depend on suitable night and severe weather roosts in sheltered timber stands located close to food sources (Peterson 1986). Roost trees on Fort Niobrara NWR are mostly mature cottonwoods with open structure and stable limbs located along the shores of the Niobrara River. No eagles nest on the Refuge; however, nesting has been documented several miles east at the confluence of the Niobrara and Keya Paha Rivers since 1996 (J. Dinan pers. comm.). Eagle mortality due to pesticide poisoning (Famphur), gunshot, and electrocution has been documented in the area with actions taken to reduce its occurrence (law enforcement, education, removal or modification of source) annually.

Whooping cranes migrate through the area in April and October. One adult whooping crane was sighted with approximately 100 sandhill cranes resting in native prairie north of Fort Niobrara on October 21, 1997. The most recent sighting of whooping cranes on the Refuge was made in October, 1993 when two adult cranes spent several days roosting and feeding on shallow, sparsely vegetated segments of the Niobrara River above Cornell Dam.

Piping plovers are occasionally sighted on the Refuge during spring and fall migrations.

Most of the exposed sandbar habitat on the Refuge is located above Cornell Dam with sandbars downstream usually exposed in July and August.

Threatened and endangered plants and animals documented in the area, but not documented on the Refuge, include blowout penstemon, western prairie fringed orchid, American burying beetle, and the interior population of the least tern.

Cultural and Paleontological Resources

Numerous significant cultural and paleontological, remains exist on the Refuge. The following summaries were taken from Cultural Resource Inventory And Assessment For Selected Areas Within Fort Niobrara National Wildlife Refuge, Valentine, Nebraska: A Final Report by Osborn 1979.

Paleontologic resources of the Niobrara River valley are unusually rich with 17 distinct fossil sites excavated on the Refuge within the wilderness area. Two fossil beds of the lower Pliocene and upper Miocene epochs provided the non-articulated skeletons and bone fragments of more than 20 extinct mammalian species including three-toed horses, camels, antelopes, rhinoceroses, rodents, and rabbits.

Archaeological remains collected in this area suggest short-term occupation by prehistoric and historic aboriginal groups for hunting and gathering. Artifacts date back through several cultures to the Paleo-Indian period of 7,500-11,500 years ago and include scattered flint chips, projectile points, other stone tools, animal bone fragments, charcoal pieces, and pottery pieces. Aboriginal occupation of this region documented in various expeditions of the middle and late 1800's was by the Dakota Sioux, Ponca, and Pawnee.

Military history of the area began in the late 1870's with the restriction of Sioux Indian tribes to the Great Sioux reservation in Dakota Territory (now western South Dakota) and establishment of Fort Niobrara Military Reservation. The Fort was established in 1879 to monitor Sioux activity and control operations of cattle rustlers and horse thieves. "Long-horned" cattle trailed from Texas were distributed to the Sioux, and the Fort served as a market for locally furnished goods and services. Soldiers were dispatched to several skirmishes although no major battles or events occurred. The Fort was closed in 1906 and retained by the War Department as a remount station until 1911 when a portion was transferred to the Department of Agriculture, Bureau of Biological Survey to be used as a preserve and breeding ground for native birds. A hay shed, constructed in 1897 by the Army, remains on the Refuge and is listed on the National Register of Historic Places.

Euro-American settlement of the Sandhills began in the late 1870's and 1880's and corresponded with the strong cattle market provided by the Military Fort. The railroad (Fremont, Elkhorn, and Missouri Valley) reached Fort Niobrara in 1883 resulting in the development of the town of Valentine. Homesteading was further encouraged by the Fort's ready market for local farm produce and labor. Several saw and flour mills were in operation along the Niobrara River by the mid-1880's. Homesteading and farming grew during the 1880's but were challenged by drought and recession in the 1890's. The 1904 Kinkaid Act encouraged more settlement; however, the Sandhills was nearly the last of the Great Plains to be homesteaded. Population in the area increased and peaked during World War I with elevated commodity prices but steadily declined to current levels (Miller 1990).

Socio-Economic and Political Environment

The Refuge is located in Cherry County approximately three miles east of the city of Valentine, the County seat and biggest city in the County with a population of approximately 2,800 (see Figure 1). Cherry County is the largest County in Nebraska with a total area of approximately 6,013 square miles. Rural population in the County is very sparse due to large ranch sizes. Predominate land-use in the County is native prairie grazing and haying with less than 10 percent of the acreage cropped or irrigated (Miller 1990). Family-owned ranching is the primary source of income in the county, although income generated from tourism is increasing. According to the County and City Data Book (U.S. Bureau of Census, 1994), for the year 1989, the median family income for Cherry County was $22,902, the median household income was $18,962 and the per capita income was $10,758. The percentage of households, for the same year, with annual income levels below $15,000 was 37.8 percent. The number of families with income below the poverty level was 286 and the number of persons was 1,386. According to the same source, Cherry County minority population (excluding women) accounted for only .4 percent of the total population (218 persons out of 6,336 in the 1992 Cherry County population).

Access to the Refuge is by Nebraska Highway 12 and a County maintained gravel road and bridge. Major highways traversing the County are US Highway 83 (north/south) and US Highway 20 (east/west). The nearest airport with scheduled passenger service is in North Platte located 136 miles south of Valentine.

Neighboring jurisdictions of Fort Niobrara include the National Park Service (Niobrara National Scenic River), Nature Conservancy (Niobrara Valley Preserve), Nebraska Game and Parks Commission (Merritt Reservoir Recreation Area, Smith Falls State Park, Bowring Ranch, Cowboy Trail, Valentine Fish Hatchery, several Wildlife Areas), Middle Niobrara Natural Resource District (Brewer Bridge Recreation Site), U.S. Forest Service (Nebraska National Forest), and Bureau of Land Management (several small tracts).

Public Uses

Public use of the Refuge occurs year-round with the greatest amount of visitation documented from mid-May to mid-October. Activities include wildlife/wildland observation, photography, interpretation/education, picnicking, hiking, floating the Niobrara River, fishing and periodic special events. A more detailed look at current levels of use can be found in the Environmental Assessment on Appendix H. NEPA Documentation, under the Current Management (No Action) Alternative discussion.

Special Management Areas
Special Legislated Designations
Wilderness Area
Definition of Wilderness

The Wilderness Act of 1964 (Public Law 88-577 [16 U.S.C. 1131-1136]) defines wilderness as follows: "A wilderness, in contrast with those areas where man and his works dominate the landscape, is hereby recognized as an area where the earth and its community of life are untrammeled by man, where man himself is a visitor who does not remain. An area of wilderness is further defined to mean in this Act an area of undeveloped Federal land retaining its primeval character and influence, without permanent improvements or human habitation, which is protected and managed so as to preserve its natural conditions and which (1) generally appears to have been affected primarily by the forces of nature, with the imprint of man's work substantially unnoticeable; (2) has outstanding opportunities for solitude or a primitive and unconfined type of recreation; (3) has at least 5,000 acres of land or is of sufficient size as to make practicable its preservation and use in an unimpaired condition; and (4) may also contain ecological, geological, or other features of scientific, educational, scenic, or historical value."

Principles Governing the Management of Wilderness Areas

Manage wilderness as a distinct resource with inseparable parts.
1. Manage the use of other resources and activities within wilderness in a manner compatible with the wilderness resource.
2. Allow natural processes to operate freely within wilderness.
3. Attain the highest level of primeval wilderness character within legal constraints.
4. Preserve wilderness air and water quality.
5. Produce human values and benefits while preserving wilderness.
6. Preserve outstanding opportunities for solitude or a primitive and unconfined recreation experience in each wilderness.
7. Control and reduce the adverse physical and social impacts of human use in wilderness through education or minimum regulation.
8. Favor wilderness-dependent activities when managing wilderness use.
9. Exclude the sight, sound, and other tangible evidence of motorized or mechanical transport wherever possible within wilderness.
10. Remove existing structures and terminate uses and activities not essential to wilderness management or not provided for by law.
11. Accomplish necessary wilderness management work with the "minimum tool."
12. Establish specific management direction with public involvement, in a Management Plan for each wilderness.
13. Harmonize wilderness and adjacent land management activities.
14. Manage wilderness with interdisciplinary scientific skills.
15. Manage special provisions provided for by wilderness legislation with minimum impact on the wilderness resource.

A 4,635 acre portion of the Refuge was designated as wilderness on October 19, 1976. This area includes a portion of the Niobrara River Valley as it straddles the River and the timbered bench land interspersed with native prairie north of the River. Designated wilderness equals 3,810 acres in one single unit. The remaining 825 acres include portions of four other habitat units and approximately five miles of Niobrara River corridor.

Section 4 (b) of the Wilderness Act of 1964 reads as follows: "Except as otherwise provided in this Act, each agency administering any area designated as wilderness shall be responsible for preserving the wilderness character of the area and shall so administer such area for such other purposes for which it may have been established as also to preserve its wilderness character. Except as otherwise provided in this Act, wilderness areas shall be devoted to the public purposes of recreational, scenic, scientific, educational, conservation, and historical use."

The Fort Niobrara Wilderness is managed according to the Wilderness Act of 1964 which requires wilderness areas to be managed in a natural condition with opportunities for solitude or a primitive and unconfined type of recreation.

The major area serves as a winter pasture for the buffalo herd; the Niobrara River corridor is fenced separately and has not been grazed for several years. The remainder of the area included in other habitat management units receives grazing use by elk and Texas longhorns. Due to use by Bison and the status of private land adjoining the Wilderness, it is necessary to maintain the boundary fence, control wild fires, and monitor and move the bison herd. Previously existing fire trails and rustic bridges are utilized for access by horseback and limited service access by motorized equipment necessary for fence maintenance and wildfire suppression.

Public use of the main portion of the Wilderness Area to the north of the River is primarily by hikers or horseback, largely for wildlife observation. Day-use is permitted, with public access by foot, horseback, or cross-country ski. The primary public users of the Niobrara River corridor portion of the Wilderness Area are River floaters, who access the area for day-use by canoe or inflatable inner tubes on the River, or by hikers on the Fort Falls Nature Trail. Virtually all of the Niobrara River used by the public on the Refuge is inside the Wilderness Area, as the Wilderness boundary is only a few hundred yards downstream from the launch point.

Wild and Scenic River
Congressional Declaration of Policy
The Wild and Scenic Rivers Act of 1968 ([Public Law 90-542, as amended], [16 U.S.C. 1271-1287]) states that: "It is hereby declared to be the policy of the United States that certain selected rivers of the Nation which, with their immediate environments, possess outstandingly remarkable scenic, recreational, geologic, fish and wildlife, historic, cultural, or other similar values, shall be preserved in free-flowing condition, and that they and their immediate environments shall be protected for the benefit and enjoyment of present and future generations. The Congress declares that the established national policy of dam and other construction at appropriate sections of the rivers of the United States needs to be complemented by a policy that would preserve other selected rivers or sections thereof in their free-flowing condition to protect the water quality of such rivers and to fulfill other vital national conservation purposes."

Designation of Sections of the
Niobrara River as Wild and Scenic
In Section 3(a) of the Wild and Scenic Rivers Act Congress states: "The following rivers and the land adjacent thereto are hereby designated as components of the national wild and scenic rivers system: "and in subsection 117 we read: "NIOBRARA, NEBRASKA. – (A) The 40-mile segment from Borman Bridge southeast of Valentine downstream to its confluence with Chimney Creek and the 30-mile segment from the River's confluence with Rock Creek downstream to the State Highway 137 bridge, both segments to be classified as scenic and administered by the Secretary of the Interior. That portion of the 40-mile segment designated by this subparagraph located within the Fort Niobrara National Wildlife Refuge shall continue to be managed by the Secretary through the Director of the United States Fish and Wildlife Service."

Review Requirements for Early Designations and Management Plans
Regarding management plans for designated wild and scenic rivers, the Wild and Scenic Rivers Act further states: "(1) For rivers designated on or after January 1, 1986, the Federal agency charged with the administration of each component of the National Wild and Scenic Rivers System shall prepare a comprehensive management plan for such River segment to provide for the protection of the River values. The plan shall address resource protection, development of lands and facilities, user capacities, and other management practices necessary or desirable to achieve the purposes of this Act. The plan shall be coordinated with and may be incorporated into resource management planning for affected adjacent Federal lands. The plan shall be prepared, after consultation with State and local governments and the interested public within three full fiscal years after the date of designation. Notice of the completion and availability of such plans shall be published in the Federal Register; (2) For rivers designated before January 1, 1986, all boundaries, classifications, and plans shall be reviewed for conformity within the requirements of this subsection within 10 years through regular agency planning processes."

Seventy-six miles of the Niobrara River which includes the nine-mile portion on the Refuge was included in the Wild and Scenic River System in 1991.

Research Natural Area
A relatively dense stand of ponderosa pine (approximately 200 acres in size) located within the Wilderness Area, was established as a Research Natural Area in 1960.

National Recreational Trail System
Five miles of the Niobrara River on the Refuge has been included in the National Recreational Trail System since 1982.

National Historic Building
The "hay barn" built in 1897 and the only building remaining of the historic military Fort Niobrara is registered as a National Historic Building.

National Register of Historic Places
Fort Niobrara was nominated to the National Register of Historic Places.

Management Direction

Refuge Management Direction: Goals, Objectives, and Strategies/Projects

Refuge Goals and Objectives

The mission and purposes of the National Wildlife Refuge System, the purpose(s) for which a refuge was established, and the existence of a wild and scenic River corridor and a designated wilderness area within the Refuge boundaries are the primary references for setting Refuge goals and objectives. The ecosystem priorities provide a secondary reference for setting Refuge goals and objectives.

Refuge goals are qualitative statements that define what outputs and outcomes a refuge must achieve to satisfy the System's mission and purposes as well as the refuge's purpose(s). Refuge objectives are benchmarks indicating progress toward achieving the mission, purposes and goals.

Fort Niobrara NWR goals and objectives are listed below. These goals and objectives were developed during the developmental stages of this Plan and refined, updated, and merged with each revision during the planning process of the Draft Comprehensive Conservation Plan and Environmental Assessment.

The goals and objectives were the benchmarks used for the development of the Preferred Alternative from among the management actions discussed in the Alternatives presented in the Draft Comprehensive Conservation Plan and Environmental Assessment (see Appendix H for more information on the alternatives considered during the draft stages of this Plan).

The Refuge planning team spent considerable time defining habitat and other objectives to further describe management actions needed to meet Refuge goals. They are presented in this Plan to provide a logical step-down from the broad purpose and mission statements to concrete management decisions.

Interrelationships of Goals and Objectives

The Refuge goals and objectives are presented separately for ease of understanding and reference. They are not, however, independent of each other. The goals and objectives and the resources and activities discussed are completely interrelated in spatial, ecological, and management considerations.

The habitat goals and objectives are the primary criteria which refuge managers will use to guide their efforts and evaluate successes. Goals and objectives for habitat, wildlife, threatened and endangered species, interpretation and recreation, and ecosystem provides additional information for managers to refine specific actions and to help in evaluating success of habitat management and use of the Refuge by the public. In order for refuge managers to achieve the mission of the Refuge fully, these objectives need to be understood holistically and applied in combination, each being a critical part of the Refuge vision.

P   Habitat Management

Goal: - Preserve, restore, and enhance the unique diversity of upland and riparian plant communities and associated water resources representative of the physiographic regions described as Sandhills Prairie, Mixed Prairie, Rocky Mountain Coniferous Forest, Eastern Deciduous Forest, and Northern Boreal Forest within the Northern Great Plains to ensure their rarity, richness, and representativeness is sustainable into the future.

The Niobrara River, numerous tributary streams, and associated riparian habitat will be maintained. Cornell Dam will be maintained to provide shallow-braided River and sandbar habitat upstream. Twelve ponds formed by damming tributary streams will continue to be held at full capacity throughout most of the year for use by waterfowl and other birds, bison and elk, and fish rearing under cooperative agreement with the Nebraska Game and Parks Commission. Breached impoundments in the wilderness area will be returned to their natural state. Nearly all of the River and associated habitat will continue to be fenced to control access by bison, elk, and, if reintroduced, bighorn sheep.

The Service will remove Texas longhorn cattle from the Refuge within one to two years of completion of this Plan. The Service will disburse the animals that compose this herd between the Wichita Mountains NWR and a non-profit organization willing to continue maintaining the genetic integrity of the herd through a management system similar to the one currently in use at the Refuge. Wichita Mountains NWR, whose purpose is to preserve the genetic integrity of another herd of these animals, will receive those animals from the Refuge herd that they request based on genetic makeup of the animals. The Service will then support or facilitate the creation of a non-profit organization to manage the remaining herd, preferably in the City of Valentine, Cherry County or State of Nebraska. The last option for disbursing the herd will be through public auction.

Efforts to improve the woodland community will focus on reduction of cedars and regeneration of native woodland species through the use of prescribed fire and other forest management practices. Management will ensure that an adequate number of mature trees are maintained for winter roosting use by bald eagles.

The Service will continue its integrated pest management program. A combination of biological, mechanical, and/or chemical control methods will continue to be used to reduce the presence of purple loosestrife and leafy spurge. Cedar control efforts will increase through the use of prescribed fire and mechanical methods. Management efforts will be implemented to reduce the presence invasive cool season grasses, sweet clover, Russian olive, and other exotic/invasive species.

Grassland Objective: Maintain the approximate 14,264 acres of Sandhill Prairie and Mixed Prairie vegetation communities in early through late successional stages to meet nesting, brooding, feeding, and/or protective cover requirements of various grassland dependent birds, fenced animals and other wildlife. Species composition on a minimum of 90 percent of the grasslands will be middle-to-late successional stage and consist of 75-85 percent grasses, 5-10 percent grass-like plants, 5-10 percent forbs, and 5 percent shrubs (dominant species as described by Kaul and Rolfsmeier 1993, Schneider *et al.* 1996, USDA Soil Conservation Service 1983). Vegetation structure will exist in a range of heights and densities with complete visual obstruction to an average height of six inches in the fall on a minimum of 50 percent of the grassland acreage (Prose 1985; Prose 1987). A minimum of 50 percent of the grasslands will not have planned burning or grazing during the native bird breeding season (April 15 - July 15).

Reduce vehicle trails on the Refuge. Identify main access trails to be maintained and discontinue use of other trails. Complete minimum trail maintenance required for Refuge vehicle access (i.e., mulch with native prairie hay).

Stabilize and encourage revegetation of blowouts located on or adjacent to boundary fence, main access trails, etc. Allow other blowouts to exist in a natural state if they provide suitable habitat for blowout penstemon.

Ponderosa Pine Savanna/Woodland Objective: Manage the approximate 3,022 acres of Rocky Mountain Coniferous Forest community to provide nesting, brooding, feeding and/or protective cover requirements of various native birds, fenced animals, and other wildlife. Approximately 85 percent of the acreage will be maintained as savanna and consist of 70 percent grasses, 10 percent grass-like plants, 5 percent forbs, 5 percent shrubs, and 10 percent trees with the remaining acreage managed as a woodland/forest. Species composition to manage for will be based on descriptions by Kaul and Rolfsmeier 1993, Schneider *et al.* 1996, USDA Soil Conservation Service 1983. A minimum of 50 percent of this community type will not have planned grazing or burning during the native bird breeding season (April 15 - July 15).

Riparian Eastern Deciduous/Northern Boreal Forest

Objective: Maintain and preserve the approximate 1,296 acres of Eastern Deciduous Forest/Northern Boreal Forest riparian community to provide nesting, brooding, feeding and/or protective cover requirements of various native birds and other wildlife. Species composition to manage for will be based on descriptions by Kaul and Rolfsmeier 1993, and Schneider *et al.* 1996. Habitat diversity will be enhanced by managing for a mix of trees (size and age classes with a minimum of 10 percent mature trees), and well-developed shrub and herbaceous layers. Strips of woodlands (150 acres) in habitat units utilized by fenced animals will be protected to the extent necessary to ensure regeneration. A minimum of 50 percent of this community type will not have planned grazing or burning during the native bird breeding season (April 15 - July 15).

Niobrara River and Associated Wetlands Objectives:

Restore and maintain the approximate 375 acres of the Niobrara River and associated wetlands with emphasis on maintaining streambed quality, stream bank stability, water flow, water temperature, and quality. Use existing data on the Niobrara River water flow, quality (sediment, nitrate, pollutants) and water temperature as minimum baseline levels and repeat at five year intervals. Ensure vegetation adjacent to the River and streams are adequate to minimize erosion, dissipate water energy and trap sediments.

Exotic and Invading Species Objective: Prevent

additional exotic plant species from becoming established and reduce the occurrence, frequency and stand density of existing invading and exotic vegetation. Target level of combined total of invading and exotic plant species is less than 5 percent of species composition. Invading and exotic plant species to manage include leafy spurge, purple loosestrife, Canada thistle, Kentucky bluegrass, smooth brome, downy brome, sweet clover, reed canary grass, eastern red cedar, Russian olive, and phragmites.

Reduce the presence of nonnative tree species in Refuge plantations by allowing natural degeneration to occur. Future replantings/plantings will include only native tree and shrub species.

P   Wildlife

Goals: Preserve, restore, and enhance the ecological diversity and abundance of migratory and resident wildlife with emphasis on native birds. Maintain representative breeding herds of nationally significant animals under reasonably natural conditions.

Between 200-350 bison (depending on herd genetic viability needs) and 70-100 elk will be managed on the Refuge under reasonably natural conditions. Bighorn sheep might be reintroduced to the Refuge and allowed to grow to a herd of 50 if this introduction is deemed feasible and in accordance with the future Bighorn Sheep Management Plan currently being prepared by the Nebraska Game and Parks Commission. Texas longhorns will no longer be managed at Fort Niobrara. In accordance with Service policy, animal numbers above winter population levels will be transferred to Native American Tribes, other refuges, sold, or donated annually. Limited Refuge hunts may be used as a tool periodically to reduce the elk and, if reintroduced, bighorn sheep populations. Sex and age ratios of the herds will approximate historic free-ranging herds. Bison, elk, and bighorn sheep populations will be managed as "open" herds with introductions or exchanges made periodically to maintain the genetic integrity of the herds and minimize the negative effects of inbreeding. Sufficient monitoring of the herds will be accomplished to ensure genetics and health of the animals are maintained and herd levels are at or below desired numbers.

Bison, elk, and, if reintroduced, bighorn sheep herds will have access to nearly all of the grasslands and ponderosa pine savanna habitats with the addition of 8-11 miles of big game fence. Some interior fence will be removed so that herds have a more natural and open movement pattern. Prescribed fire, water, and salt will be used to influence habitat use. The prescribed fire program will increase with up to 1,000 acres treated annually to invigorate native prairie, influence big game use, control cedars, and encourage regeneration of unique forest types. Other annual management actions will include one or more years of rest on approximately 10 percent of the acreage and suppression of all wildfires. A Habitat Management Plan will be developed and an adaptive management approach will be used to measure achievement toward the grassland habitat objectives.

A large ungulate herd will consume and/or remove by trampling an estimated 3,400 - 5,900 AUMs of forage a year which is approximately 16 to 28 percent of total plant production, leaving approximately 72 to 84 percent of the vegetation for plant vigor and use by other wildlife (Waller *et al.* 1986, USDA Natural Resources Conservation Service 1996). Exhibition herds and government horses will be supplemented during the winter as conditions warrant with approximately 40 tons of prairie hay harvested from Valentine NWR.

Maintaining long-term population genetic variability of the bison, elk, and bighorn sheep herds, which affects population fitness or health, will be addressed through population size, sex, and age ratio and addition of animals from other populations. Elk and bighorn sheep will be maintained below minimum population levels; therefore, periodic introductions of animals from other populations will be accomplished to minimize inbreeding. Maintaining the bison herd at 350 animals along with sex and age ratio of historic herd will provide the effective population size required for maintaining levels of genetic variability that commensurate with accepted standards of conservation biology (Berger 1996, Berger and Cunningham 1994). Should the bison herd level exist below 350, periodic introduction will be needed to minimize inbreeding.

In addition to implementing habitat management actions that improve and maintain the diverse native plant communities, the Service will consider and implement management regimes that meet various native bird requirements. Biological monitoring of native birds and other wildlife will increase to better document population trends and effects of management.

Refuge acreage inhabited by prairie dogs will be allowed to expand to a manageable size. Population and disease monitoring actions will be implemented. Prairie dogs will be excluded from areas where their presence creates a safety hazard or conflicts with management objectives.

Alternative summer roosting habitat will be provided for the maternity colony of big brown bats currently using the historic barn. The barn will then be appropriately sealed to prevent further degradation.

Prairie Grouse Objective: Maintain a five-year average density of one prairie grouse lek/1.4 sq. mile with an annual target of 100 sharp-tailed grouse and 65 prairie chicken breeding males in the grasslands (approximately 12,271 acres) south and east of the Niobrara River (USFWS, unpublished Refuge data).

Native Birds Objective: Maintain or increase breeding and migration use on Fort Niobrara by Species of Management Concern, U.S. Fish and Wildlife Service, Region 6, including northern harrier, ferruginous hawk, upland sandpiper, long-billed curlew, burrowing owl, short-eared owl, red-headed woodpecker, loggerhead shrike, dickcissel, lark bunting, grasshopper sparrow, chestnut-collared longspur, eastern meadowlark, and other habitat sensitive migratory birds such as western meadowlark, bobolink, clay-colored sparrow, belted kingfisher, willow flycatcher, and yellow-breasted chat. Monitor and document migration use by peregrine falcons as it occurs. Use existing data as minimum baseline levels and implement monitoring procedures that provide an index to overall species richness/diversity and document population trends of selected species over a five year period.

Bison and Elk Objective: Preserve and maintain breeding populations of bison and elk with age and sex composition approximating historic herds. Implement management actions that maintain or increase levels of genetic variability to assure viable, sustainable populations according to accepted standards of conservation biology (Berger 1996, Berger and Cunningham 1994). This objective is intended not as an end in itself but as a means to attain the Refuge's goals and objectives for native avian species while conserving essential populations of these important prairie ungulates.

Incrementally remove some interior fence where feasible and construct 8-11 miles of big game boundary fence.

Rocky Mountain Bighorn Sheep Objective: Reintroduce, if feasible and in accordance with the State's future Bighorn Sheep Management Plan, Rocky Mountain bighorn sheep to the Refuge to restore an indigenous species into its historic range and aid in habitat management goals.

Prairie Dog Objective: Allow the expansion of the existing black-tailed prairie dog town in the Refuge to a manageable size to enhance Refuge biological diversity and attain stated goals and objectives for native and migratory avian species.

Other Indigenous Wildlife Objective: Ensure the diversity and abundance of other indigenous mammals, reptiles, amphibians, fish, and invertebrates continues. Use existing data as minimum baseline levels and monitor periodically to document population trends. (Bogan, 1995)

P   Threatened and Endangered Species

Goal: Contribute to the preservation and restoration of threatened and endangered flora and fauna that occur or have historically occurred in the area of Fort Niobrara NWR.

In addition to continuing to provide for wintering bald eagle use, the Service will conduct an American burying beetle survey, introduce blowout penstemon into suitable habitat for this species, and continue to provide migration habitat for whooping cranes, plovers, and terns in the braided River channel habitat upstream of Cornell Dam.

Blowout Penstemon Objective: Evaluate the Refuge for blowout penstemon habitat. If suitable habitat exists, establish plants in at least two sites

Bald Eagle Objective: Maintain a minimum of 10 percent of the woodlands within the Niobrara River corridor in mature or old-growth timber with an open and discontinuous canopy to provide undisturbed roosting habitat for wintering populations of bald eagles. Monitor and document eagle use on the Refuge and mortality in the area.

Whooping Crane, Piping Plover, and Least Tern Objective: Maintain the shallow braided River habitat above Cornell Dam for use by whooping cranes, piping plovers, and least terns during migration. Keep use areas free from human disturbance. Monitor and document migration use by whooping cranes, piping plover, and least terns as it occurs.

American Burying Beetle Objective: Determine if American burying beetles inhabit the Refuge. Implement appropriate management strategies if a population exists.

P   Interpretation and Recreation

Goal: Provide the public with quality opportunities to learn about and enjoy the ecological diversity, wildlands, wildlife, and history of the Refuge in a largely natural setting and in a manner compatible with the purposes for which the Refuge was established.

River Use

The Service will address overcrowding on the portion of the Niobrara River that flows along the designated Wilderness Area of the Refuge on summer weekends as a result of people floating the River by developing, with participation from other interested parties, a detailed River Management Plan within two years. This overcrowding could be affecting not only Federal Trust Resources but the recreational experience of Refuge visitors that seek a wild and scenic river and wilderness experience. In the interim, no new outfitters will be issued permits to launch canoes or tubes on the Refuge. River use on weekends in the summer will be capped at 1998 levels.

Data collection during a social carrying capacity study of the River conducted in 1998 along with future monitoring of River use, habitat, wildlife, erosion, and other factors will be used to set upper limits of use for summer weekends during the summer, and the remainder of the year. Actions to be taken when peak use levels have been reached will be defined in detail.

A user fee of $2.00 per vessel per day or $25.00 per year that was implemented in 1998 will be continued. Monies collected from the fee program have been used to pump rest rooms, for signs, for costs related to collection, law enforcement and other related costs. The Service will make adjustments to the user fee as necessary to ensure that a safe and quality experience is provided to the public.

Bans on possession of alcohol, high volume radios (normally known as boom boxes), or any device capable of shooting or directing a projectile or liquid at another person to include, but not limited to, water balloons, high pressure water guns (normally known as water cannons), paint ball guns, potato guns, and sling shots will be implemented. No more than five tubes will be allowed to be tied together, and River floating will only be allowed downstream of Cornell Dam. River floaters will be encouraged to follow a code of ethics developed by the Niobrara Scenic River Council.

The Service's Regional Dam Safety Officer will continue to inspect Cornell Dam periodically to ensure compliance with applicable laws, policies, directives, and technical recommendations governing Federal safety of dams. Furthermore, this Officer will provide technical assistance should determination be made that the Dam is no longer safe and needs to be removed.

Hunting and Fishing

Limited Refuge hunts may be used as a tool periodically to reduce elk and, if reintroduced, bighorn sheep populations.

The Service will allow fishing on the Niobrara River and Minnichaduza Creek. Special events, such as youth fishing day, will continue.

Other Public Uses

The Service will seek funds to construct and staff a new environmental education/visitor center to improve environmental education and interpretation of wildlife, cultural, and historic resources on the Refuge. A Site Plan, being developed, will include a concept design for an environmental education/visitor center. The Site Plan will also contain suggestions for improving the existing visitor center until such time as a new center is constructed.

Wildlife/wildland observation opportunities will be expanded and include an access point for hiking and horseback riding in the Wilderness Area and construction of a trail to a scenic overlook of the Niobrara River Canyon.

Viewing of bison and elk will continue to be available year round in an exhibition habitat unit. Current facilities and wildlife observation and photography uses will remain open. Access to the main herds will be allowed through a concessionaire during peak public use periods, mainly the summer months.

Cultural and Paleontological Resources

The Service will develop a Cultural Resource/ Paleontological Management Plan. The Plan will include Refuge-wide cultural resource inventory and paleontological resource inventory strategies. It will also include increased interpretation, protection, and education about the cultural and paleontological resources on the Refuge. The historic hay shed will be protected from further degradation by sealing the building and relocating the bat colony.

Interpretation, Wildlife Observation and Photography, and Environmental Education Objectives: Provide visitors with quality interpretation, environmental education, wildlife observation and photography opportunities.

Ensure a safe, quality river-floating experience on the Wild and Scenic Niobrara River that follows the standards of the National Wild and Scenic Rivers Act, National Wildlife Refuge System and maintains the integrity of the Fort Niobrara Wilderness Area.

Protect and interpret Refuge cultural and paleontological sites.

Fishing Objective: Provide opportunities for warm water fishing in the Niobrara River and Minnichaduza Creek.

Hunting Objective: Offer ethically sound, limited and strictly controlled hunting opportunities for elk and, if reintroduced, for bighorn sheep to facilitate removal of herd excess.

P   Ecosystem (Partners)

Goal: Promote partnerships to preserve, restore, and enhance a diverse, healthy, and productive ecosystem of which the Fort Niobrara and Valentine NWR's are part.

Ecosystem Objectives/Strategies for the Fort Niobrara/Valentine NWR Complex: Support the National Scenic River, the National Park Service and other management entities to meet desired future conditions of the Niobrara Scenic River.

Support the Sandhills Management Plan through Partners for Wildlife Program to enhance wildlife habitat on private lands.

Support use of Refuges as research areas for relevant natural resource studies. Conduct applied research on management of threatened and endangered plant and animal populations.

Develop an effective outreach program that results in two wildlife habitat/public use projects completed annually with nongovernmental organizations.

Develop greater cooperation with state and local governments that result in completion of at least two projects annually. Projects are to benefit area wildlife resources or enhance public use opportunities such as fish rearing in Refuge ponds.

Use this Plan to help in marketing Refuge needs through grant writing and networking with other entities.

Support the National Scenic River; coordinate and cooperate as appropriate with River management partners including the National Park Service, Natural Resource Districts, etc., to meet desired future conditions of the Niobrara Scenic River and related resources.

Implementation and Monitoring

Funding and Personnel
Staffing Needed to Implement This Plan

The following Staff Chart shows current staff and proposed additional staffing needed to fully implement this Plan. If all positions were filled, the Refuge Complex would be able to carry out all aspects of this Plan to a high standard. If some positions are not filled, all aspects of this Plan may not be able to be completed or those completed may be done over a longer period of time. Staffing and funding are expected to come over the 15-year life of this Plan. Positions marked with an * are shared with Valentine NWR. The new refuge operations specialist position would be responsible for the Partners For Wildlife Program, Holt Creek WMA, and Tower WMA. (✔ = filled; ✘ = vacant)

Position	Current	Proposed
Refuge Manager*	✔	✔
Refuge Operations Specialist	✔	✔
Refuge Operations Specialist*	✘	✔
Outdoor Recreation Planner*	✘	✔
Law Enforcement Officer*	✔	✔
Administrative Officer*	✔	✔
Office Automation Clerk*	✔	✔
Wildlife Biologist	✔	✔
Bio. Technicians/Seasonal (2)	✘	✔
Heavy Equipment Operator*	✔	✔
Maintenance Worker (2)	✔	✔
Maintenance Laborer/Seasonal(2)	✘	✔
Asst. Fire Management Officer*	✔	✔
Range Technician (Fire)	✔	✔
Firefighters/Seasonal (3)	✔	✔

Funding Needed to Implement This Plan

Currently, a large backlog of maintenance needs exists on the Refuge. The needs are recorded in a national Maintenance Management System (MMS). In 1997, under current management plans, the backlog for Fort Niobrara NWR was $3,830,000. Most of these needs would also need to be met under this Plan. A synopsis of these needs is listed below:

Vehicles and Equipment	$ 708,000
Fences, Corrals, and Wells	$ 943,000
Water Control Structures and Dikes	$ 197,000
Roads and Bridges	$ 292,000
Public Use Facilities	$ 709,000
Buildings and Maintenance Facilities	$ 821,000
Residences	$ 160,000
TOTAL	**$3,830,000**

The System uses another database, the Refuge Operating Needs System (RONS), to document proposed new projects that will implement a Plan, implement ecosystem or federally listed species goals or meet legal mandates. The total cost to implement this Plan is $3,908,000. A synopsis of these needs is listed below:

Biological Monitoring and Studies	$ 110,000
Habitat Management	$ 443,000
Possible Reintroduction of Bighorn Sheep	$ 20,000
Resource Protection	$ 393,000
Public Education and Recreation	$ 742,000
Environmental Education Center	$2,200,000
TOTAL	**$3,908,000**

CCP Implementation and Step-down Management Plans

This section is intended to provide additions to the Refuge Management Direction section above. Where possible, time frames are delineated, specific strategies and actions are stated, and a list of projects is presented.

The Service has traditionally used a Refuge Manual to guide field station management actions. The policy direction provided through the Manual has been used to prepare annual work schedules, budget, land management plans (i.e., prescribed fire, grazing, haying), sale of surplus animals, biological monitoring, public use, safety, and other aspects of public land management in the Refuge.

This CCP is intended as a broad umbrella plan that provides general concepts, specific wildlife and habitat objectives, federally listed species, public use, and partnership objectives. Depending on the Refuge needs, these may be very detailed or quite broad. The purpose of step-down management plans is to provide greater detail to managers to implement specific actions authorized by the CCP. Step-down management planning is the formulation of detailed plans that describe management activities necessary to implement strategies identified in this CCP. Step-down plans describe the specific management actions to be followed, "stepping down" from general goals, objectives, and strategies

Step-down plans provide a detailed assessment and strategy that is based upon and complement the Fort Niobrara NWR CCP. While many potential topics for step-down plans exist, the most critical ones include Habitat Management, Wilderness Management Plan, Wildlife Inventory, River Use, and Public Use Plans. The objectives and implementation strategies in each step-down plan will dovetail with each other and the CCP.

The Refuge, within a reasonable amount of time, will prepare all the necessary Step-down Management Plans to attain the goals and objectives described in this CCP: for example, a Niobrara River Use Management Plan (in approximately two years), a Public Use Plan, and a Fishing Management Plan.

Habitat Management and Monitoring

A step-down Habitat Management Plan for the Refuge will include an assessment of the current status and distribution of plant communities and wildlife habitat, and a prescription and strategy for habitat management that will achieve long-term habitat, wildlife population, and ecosystem goals for the Refuge and surrounding landscape. The habitat prescription, or objectives (how much of what kind located where), will be based on: (1) Refuge resource priorities identified locally, regionally, and nationally; (2) potential contribution of a site to resource priorities (rare species/communities, other priority species, ecosystem function); and (3) historical, current, and potential plant community types for particular site in the Refuge area.

The habitat objectives will be combined with an implementation strategy to produce a Habitat Management Plan. Habitat strategies will include site-specific manipulations to achieve site objectives and evaluations of the manipulations. Manipulations include standard practices of wetland, grassland, or forest restoration and management, prescribed burning, moist soil and water management, and allowing natural ecosystem processes to dictate the ecological community type. The cycle time for some of the habitat management strategies is very long-term. However, many habitat management actions may be initiated immediately, if staff and dollars are available.

An overall Habitat Management Plan will be developed to guide all aspects of habitat management including but not limited to: annual grazing by large animal herds, the use of prescribed fire, prairie dog colony growth and management, other wildlife (i.e., bison, elk, bighorn sheep), and rest required by habitat for native birds.

The Refuge staff will develop and implement an updated Wilderness Management Plan, taking into consideration wilderness values (in compliance with the Wilderness Act), Service policy, adjoining land uses, and comments and concerns addressed in the CCP, and providing a basis for other related plans.

Develop and implement a monitoring program that assesses landscape and individual habitat variables such as vegetation species composition, grassland structure (density, height) and ground cover, woodland structure (percent tree, shrub, herbaceous, bare ground, canopy cover; basal area, diameter and height, age, snags), and utilization by large ungulates. Procedures will be completed annually or at three- to five-year intervals depending upon available staff and technique requirements.

Fire-funded personnel will develop and implement a fire effects monitoring program that integrates with other Refuge biological monitoring activities.

Wildlife Management and Monitoring

Continue to conduct sharp-tailed grouse and greater prairie chicken lek counts. Obtain prairie grouse lek data from the Nebraska Game and Parks Commission and harvest data from Valentine NWR for general comparison to Fort Niobrara NWR population trends.

Implement nongame bird monitoring techniques in the grasslands and woodlands to document population trends and species richness/diversity.

Conduct a graduate research project that documents native bird response pre- and post-change in management from current habitat management emphasizing fenced animals to a more natural, less-controlled management regime emphasizing native birds. Conduct a graduate research project that compares native bird use within the River corridor during high and low public use periods.

Continue to maintain a general observation log of bird sightings to document presence/absence, relative abundance, and use areas.

Maintain the bison herd at its current winter population level of 350 animals. The population level may vary between 200-350 animals depending on habitat, native bird, and bison herd genetic viability needs and objectives. Surplus bison will be disbursed to Native American Tribes (in accordance with Service policies and agreements), donations to tax supported entities, other Service herds, with the remaining going to public auction.

Continue to implement fenced animal management practices that ensure long-term health and survival of the herds. Actions to be taken include periodic animal introductions to minimize inbreeding, disease testing and vaccination, and mineral supplementation. Geneticists and health care professionals will be consulted on a regular basis regarding recommended practices and/or requirements.

Consult with population ecologists and/or bison geneticists regarding genetic management recommendations/options for the Fort Niobrara NWR bison gene pool. Collect and analyze bison genetic material to establish baseline for future comparison.

Conduct seasonal population surveys of bison, elk, and, if reintroduced, bighorn sheep to document numbers by age and sex, mortality, natality, and general health/condition. Annually test excess animals for various diseases and ensure that animals introduced to the Refuge meet all health test requirements. Complete genetic testing of the herds at intervals recommended by geneticists to assess if fenced animals are being managed appropriately.

Allow the black-tailed prairie dog colony to increase to a manageable size. Manage predator populations and vegetation to hold prairie dogs to designated acreage with other control measures implemented as necessary.

Relocate big brown bat colony by sealing historic hay barn and maintain/enhance natural artificial bat roost sites.

Complete surveys of small mammals, reptiles, amphibians, and fish at five year intervals.

Threatened and Endangered Species Management and Monitoring

Identify habitat suitable for blowout penstemon and, if it exists, introduce plants at a minimum of two sites with assistance from University of Nebraska-Lincoln. Implement management actions that result in a sustainable population of blowout penstemon.

Conduct an American burying beetle survey.

Continue to conduct biweekly eagle surveys October-April. Monitor bald eagle mortality and submit carcasses to the National Health Lab for analysis. Implement appropriate protection measures. Conduct an aerial survey of the Niobrara River every two years to document proximity of or possible nesting activity on the Refuge.

Conduct periodic surveys of the Niobrara River to document use or non-use by whooping cranes, least terns, and piping plovers. Document habitat selection, usage, and distribution. Implement appropriate protection measures.

Interpretation and Recreation Resources Management and Monitoring

Niobrara River Use Management and Monitoring

The Service will prepare a Fishing Plan to provide a basis for special regulations concerning this use on the Niobrara River and Minnichaduza Creek. Sport fishing regulations will follow those of the Nebraska Game and Parks Commission except that taking of frogs, turtles, and minnows will be prohibited. No motorized boats will be permitted.

The Service will develop and implement a Niobrara River Management Plan, within two years of the issuance of this Plan, and will invite the participation of other Federal and State agencies, local and county government representatives, River outfitter groups, environmental groups, and other groups or individuals.

This Management Plan will ensure that this use is compatible with the six wildlife-dependent uses of the System, it protects the natural resources of this riparian corridor, and it preserves the characteristics for which it was designated a Wild and Scenic River area. Furthermore, this Management Plan will also ensure that the wilderness area that this stretch of the River crosses is not adversely impacted by recreational uses. This Management Plan will be subordinate to the statutes and requirements of the Wild and Scenic River Act and the Wilderness Act that have jurisdiction over the Niobrara River as it flows through the Fort Niobrara NWR.

Bans on possession of alcohol, high volume radios (normally known as boom boxes), or any device capable of shooting or directing a projectile or liquid at another person to include, but not limited to, water balloons, high pressure water guns (normally known as water cannons), paint ball guns, potato guns, and sling shots will be implemented. No more than five tubes will be allowed to be tied together, and River floating will only be allowed downstream of Cornell Dam. River floaters will be encouraged to follow a code of ethics developed by the Niobrara Scenic River Council.

During the period of development of this River Management Plan, the Service will not increase the number of Special Use Permits issued until the environmental effects of this use are assessed, and the Management Plan can be implemented and incorporated into the Refuge goals and strategies. The Service will continue to study and monitor the environmental effects of the current uses of the Niobrara River by River floaters and other to riparian and upland Refuge resources. With the River Management Plan, the refuge manager will have specific information and data on which to base sound scientific decisions for the future management of this important resource.

Permits will be required for Scout, church, educational and other such groups floating the River that want to tie more than five tubes together.

Public Use Management and Monitoring

The Service will seek funds to construct and staff a new environmental education/visitor center to improve environmental education and interpretation of wildlife, cultural, and paleontological resources on the Refuge. A Site Plan, being developed, will include a concept design for the new center and suggestions for improving the existing visitor center until such time as a new center is constructed. Interim projects to complete include updating exhibits and broaden themes to include wildlife and their habitats; unusual ecological diversity; cultural and paleontological resources; and management. Investigate the possibility of a shared environmental education/visitor center with the Nebraska Game and Parks Commission, National Park Service, Forest Service, The Nature Conservancy, Valentine Chamber of Commerce, and others.

Fort Falls Nature Trail will be maintained for public enjoyment. The self-guiding interpretative brochure will be updated.

Provide a wilderness access point for hiking and horseback riding. Use will be limited to three groups at one time with a maximum group size of 5 horses or 10 people. An outfitter, selected by lottery, will be allowed to guide a maximum of one group per day and will pay a fee and/or a certain percent of gross receipts to the Refuge.

Construct a trail to a scenic overlook of the Niobrara Canyon and provide appropriate interpretation.

Establish a concessionaire contract to view and interpret the bison and elk herds during the summer tourist season.

Continue to improve the main auto tour route by resurfacing with gravel and closing/revegetating numerous side trails. Expand the display habitat unit and provide more natural and aesthetic setting by removing and/or relocating fence.

Staff and expand the hours of operation of the visitor/ environmental education center.

Maintain the visitor center, information kiosks/leaflet dispensers, education panels, other signs, picnic tables, and rest rooms in clean, orderly, well cared for condition.

Update Refuge brochures to new Service standards.

Develop a Refuge specific environmental education curricula for teachers to use independently.

Continue to prepare periodic news releases and send to newspapers, radio, and television to inform the public about Refuge events and issues.

Ecosystem (Partners) Management and Monitoring

Maintain a contaminant database on the Niobrara River. Cooperate with various entities (i.e., USFWS Ecological Services; State of Nebraska) to collect data on flow, temperature, sediment, nitrates, and other pollutants.

Work with Boy Scouts, Girl Scouts, 4-H, National Audubon Society, Niobrara Outfitters Association, Fort Niobrara Natural History Association, Cherry County Schools, and others to complete at least two wildlife/public use projects a year.

Contact and seek cooperation/partnership with universities regarding a paleontological inventory of the Refuge. Consider acquisition of nondevelopment easements from willing adjacent landowners to protect Refuge integrity.

Contact and seek cooperation/partnership with International Safari Club, Rocky Mountain Elk Foundation, and others regarding large ungulate projects. Participate on NPS working group to develop general management plan for Niobrara National Scenic River to include biological monitoring at an ecosystem level.

Work with USDA Natural Resources Conservation Service (NRCS), Nebraska Game and Parks Commission, U.S. Forest Service, National Park Service, Middle Niobrara Natural Resource District, and others to complete at least two wildlife habitat and/or public use projects a year.

Continue to cooperate with NRCS on soil mapping and data digitizing of Service lands, review and comment on revised National Range and Pasture Handbook, participation in range judging contests, range condition surveys, and provide technical assistance on wildlife/wildland concerns.

Continue to cooperate with the Nebraska Game and Parks Commission on wildlife surveys and fish rearing in Refuge ponds.

Write a minimum of three grant proposals a year to seek outside funding.

Work with State of Nebraska Veterinarian, Nebraska Game and Parks Commission, National Park Service, and others on management of fenced and free-ranging elk.

Work with veterinarians for the State of Nebraska, neighboring states, USDA-APHIS, and private sector on disease/health issues, regulations, etc.

Cultural and Paleontological Resources Management and Monitoring

A Cultural Resource and Paleontological Resources Management Plan to provide a basis for research and enactment of special regulations concerning protection of these resources on the Refuge will be prepared by the Service.

Complete a Refuge-wide cultural resource survey and develop a management plan based on results. The Plan will include management strategies for the historic hay shed based on future objectives and possible uses (i.e., storage, environmental education) for the designated historic site.

Relocate the big brown bat colony away from the historic barn and complete appropriate bat proofing and renovations according to future management plans.

Conduct a Refuge-wide paleontological inventory.

Display and interpret cultural and paleontological specimens.

Partnership Opportunities

Only with public support will the Service succeed in its mission. That support comes through outreach: fostering education, understanding, and communicating the importance of the Service commitment to protecting habitat upon which wildlife depends. Outreach includes a broad array of activities and services focused on building relationships and communication. The Service is committed to getting its message to both traditional and nontraditional groups.

The Service continues to seek opportunities to work with various conservation groups, State and local agencies, and private corporations and organizations to advance the Fort Niobrara NWR mission. Generally, the Fort Niobrara NWR and Valentine NWR Complex will strive to combine resources with appropriate entities to expedite and carry out planning projects.

The Service will continue to cooperate with Nebraska Game and Parks Commission for rearing of brood fish in tributary impoundments. Agreements in place for wildlands wildfire suppression efforts, excess bison for the Inter Tribal Bison Council, participation in the Niobrara Council, and other common coordination efforts with other agencies and landowners will continue. The Service will continue to uphold and develop partnerships with the National Park Service on many issues, including use and protection of the wild and scenic portion of the Niobrara River, and will seek to increase partnerships with others as well.

The Service will seek to develop outside funding sources and support for implementing some aspects of this Plan. Examples would be construction of the environmental education center, big game fence, and possible acquisition of nondevelopment easements on the Refuge's north and west borders.

Partnerships require extensive time to coordinate, develop, and nurture. This must be accounted for in the development of budgets and annual work plans.

Monitoring and Evaluation

Adaptive management is a flexible approach to long-term management of biotic resources that is directed over time by the results of ongoing monitoring activities and other information. Biological management techniques and specific objectives will be regularly evaluated in light of monitoring results and other new information. These periodic evaluations will be used over time to adapt both the management objectives and techniques to better achieve management goals.

Monitoring is an essential component of this Plan, and specific monitoring strategies have been integrated into the goals and objectives outlined above. All habitat management activities will be monitored to assess whether the desired effect on wildlife and habitat components has been achieved. Monitoring the number of breeding pairs and the reproductive parameters of native and neotropical bird species will follow established Federal and statewide protocols, at a minimum. Baseline surveys will be established for other species of wildlife for which existing or historical numbers are not well known. It also will be important to begin studies to monitor the response of wildlife to increased public use in the form of observation and environmental education.

This Plan is designed to be effective for a 15-year period. Periodic review of the Plan will be required to ensure that established goals and objectives are being met and that the Plan is being implemented as scheduled. To assist this review process, an ongoing monitoring and evaluation program will be implemented, focusing on issues involving public use activities, wildlife-dependent recreational activities, and habitat and population management.

Monitoring of public use programs will involve the collection and compilation of visitation figures and activity levels. In addition, research and monitoring programs will be established to assess the impacts of public use activities on wildlife and wildlife habitat. The Refuge will strive to establish the collection of baseline data on all wildlife populations. This data will be used to update existing records of wildlife species using the Refuges, their habitat requirements, and seasonal use patterns. This data will also be used to evaluate the effects of public use and habitat management programs on wildlife populations.

Refuge habitat management programs will be continually monitored for positive and negative impacts on wildlife and wildlife habitat, and to determine if these management tools are helping to meet Refuge goals and objectives. Monitoring will focus on habitat changes and the associated changes in the wildlife community.

The establishment of a monitoring and evaluation program is important to support the direction of the Plan. The information gathered through this program will provide necessary data to ensure that goals and objectives established in the Plan are being met.

The Service will conduct, at the very minimum, the following monitoring actions:

! wildlife herd monitoring sufficient to maintain age and sex ratios, health, genetic diversity, and annual excess removal
! native bird species monitoring to supply trend information on prairie grouse, species of management concern, grassland neotropical migrants, biodiversity trend indexes
! monitor habitat parameters (i.e., vegetation composition and structure, tree canopy, etc.) sufficient to ensure that habitat objectives are being measured and determined successful according to a Habitat Management Plan and the adaptive management process
! water quality parameters on the Niobrara River
! federally listed species monitoring, American burying beetle survey
! monitoring/research on River use through the Wilderness Area and it's wildlife and social impacts
! monitoring fire effects as part of the prescribed burning program.

Plan Amendment and Revision

This Refuge CCP is a dynamic Plan. While it will serve as a guide for overall Refuge direction, it will be adjusted to consider new and better information, ensuring that Refuge activities best serve the intended purpose for which this Refuge was established and the mission of the National Wildlife Refuge System. The CCP will be reviewed every five years, and monitored continuously to ensure the management actions developed support the goals and objectives of the Fort Niobrara NWR.

This Plan will be informally reviewed by Refuge staff while preparing annual work plans and updating the Refuge Management Information System (RMIS) database. It may also be reviewed during routine inspections or programmatic evaluations. Results of the reviews may indicate a need to modify the Plan. The monitoring of objectives is an integral part of the Plan, and management activities may be modified if desired results are not achieved. If minor changes are required, the level of public involvement and associated NEPA documentation will be determined by the project leader. This CCP will be formally revised at least every 15 years.

Appendix A. Glossary
(including acronyms and abbreviations)

Adaptive Management: Refers to the process in which policy decisions are implemented within a framework of scientifically driven experiments to test predictions and assumptions inherent in management plans. Analysis of results help managers to determine whether current management should continue as is or it should be modified to achieve desired conditions.

Alternative: 1) A reasonable way to fix the identified problem or satisfy the stated need (40 CFR 1500.2); 2) Alternatives are different means of accomplishing refuge purposes and goals and contributing to the System mission (Draft Service Manual 602 FW 1.5).

AUM or Animal Unit Month: A measure of the quantity of livestock forage. Equivalent to the forage sufficient to sustain a 1,000 pound animal (or 1 cow/ calf pair) for 1 month during the normal range season.

Biological Control: The use of organisms or viruses to control weeds or other pests.

Biological Diversity: The variety of life and its processes, including the variety of living organisms, the genetic differences among them, and the communities and ecosystems in which they occur.

CCP or Plan: Comprehensive Conservation Plan

Compatible Use: A wildlife-dependent recreational use or any other use of a refuge that, in the sound professional judgment of the Director, will not materially interfere with or detract from the fulfillment of the mission of the System or the purposes of the refuge.

Comprehensive Conservation Plan, Plan, or CCP: A document that describes the desired future conditions of the refuge and provides long-range guidance and management direction for the refuge manager to accomplish the purposes of the refuge, contribute to the mission of the System, and to meet other relevant mandates.

EA or Environmental Assessment: A concise public document, prepared in compliance with the National Environmental Policy Act, that briefly discusses the purpose and need for an action, alternatives to such action, and provides sufficient evidence and analysis of impacts to determine whether to prepare and Environmental Impact Statement (EIS) or a Finding of No Significant Impact (FONSI).

Ecosystem: Dynamic and interrelated complex of plant and animal communities and their associated nonliving environment.

Ecosystem Approach: Protecting or restoring the natural function, structure, and species composition of an ecosystem, recognizing that all components are interrelated.

Endangered Species (Federal): A plant or animal species listed under the Endangered Species Act that is in danger or becoming extinct throughout all or a significant portion of its range.

Endemic Species: Plants or animals that occur naturally in a certain region and whose distribution is relatively limited to a particular locality.

Exotic and Invading Species (Noxious Weeds): Plant species designated by Federal or State law as generally possessing one or more of the following characteristics: aggressive or difficult to manage; parasitic; a carrier or host of serious insects or disease; or nonnative, new, or not common to the United States, according to the Federal Noxious Weed Act (PL 93-639), a noxious weed is one that causes disease or has adverse effects on man or his environment and therefore is detrimental to the agriculture and commerce of the United States and to the public health.

Fauna: All the vertebrate and invertebrate animal species of a determined area.

Federal Trust Resources: A trust is something managed by one entity for another who holds the ownership. The Service holds in trust many natural resources for the people of the United States of America as a result of Federal Acts and Treaties. Examples are species listed under the Endangered Species Act, migratory birds protected by the Migratory Bird Treaty Act and other international treaties, and native plant or wildlife species found on the System.

Flora: All the plant species of a determined area.

FONSI or Finding of No Significant Impact: A document prepared in compliance with the National Environmental Policy Act, supported by an environmental assessment, that briefly presents why a Federal Action will have no significant effects on the human environment and for which an Environmental Impact Statement, therefore, will not be prepared (40 CFR 1508.13).

Fragmentation: The process of reducing the size and connectivity of habitat patches.

Goal: Descriptive, open-ended, and often broad statement of desired future conditions that conveys a purpose but does not define measurable units (Draft Service Manual 620 FW 1.5).

Habitat: Suite of existing environmental conditions required by an organism for survival and reproduction. The place where an organism typically lives.

Habitat Restoration: Management emphasis designed to move ecosystems to desired conditions and processes, and/or to healthy forestlands, rangelands, and aquatic systems.

Integrated Pest Management: Methods of managing undesirable species, such as weeds, including: education; prevention, physical or mechanical methods of control; biological control; responsible chemical use; and cultural methods.

Issue: Any unsettled matter that requires a management decision; i.e., a Service initiative, opportunity, resource management problem, threat to the resources of the unit, conflict in uses, public concern, or the presence of an undesirable resource condition (Draft Service Manual 602 FW 1.5).

Migration: The seasonal movement from one area to another and back.

Mission Statement: A succinct statement of a unit's purpose and reason for being.

Mitigation: Measures designed to counteract environmental impacts or to make impacts less severe.

Monitoring: The process of collecting information to track changes of selected parameters over time.

National Wildlife Refuge (Refuge): A designated area of land or water or an interest in land or water within the System, including national wildlife refuges, wildlife ranges, wildlife management areas, waterfowl production areas, and other areas (except coordination areas) under Service jurisdiction for the protection and conservation of fish and wildlife. A complete listing of all units of the Refuge System may be found in the current "Annual Report of Lands Under Control of the U.S. Fish and Wildlife Service."

National Wildlife Refuge System, Refuge System, or System: Various categories of areas that are administered by the Secretary for the conservation of fish and wildlife, including species that are threatened with extinction; all lands, waters, and interests therein administered by the Secretary as wildlife refuges; areas for the protection and conservation of fish and wildlife that are threatened with extinction; wildlife ranges; game ranges; wildlife management or waterfowl production areas.

Native Species: Species that normally live and thrive in a particular ecosystem.

Neotropical Migratory Bird or Neotropicals: A bird species that breeds north of the U.S. - Mexican border and winters primarily south of this border.

NEPA: National Environmental Policy Act of 1969

No Action Alternative: An alternative under which existing management would be continued.

Non-Priority Public Uses: Any use other than a compatible wildlife-dependent recreational use.

NWR: National Wildlife Refuge

Objective: A concise statement of what will be achieved, how much will be achieved, when and where it will be achieved, and who is responsible for the work. Objectives are derived from goals and provide the basis for determining management strategies, monitoring refuge accomplishments, and evaluating the success of the strategies. Objectives should be attainable and time-specific and should be stated quantitatively to the extent possible. If objectives cannot be stated quantitatively, they may be stated qualitatively (Draft Service Manual 602 FW 1.5).

Opportunities: Potential solutions to issues.

Planning Team: A team or group of persons working together to prepare a document, such as this Comprehensive Conservation Plan. Planning teams are interdisciplinary in membership and function. Teams generally consist of a planning team leader; refuge manager and staff; biologists; staff specialists or other representatives of Service programs, ecosystems or regional offices; and other Federal and State governmental agencies as appropriate.

Plant Community: An assemblage of plant species unique in its composition; occurs in particular locations under particular influences; a reflection or integration of the environmental influences on the site – such as soils, temperature, elevation, solar radiation, slope, aspect, and rainfall; denotes a general kind of climax plant community, i.e., ponderosa pine or bunchgrass.

PILT: Payment-in-Lieu-of-Taxes

Prairie Grouse: Both sharp-tailed grouse and prairie chickens.

Preferred Alternative: This is the alternative determined (by the decision maker) to best achieve the Refuge purpose, vision, and goals; contributes to the Refuge System mission, addresses the significant issues; and is consistent with principles of sound fish and wildlife management. The Service's selected alternative at the Draft CCP stage.

Prescribed Fire: The skillful application of fire to natural fuels under conditions of weather, fuel moisture, soil moisture, etc., that allows confinement of the fire to a predetermined area and produces the intensity of heat and rate of spread to accomplish planned benefits to one or more objectives of habitat management, wildlife management, or hazard reduction.

Prescribed Natural Fire: A fire ignited by natural processes (usually lightning) and allowed to burn within specified parameters of fuels, weather, and topography to achieve specified resource management objectives.

Priority Public Uses: Compatible wildlife-dependent recreational uses (hunting, fishing, wildlife observation and photography, and environmental education and interpretation) are the priority general public uses of the System and shall receive priority consideration in refuge planning and management.

Proposed Action: The Service's proposed action for Comprehensive Conservation Plans is to prepare and implement the CCP.

Public: Individuals, organizations, and groups; officials of Federal, State, and local government agencies; Indian tribes; and foreign nations. It may include anyone outside the core planning team. It includes those who may or may not have indicated an interest in Service issues and those who do or do not realize that Service decisions may affect them.

Public Involvement: The process by which interested and affected individuals, organizations, agencies, and governmental entities are offered an opportunity to become informed about, to express their opinions and participate in the planning and decision making process of Service actions and policies. In this process, these views are studied thoroughly and thoughtful consideration of public views is given in shaping decisions for refuge management.

Purposes of the Refuge: The purposes specified in or derived from the law, proclamation, executive order, agreement, public land order, donation document, or administrative memorandum establishing, authorizing, or expanding a refuge, refuge unit, or refuge sub-unit.

ROD or Record of Decision: A concise public record of decision prepared by the Federal agency, pursuant to the National Environmental Policy Act, that contains a statement of the decision, identification of all alternatives considered, identification of the environmentally preferable alternative, a statement as to whether all practical means to avoid or minimize environmental harm from the alternative selected have been adopted (and if not, why they were not adopted), and a summary of monitoring and enforcement where applicable for any mitigation (40 CFR 1505.2).

RMIS: Refuge Management Information System database

Refuge: short for Fort Niobrara National Wildlife Refuge

Refuge Operating Needs System or RONS: National database containing the unfunded operational needs of each refuge. Projects included are those required to implement approved plans, and meet goals, objectives, and legal mandates.

Refuge Use: Any activity on a refuge, except administrative or law enforcement activity carried out by or under the direction of an authorized Service employee.

Refuge Purposes: The purposes specified in or derived from the law, proclamation, executive order, agreement, public land order, donation document, or administrative memorandum establishing, authorizing, or expanding a refuge, a refuge unit, or refuge subunit (Draft Service Manual 602 FW 1.5)

Refuge Revenue Share Program or RRSP: provides payments to counties in lieu of taxes using revenues derived from the sale of products from refuges (see Appendix G: Refuge Revenue Sharing Act of 1935, as amended (16 U.S.C. 715s) for more details).

Reserve Acres: Lands that were Public Domain lands when first withdrawn to create the Refuge.

Riparian: Refers to an area or habitat that is transitional from terrestrial to aquatic ecosystems; including streams, lakes, wet areas, and adjacent plant communities and their associated soils which have free water at or near the surface; and area whose components are directly or indirectly attributed to the influence of water; of or relating to a river; specifically applied to ecology, "riparian" describes the land immediately adjoining and directly influenced by streams. For example, riparian vegetation includes any and all plant-life growing on the land adjoining a stream and directly influenced by the stream.

Secretary: short for Secretary of Interior

Service or USFWS: Short for U.S. Fish and Wildlife Service

Strategy: A specific action, tool, or technique or combination of actions, tools, and techniques used to meet refuge objectives.

Step-down Management Plan: A plan that provides the details necessary to implement management strategies identified in the CCP (Draft Service Manual 602 FW 1.5).

Sound Professional Judgement: A finding, determination, or decision that is consistent with principles of sound fish and wildlife management and administration, available science and resources, and adherence to the requirements of the Refuge Administration Act and other applicable laws.

Strategy: A specific action, tool, or technique or combination of actions, tools, and techniques used to meet unit objectives (Draft Service Manual 602 FW 1.5).

System or Refuge System: National Wildlife Refuge System

Threatened Species (Federal): Species listed under the Endangered Species Act that are likely to become endangered within the foreseeable future throughout all or a significant portion of their range.

Trust Species: Species for which the U.S. Fish and Wildlife Service has primary responsibility, including, most federally listed threatened and endangered species, anadromous fishes once they enter inland U.S. waterways, migratory birds, and certain marine mammals.

USFWS or Service: Short for U.S. Fish and Wildlife Service

Vegetation Type or Habitat Type: A land classification system based upon the concept of distinct plant associations.

Vision Statement: A concise statement of the desired future condition of the planning unit, based primarily upon the System mission, specific refuge purposes, and other relevant mandates (Draft Service Manual 602 FW 1.5).

Wetland: includes lakes, marshes, temporary wetlands, fens, rivers, and creeks but not subirrigated meadows.

Wilderness Area (or Designated Wilderness Area): An area designated by the U.S. Congress to be managed as part of the National Wilderness Preservation System (Draft Service Manual 602 FW 1.5).

Wildfire: A free-burning fire requiring a suppression response; all fire other than prescribed fire that occurs on wildlands (Draft Service Manual 602 FW 1.5).

Wildland: lands characterized by natural vegetation and landscapes where man-made structures and alterations are not evident.

Wildland Fire: Every wildland fire is either a wildfire or a prescribed fire (Draft Service Manual 602 FW 1.5).

Wildlife: Wild animals and vegetation, especially animals living in a natural, undomesticated state.

Wildlife Corridor: A landscape feature that facilitates the biologically effective transport of animals between larger patches of habitat dedicated to conservation functions. Such corridors may facilitate several kinds of traffic, including frequent foraging movement, seasonal migration, or the once in a lifetime dispersal of juvenile animals. These are transition habitats and need not contain all the habitat elements required for long-term survival or reproduction of its migrants.

Wildlife-Dependent Recreation/Wildlife-Dependent Recreational Use: A use of a refuge involving hunting, fishing, wildlife observation and photography, or environmental education and interpretation. The National Wildlife Refuge System Improvement Act of 1997 specifies that these are the six priority general public uses of the System.

Appendix B.
Bibliography

Armstrong, D.M., Choate, J.R., and Jones, J.K., Jr. 1986. Distributional patterns of mammals in the plains states. Occasional Papers of Museum of Texas Tech Univ., v.105, pp 1-27.

Aughey, S. 1880. Sketches of the physical geography and geology of Nebraska. Daily Republican Book and Job Office, Omaha. 346 pp.

Bentall, R. 1990. Streams. Pages 93-114 in A. Bleed and C. Flowerday, editors. An atlas of the Sand Hills. Resource Atlas No. 5a. Conserv. and Survey Div., Inst. Agr. Nat. Res., Univ. Nebraska, Lincoln. 265 pp.

Berger, J. 1996. Scenarios involving genetics and population size of bison in Jackson Hole. Unpublished report to Grand Teton National Park, Moose, Wyoming. 21 pp.

_____, and C. Cunningham. 1994. Bison: mating and conservation in small populations. Columbia Univ. Press, New York. 330 pp.

Bogan, M.A. and C.A. Ramotnik. 1995. Mammals. Pages 140-186 in M.A. Bogan, editor. A Biological Survey of Fort Niobrara and Valentine National Wildlife Refuges. U.S. Nat. Biol. Serv., Midcont. Ecol. Sci. Cen. 193 pp.

_____.1995. A Biological Survey of Fort Niobrara and Valentine National Wildlife Refuges. U.S. Nat. Biol. Serv., Midcont. Ecol. Sci. Cen. 193 pp.

Bragg, T.B. and A.A. Steuter. 1996. Prairie ecology - the Mixed Prairie. Pages 53-65 in Samson, F.B. and F.L. Knopf, editors. Prairie conservation: preserving North America's most endangered ecosystem. Island Press, Washington, D.C. 339 pp.

Burgett, G.R. and R.K. Nickel. 1999. Archeological Overview and Assessment for Lacreek, Fort Niobrara and Valentine National Wildlife Refuges. Midwest Archeological Center, National Park Service. 41 pp.

Case, R.M. 1986. Wetlands, wildlife part of Sandhills. I.A.N.R. Quart. 32:20-21.

Churchill, S.P., C.C. Freeman and G.E. Kantak. 1988. The vascular flora of the Niobrara Valley Preserve and adjacent areas in Nebraska. Trans. Nebr. Acad. Sci., XVI:1-15.

Corn, P.S., M.L. Jennings and R.B. Bury. 1995. Amphibians and Reptiles. Pages 32-59 in M.A. Bogan, editor. A biological survey of Fort Niobrara and Valentine National Wildlife Refuges. U.S. Nat. Biol. Serv., Midcont. Ecol. Sci. Cen. 193 pp.

Constanza, Robert, Ralph d'Arge, Rudolf de Groot, Stephen Faber, Monica Grasso, Bruce Hannon, Karin Limberg, Shahid Naeem, Robert O'Neill, Jose Paruelo, Robert Raskin, Paul Sutton, and Marjan van den Belt, *The Value of the World's Ecosystem Services and Natural Capital* in Nature, Vol. 387, May 15, 1997

Dinan, J. 1998. Wildlife biologist, Nebraska Game and Parks Commission. Personal communication.

Dobie, J.F. 1994. The longhorns. Univ. Texas Press, Austin. 388 pp.

Farrar, J. 1983. Nebraska Rivers. NEBRASKAland Magazine, Nebr. G&P Comm. 146 pp.

Freeman, P. 1990. Mammals. Pages 181-188 in A. Bleed and C. Flowerday, editors. An atlas of the Sand Hills. Resource Atlas No. 5a. Cons. and Sur. Div., Insti. Agr. Nat. Resour., Univ. Nebraska, Lincoln. 265 pp.

_____. 1990. Amphibians and Reptiles. Pages 157-160 in A. Bleed and C. Flowerday, editors. An atlas of the Sand Hills. Resource Atls No. 5a. Cons. and Sur. Div., Insti. Agr. Nat. Res., Univ. Nebraska, Lincoln. 265 pp.

Halloran, A. 1964. The heritage of the longhorn. Oklahoma Cowman 7 (9):18 & 38.

Higgins, K.F., A.D. Kruse and J.L. Piehl. 1986. Effects of fire in the northern Great Plains. SDSU Ext. Circ. EC 761. 47pp.

Hrabik, R.A. 1990. Fishes. Pages 143-154 in A. Bleed and C. Flowerday, editors. An atlas of the Sand Hills. Resource Atlas No. 5a, Cons. and Sur. Div., Inst. Agr. Nat. Res., Univ. Nebraska, Lincoln. 265 pp.

Jones, J.K., Jr., 1964. Distribution and taxonomy of mammals of Nebraska. Univ. Kansas Publ., Mus. Nat. Hist. 16:1-356.

_____., D.M. Armstrong, R.S. Hoffman, and C. Jones. 1983. Mammals of the northern Great Plains. Univ. Nebraska Press, Lincoln. 379 pp.

Kantak, G.E. 1995. Terrestrial plant communities of the Middle Niobrara Valley, Nebraska. Southwest. Nat. 40 (2):129-138.

Kaul, R.B. and S.B. Rolfsmeier. 1993. Native vegetation of Nebraska. Cons. and Sur. Div., Univ. Nebraska, Lincoln. (map 1:1,000,000).

Kaul, R.B. 1990. Plants. Pages 127-142 *in* A. Bleed and C. Flowerday, editors. An atlas of the Sand Hills. Resource Atlas No. 5. Cons. and Sur. Div., Inst. Agr. Nat. Res., Univ. Nebraska, Lincoln. 265 pp.

Knopf, F.L. 1994. Avian assemblages on altered grasslands. Studies in Avian Bio. 15:247-257.

Labedz, T.E. 1990. Birds. Pages 161-180 *in* A. Bleed and C. Flowerday, editors. An atlas of the Sand Hills. Resource Atlas No. 5a. Cons. and Sur. Div., Insti. Agr. Nat. Resour., Univ. Nebraska, Lincoln. 265 pp.

Layton, M.H. 1956. Soil survey of Cherry County, Nebraska. USDA Series 1940, No. 21. 91 pp.

Leenhouts, B. 1995. Presettlement fire and emission production estimates: a framework for understanding potential system change. Poster session paper presented at the Environmental Regulation and Prescribed Fire Conference, March 14-17, 1995, Tampa, Florida.

Miller, S.M. 1990. Land development and use. Pages 207-226 *in* A. Bleed and C. Flowerday, editors. An atlas of the Sand Hills. Resource Atlas No. 5a. Cons. and Sur. Div., Insti. Agr. Nat. Res., Univ. Nebraska, Lincoln. 265 pp.

Mitchell, L. and C. Wolfe. 1984. Prairie grouse in Nebraska. NEBRASKALand Magazine, Nebr. G & P Comm. 15 pp.

NOAA National Climatic Data Center. 1996. Local climatological data - annual summary with comparative data for Valentine, Nebraska. 8 pp.

Osborn, A.J. 1979. Cultural resource inventory and assessment for selected areas within the Fort Niobrara National Wildlife Refuge, Valentine, Nebraska: A final report. Univ. Nebraska, Lincoln. Tech. Rep. No. 79-07. 181 pp.

Peterson, A. 1986. Habitat suitability index model: Bald eagle (breeding season). U.S. Fish Wildl. Serv. Biol. Rep. 82 (10.126).

Prose, B.L. 1985. Habitat suitability index models: Greater prairie chicken (multiple levels of resolution). U.S. Fish Wildl. Serv. Biol. Rep. 82 (10.102). 33pp.

_____. 1987. Habitat suitability index models: plains sharp-tailed grouse. U.S. Fish Wildl. Serv. Biol. Rep. 82 (10.142). 31 pp.

Ruth, C. 1938. Fort Niobrara Game Preserve, Nebraska. USDA Bur. Biol. Sur. Wildl. Manag. Publ. BS-109. 6 pp.

Schneider, R.E., D. Faber-Langendoen, R.C. Crawford and A.S. Weakley. 1996. The status of biodiversity in the Great Plains: Great Plains vegetation classification. Supplemental Document I *in* W.R. Ostlie, R.E. Schneider, J.M. Aldrich, T.M. Faust, R.L.B. McKim and S.J. Chaplin. The status of biodiversity in the Great Plains. The Nature Conservancy. Arlington, VA.

Sedgwick, J.A. 1995. Occurrence, diversity, and habitat relationships of birds. Pages 60-139 *in* M.A. Bogan, editor. A biological survey of Fort Niobrara and Valentine National Wildlife Refuges. U.S. Nat. Biol. Serv., Midcont. Ecol. Sci. Cen. 193 pp.

Steuter, A.A. 1991. Human impacts on biodiversity in America: Thoughts from the grassland biome. J. Conser. Biol. 5(2):136-137.

USDA Natural Resources Conservation Service. 1996. Range Inventory Summary and Suggestive Initial Stocking Rates Based on Present Range Condition for Fort Niobrara National Wildlife Refuge. 8 pp.

USDA Soil Conservation Service. 1983. Nebraska range site descriptions and guide for determining range condition and suggested initial stocking rates. Lincoln, Nebraska.

U.S. Bureau of Census, *County and City Data Book: 1994*, 12th Edition, Washington, DC

U.S. Fish and Wildlife Service, *An Ecosystem Approach to Fish and Wildlife Conservation*, March 1994

U.S. Fish and Wildlife Service, *Fort Niobrara National Wildlife Refuge Draft Comprehensive Conservation Plan and Environmental Assessment*, April 1999, 74 pp.

Waller, S.S., L.E. Moser, and B. Anderson. 1986. A guide for planning and analyzing a year-round forage program. Univ. Nebraska Coop. Ext. Serv. EC86-113. 19 pp.

Appendix C.
Refuge Operating Needs
System (RONS) List

HQ: Fort Niobrara NWR   CD: NE03

Project no.: 99001   Type: NWR   District: NE,KS,CO,UT

     Main ecosystem: Platte/Kansas Rivers

Also includes work on Sier National Wildlifge Refuge

ACTIVITY: *MONITORING & STUDIES*   *Wildlife*

          1.a.   Surveys & Censuses

MEASURES   5 wildlife surveys will be conducted

                      5 habitat surveys will be conducted

                      0 % of survey will be off-refuge

               100

TITLE: Refuge Manager for newly acquired Sier National Wildlife Refuge

DESCRIPTION:

In 1999 the Sier National Wildlife Refuge will become part of the National Wildlife Refuge System as a result of a generous donation by the Sier family. The refuge is about 2,000 acres in size and located 90 miles from the Fort Niobrara/Valentine NWR Complex Headquarters. An on site manager, GS -11, will be hired to prepare a comprehensive conservation plan, protect refuge resources, conduct initial wildlife and habitat surveys, and manage habitat, wildlife, and public use programs.   Sound initial planning and management will insure that this generous donation of land and resources is best managed for wildlife and the public and serve as an example of how the US Fish and Wildlife Service can manage donated lands.

FUNDS NEEDED ($1000s):	One-Time	Recurring Base	First Year Need
Construction Appropriation Costs..............			
Operations: Personnel Cost..........		$58	
Equipment Cost.........	$35		
Facility Cost..........			
Services/Supplies.......	$20	$5	
Miscellaneous Costs.....	$64	$5	
TOTAL Operations Cost..	$119	$68	$187

HQ: Fort Niobrara NWR   CD: NE03

Project no.: 97001   Type: NWR   District: NE,KS,CO,UT

   Main ecosystem: Platte/Kansas Rivers

Also includes work on Valentine NWR

ACTIVITY: *MONITORING & STUDIES*   *Wildlife*

   1.a   Surveys & Censuses

MEASURES   8 wildlife surveys will be conducted

                  0 habitat surveys will be conducted

                  0 % of survey will be off-refuge

TITLE: Endangered Species

DESCRIPTION:

Valentine NWR has endangered or threatened prairie fringed orchids, blowout Penstemon and American burying beetles. The locations and abundance of these species is not known as complete surveys have not been conducted. Surveys need to be conducted to establish baselines, determine suitable habitat and management actions. The refuge could play an important role in recovery of these listed species. As information is gathered, habitat management will be altered to enhance the presence of these species. It is also possible that these species and suitable habitat are present at Fort Niobrara NWR and would be included in the assessment.

FUNDS NEEDED ($1000s):	One-Time	Recurring Base	First Year Need
Construction Appropriation Costs.................			
Operations: Personnel Cost..........			
Equipment Cost.........			
Facility Cost...........			
Services/Supplies......	$20	$5	
Miscellaneous Costs.....	$32	$3	
TOTAL Operations Cost.	$82	$8	$90

64520   Fort Niobrara NWR   NE

HQ: Fort Niobrara NWR   CD: NE03

Project no.: 96011   Type: NWR   District: NE,KS,CO,UT

    Main ecosystem: Platte/Kansas Rivers

Also includes work on Valentine NWR; Holt Creek WMA; Yellowthroat WMA

ACTIVITY: *MONITORING & STUDIES*   *Wildlife*

        1.a.   Surveys & Censuses

MEASURES   0 wildlife surveys will be conducted

              10 habitat surveys will be conducted

              10 % of survey will be off-refuge

TITLE: Consolidate Habitat Data for Complex

DESCRIPTION:

Obtain and consolidate habitat related data for Ft. Niobrara and Valentine NWRs, Holt Creek and Yellowthroat WMA's based on use of USDA-NRCS digitized soils data being developed. Overlay GIS information on habitat; obtain and incorporate new updated aerial infrared photography. With this project, Service resource management would be more efficient and effective. Without the project, Service ability to utilize new data and technology being developed by Partners including NRCS, Nebraska Game and Parks, etc, is limited.

FUNDS NEEDED ($1000s):	One-Time	Recurring Base	First Year Need
Construction Appropriation Costs...............	....		
Operations: Personnel Cost..........	............$20	....	
Equipment Cost..........	............$12		
Facility Cost..........	....		
Services/Supplies.......	............$15	............$5	
Miscellaneous Costs.....	............$10	............$5	
TOTAL Operations Cost..	............$57	............$10	............$67

> Also includes work on Valentine NWR, Yellowthroat WMA, Holt Creek WMA

ACTIVITY: *PUBLIC EDUCATION & RECREATION*   *People*

        7.a.   Provide Visitor Services

MEASURES   30,000 new visitors will be served

        30,000 existing visitors will be served

        100 % will support the top 6 priority public uses

        0 % will support non-priority public uses

TITLE: Public Information Materials

DESCRIPTION:

Provide current and adequate public education and informational leaflets including hunting and fishing, general information, nature trail, bird lists, wildlife lists, auto and nature trail leaflets for Valentine and Fort Niobrara NWRs and Yellowthroat and Holt Creek WMA's. Shortfalls in budgets have resulted in old, outdated or near-obsolete informational materials, and in limiting distribution of the materials available. No leaflets are current with the new USFWS standards Neither WMA has any kind of information leaflet. Without adequate funding, limited or no and lesser quality materials will continue to be distributed, resulting in a reduced understanding of the Service and its mission and in increased uninformed violation of rules and regulations.

FUNDS NEEDED ($1000s):	One-Time	Recurring Base	First Year Need
Construction Appropriation Costs...............			
Operations: Personnel Cost..........	$8		
Equipment Cost..........			
Facility Cost..........			
Services/Supplies.......	$40	$10	
Miscellaneous Costs.....	$10	$2	
TOTAL Operations Cost.	$58	$12	$70

64520	Fort Niobrara NWR		NE

64520　　Fort Niobrara NWR　　　　　　　　　　　　　　　NE

HQ: Fort Niobrara NWR　　　　　　　　　　CD: NE03

Project no.: 97007　　　　Type:　NWR　　　District:　NE,KS,CO,UT

　　Main ecosystem: Platte/Kansas Rivers

ACTIVITY:　*RESOURCE PROTECTION*　　　　　　　　　　　　　*People*

　　　　6.e.　Cultural Resource Management

MEASURES　　　　　1　investigations will be conducted

　　　　　　　　　20　sites will be documented

　　　　　　　　　　0　museum property items will be maintained

TITLE:　Conduct Cultural Resource Inventory at Fort Niobrara NWR

DESCRIPTION:

Fort Niobrara NWR contains numerous known or documented sites of cultural, archaeological or paleontological significance; however, no complete review of the resources exists. This project would facilitate compilation of known information, as well as inventory of non-documented areas. This project is necessary to the efficient and prudent planning and long term management of the Refuge. Failure to complete the project will result in a inability to properly implement the CMP or future management plans in an appropriate and economical manner.

FUNDS NEEDED ($1000s):	One-Time	Recurring Base	First Year Need
Construction Appropriation Costs.................			
Operations: Personnel Cost..........			
Equipment Cost..........			
Facility Cost...........			
Services/Supplies.......	$60	$5	
Miscellaneous Costs.....	$16	$3	
TOTAL Operations Cost.	$76	$8	$84

ACTIVITY: *PUBLIC EDUCATION & RECREATION*   *People*

7.a   Provide Visitor Services

MEASURES   20,000 new visitors will be served

6,000 existing visitors will be served

0 % will support the top 6 priority public uses

0 % will support non-priority public uses

TITLE: Staff Refuge Visitor Center

DESCRIPTION:

Seasonal staff will operate Visitor Environmental Education Center during peak tourist season, Mid-May through early September. With present staffing, the Visitor Center is staffed with volunteers on weekends. This project would allow better contact with the public on weekends and better service on weekdays throughout the summer.

FUNDS NEEDED ($1000s):	One-Time	Recurring Base	First Year Need
Construction Appropriation Costs.............	....		
Operations: Personnel Cost..........	....	...............$24	
Equipment Cost..........	....		
Facility Cost.........	....		
Services/Supplies.......	...............$5	...............$10	
Miscellaneous Costs	...............$9	...............$5	
TOTAL Operations Cost..	...............$14	...............$39	...............$53

64520   Fort Niobrara NWR   NE
HQ: Fort Niobrara NWR   CD: NE03
Project no.: 96001   Type: NWR   District: NE,KS,CO,UT
     Main ecosystem: Platte/Kansas Rivers

ACTIVITY: *PUBLIC EDUCATION & RECREATION*   *People*
          7.a.   Provide Visitor Services
MEASURES   20,000 new visitors will be served
                6,000 existing visitors will be served
                   95 % will support the top 6 priority public uses
                    5 % will support non-priority public uses

TITLE: Expand, improve and staff Ft. Niobrara Visitor Center / Education facility.

DESCRIPTION:

This project will enhance public education by expanding the existing Visitor Center and education facility to allow proper storage, display and interpretation of artifacts and fossils currently stored in a closed, unheated, non-climate controlled building. The project includes an addition to the interpretive wing of the existing Visitor Center building, displays, storage space, and seasonal interpretive staffing to operate the center. Without funding, the public will continue to have a diminished educational experience and will not have access to the fossils and artifacts currently in storage; the museum pieces will continue to be stored in an unsatisfactory manner.

FUNDS NEEDED ($1000s):	One-Time	Recurring Base	First Year Need
Construction Appropriation Costs...............			
Operations: Personnel Cost.........	$30	$32	
Equipment Cost..........	$10		
Facility Cost...........	$265		
Services/Supplies.......	$10		
Miscellaneous Costs.....	$33		
TOTAL Operations Cost..	$348	$32	$380

HQ: Fort Niobrara NWR   CD: NE03

Project no.: 96027b   Type: NWR   District: NE,KS,CO,UT

Main ecosystem: Platte/Kansas Rivers

ACTIVITY: *MONITORING & STUDIES*   *Wildlife*

1.a.   Surveys & Censuses

MEASURES   2   wildlife surveys will be conducted

0   habitat surveys will be conducted

0   % of survey will be off-refuge

TITLE: Conduct Wildlife and Wild Land Monitoring

DESCRIPTION:

We will monitor native grassland, wetland, riparian areas, and wildlife. One seasonal biological technician will conduct field monitoring of vegetation on the 19,122 acre Ft. Niobrara NWR. This project is critical to the managing the refuge, providing biological information for sound habitat and wildlife management, public use, and overall management planning and decision making. Without this project, critical future management decisions effecting all resources on the refuge will be made with limited biological information.

FUNDS NEEDED ($1000s):

	One-Time	Recurring Base	First Year Need
Construction Appropriation Costs...............			
Operations: Personnel Cost..........		$32	
Equipment Cost.........	$30		
Facility Cost..........			
Services/Supplies.......	$5	$5	
Miscellaneous Costs.....	$9	$3	
TOTAL Operations Cost..	$44	$40	$84

ACTIVITY: *PUBLIC EDUCATION & RECREATION*   *People*

     7.a   Provide Visitor Services

MEASURES   1,500 new visitors will be served

            1,500 existing visitors will be served

              90 % will support the top 6 priority public uses

              10 % will support non-priority public uses

TITLE: Develop public information, interpretation and access point for the Ft. Niobrara Wilderness

DESCRIPTION:

This project would develop a new all weather access point for the public adjacent to the Ft. Niobrara Wilderness Area. It would include a parking area, overlook, information center, and trail head providing access to the north portion of the Ft. Niobrara Wilderness Area and Niobrara Scenic River corridor.

FUNDS NEEDED ($1000s):	One-Time	Recurring Base	First Year Need
Construction Appropriation Costs...............	....		
Operations: Personnel Cost..........	....	....	
Equipment Cost..........	....		
Facility Cost...........	$175		
Services/Supplies.......	....	....	
Miscellaneous Costs....	$26	$15	
TOTAL Operations Cost..	$201	$15	$216

HQ: Fort Niobrara NWR   CD: NE03

Project no.: 96018   Type: NWR   District: NE,KS,CO,UT

    Main ecosystem: Platte/Kansas Rivers

ACTIVITY: *PUBLIC EDUCATION & RECREATION*   *People*

        7.a   Provide Visitor Services

MEASURES   20,000   new visitors will be served

         6,000   existing visitors will be served

           0   % will support the top 6 priority public uses

           0   % will support non-priority public uses

TITLE: Fort Niobrara History Kiosk

DESCRIPTION:

Develop, install, and maintain an informational kiosk on the Ft. Niobrara vehicle tour route to interpret the military and frontier history of Ft. Niobrara.

FUNDS NEEDED ($1000s):	One-Time	Recurring Base	First Year Need
Construction Appropriation Costs.........			
Operations: Personnel Cost.........			
Equipment Cost.........			
Facility Cost.........	$45		
Services/Supplies.......	$15	$10	
Miscellaneous Costs.....	$17	$10	
TOTAL Operations Cost.	$77	$20	$97

Appendix D.
Maintenance
Management System
(MMS) List

RMIS - Maintenance Management System (MMS)
Record View

Station: Fort Niobrara NWR   HQ: Fort Niobrara NWR

Main ecosys: Platte/Kansas Rivers

Org code: 64520   State: NE   Cong dist: NE03

Project no.: 67024   Project no. subelement: H (67024-h)

Prop desc: Big Game Corrals   Prop #: 95

Project title: Rehab deteriorated big game handling facilities, Phase H: FY-2000

Project desc: Continue rehab of deteriorated big game corrals by replacing rotted wood posts, planks, walkways, handrails with steel; all materials and design upgraded to meet OSHA and Safety guidelines. Corrals were built in 1930's, rebuilt 1950's. Project is critical to insure safety of staff working with Bison, elk, and public observing. Project is being phased and done by Service personnel to insure annual usability

Measures: Number of 1
                      structures/facilities

Cost estimate: $75   Engineering cost included in cost est: $0

Cost est date: 1999   Cost est method: Historical/Manager   FY group: 2000
                                        estimate

Backlog: $75   FY completed: FY obligations: $0
                                         Cumulative obligations: $0

Fund source: R = Resource Management   Percent complete: 0%

Other possible   o TEA21 (Refuge Roads) o Fire   o Contaminants
fund source: o TEA21 (Other)   o Quarters   o Supplemental
                 o Title V   o RecFee   o Other

Fix type: ⊙ Repair/rehab o Replace o Remove   Condition assessment: Poor

Emphasis: CHS CRP CM OI TOT   Type: DM CI TOT   Safety? ⊠ C
           100 0   0   0   100   100 0   100

           ES   WF OMB HEC IAF SDA RW FAR PED PRC TOT
Outcomes: 0   0   0   20   0   0   60 0   10   10   100

Maint code: 567 = Other Structures/Facilities

Station rank: 1   Dist rank: Reg rank: 999   Nat rank:
                                                          DOI rank: 1000

RO support needs: □ Engineering □ Contracting ⊠ Force Account □ Hold

Project notes:

Phase H: rehab runway and east pens.
NOTE: Corrals and handling facilities MUST be usable for animal handling through May, and by September: ALL rehab must be completed by prefab oe on site June - August. Any contracting of prefab, etc, must meet this need. All on site work will be done by Refuge employees (regular or seasonal) to insure meeting of this time table.

Updated 12/17/97

RMIS - Maintenance Management System (MMS)
Record View

Station: Fort Niobrara NWR   HQ: Fort Niobrara NWR

Main ecosys: Platte/Kansas Rivers

Org code: 64520   State: NE   Cong dist: NE03

Project no.: 90006   Project no. subelement: A (90006-a)

Prop desc: Cornell Dam Power plant   Prop #: 140

Project title: Remove abandoned power plant building

Project desc: Remove abandoned power plant building and facilities, asbestos panels, etc. Naturalize the site following demolition. The Service was given the Cornell Dam and abandoned power plant, adjacent to high public use area on Niobrara River. The building is barricaded to prevent access and protect the public. This project would remove a safety hazard from along the National Scenic River.

Measures: Number of buildings: 1

Cost estimate: $430   Engineering cost included in cost est: $75

Cost est date: 1989   Cost est method: Historical/Manager Estimate   FY group: 2001

Backlog: $430   FY completed: FY obligations: $0

Cumulative obligations: $0

Fund source: R = Resource Management   Percent complete: 0%

Other possible fund source:
o TEA21 (Refuge Roads)   o Fire   o Contaminants
o TEA21 (Other)   o Quarters   o Supplemental
o Title V   o RecFee   o Other

Fix type: o Repair/rehab o Replace ● Remove   Condition assessment: Poor

Emphasis:	CHS	CRP	CM	OI	TOT	Type:	DM	CI	TOT	Safety? ☒	C
	50	0	0	50	100		100	0	100		

Outcomes:	ES	WP	OMB	HEC	IAF	SDA	RW	FAR	PED	PRC	TOT
	0	0	0	20	0	40	0	0	20	20	100

Maint code: 110 = Other Buildings

Station rank: 1   Dist rank: Reg rank: 999   Nat rank: 432

DOI rank: 650

RO support needs: ☒ Engineering ☒ Contracting ☐ Force Account ☐ Hold

Project notes:

Area is posted and building is barricaded; however, break ins and vandalism have occurred in the past. Contaminant filled switch canisters were mitigated in 1995 by Electric Cooperative and FWS. Local contractor estimated $250,000+ to demolish and mitigate site in 1990. Anticipate more than one year process.

Updated 12/17/97

RMIS - Maintenance Management System (MMS)
Record View

Station: Fort Niobrara NWR   HQ: Fort Niobrara NWR

Main ecosys: Platte/Kansas Rivers

Org code: 64520   State: NE   Cong dist: NE03

Project no.: 98004   Project no. subelement:

Prop desc: Complex Communication Sys   Prop #: 144

Project title: Replace deteriorated communications wiring and components

Project desc: Replace or repair aged communications system and radio system.
System used in law enforcement work, fire management and visitor
assistance. Includes separation of radio and telephone wires to
meet telephone company requirements and enable reestablishment of
radio-telephone link.

Measures: Number of systems: 1

Cost estimate: $54   Engineering cost included in cost est: $10

Cost est date: 1999   Cost est method: Historical/Manager Estimate   FY group: 2001

Backlog: $54   FY completed: FY obligations: $0

Cumulative obligations: $0

Fund source: R = Resource Management   Percent complete: 0%

Other possible fund source:
- ○ TEA21 (Refuge Roads)
- ○ TEA21 (Other)
- ○ Title V
- ○ Fire
- ○ Quarters
- ○ RecFee
- ○ Contaminants
- ○ Supplemental
- ○ Other

Fix type: ○ Repair/rehab ◉ Replace ○ Remove   Condition assessment: Fair

Emphasis:

CHS	CRP	CM	OI	TOT	Type:	DM	CI	TOT	Safety? ☒	C
50	0	50	0	100		100	0	100		

Outcomes:

ES	WF	OMB	HEC	IAF	SDA	RW	FAR	PED	PRC	TOT
10	10	10	10	0	20	10	10	10	10	100

Maint code: 217 = Communication Systems

Station rank: 2   Dist rank: 999   Reg rank: 63   Nat rank: 286

DOI rank: 700

RO support needs: ☒ Engineering ☒ Contracting ☐ Force Account ☐ Hold

Project notes:

Includes replacing 1950's telephone lines serving FTN HQ, 1970's lines
serving VLT, and bringing physical installation up to code to permit proper
function of telecommunication and computer systems; installation of up to
date telephone answering and intercom system to serve Complex. Also includes
separation of radio and telephone wires to meet telephone company
requirements and enable reestablishment of radio-telephone link. Project may
be cost shared with Fire Program.

RMIS - Maintenance Management System (MMS)
Record View

Station: Fort Niobrara NWR   HQ: Fort Niobrara NWR

Main ecosys: Platte/Kansas Rivers

Org code: 64520   State: NE   Cong dist: NE03

Project no.: 90006   Project no. subelement: B (90006-b)

Prop desc: Cornell Dam   Prop #: 141

Project title: Rehab Cornell Dam Site

Project desc: Rehab area adjacent to Cornell Dam; stabilize deteriorated wing walls, place rip rap below raceway to prevent erosion, and restore disturbed terrain and vegetation adjacent to the dam. The Service was given Cornell Dam, immediately upstream from the main public canoe launch area on the Niobrara River. The project would stabilize and improve the appearance of an eyesore along the National Scenic River.

Measures: Number of dams: 1

Cost estimate: $202   Engineering cost included in cost est: $35

Cost est date: 1999   Cost est method: Historical/Manager Estimate   FY group: 2002

Backlog: $202   FY completed: FY obligations: $0

Cumulative obligations: $0

Fund source: R = Resource Management   Percent complete: 0%

Other possible fund source:
- ☐ TEA21 (Refuge Roads)
- ☐ TEA21 (Other)
- ☐ Title V
- ☐ Fire
- ☐ Quarters
- ☐ RecFee
- ☐ Contaminants
- ☐ Supplemental
- ☐ Other

Fix type: ⊙ Repair/rehab   ○ Replace   ○ Remove   Condition assessment: Fair

Emphasis:

CHS	CRP	CM	OI	TOT
0	0	0	100	100

Type:

DM	CI	TOT
100	0	100

Safety? ☒

Outcomes:

ES	WF	OMB	HEC	IAF	SDA	RW	FAR	PSD	PRC	TOT
0	0	0	0	0	50	0	0	10	40	100

Maint code: 434 = Low Hazard (Inventory) Dams

Station rank: 2   Dist rank: 999   Reg rank: 999   Nat rank:

DOI rank: 300

RO support needs: ☒ Engineering ☒ Contracting ☐ Force Account ☐ Hold

Project notes:

Updated 5/7/99

RMIS - Maintenance Management System (MMS)
Record View

Station: Fort Niobrara NWR   HQ: Fort Niobrara NWR

Main ecosys: Platte/Kansas Rivers

Org code: 64520   State: NE   Cong dist: NE03

Project no.: 91029   Project no. subelement: [ ]

Prop desc: Shop / office - FTN   Prop #: T09

Project title: Rehab shop work space and ventilation system, Ft. Niobrara NWR shop

Project desc: Rehabilitate work space and ventilation system to reduce dust and smoke in main shop. Virtually all vehicle and equipment repairs, as well as metal and wood fabrication are done here. Current layout and ventilation allow dust and fumes from welding or painting to build up in the building. This project will protect Government employees and equipment from injury and damage from dust and fumes.

Measures: Number of buildings: 1

Cost estimate: $25   Engineering cost included in cost est: [ ]

Cost est date: 4   Cost est method: Historical/Manager Estimate   FY group: 2002

Backlog: $25   FY completed: [ ]   FY obligations: $0
                                      Cumulative obligations: $0

Fund source: R - Resource Management   Percent complete: 0%

Other possible fund source:
- [ ] TEA21 (Refuge Roads)   [ ] Fire   [ ] Contaminants
- [ ] TEA21 (Other)   [ ] Quarters   [ ] Supplemental
- [ ] Title V   [ ] RecFee   [ ] Other

Fix type: (•) Repair/rehab ( ) Replace ( ) Remove   Condition assessment: Poor

Emphasis:

CHS	CRP	CM	OI	TOT	Type:	DM	CI	TOT	Safety? ☒	C
100	0	0	0	100		100	0	100		

Outcomes:

ES	WF	OMB	HBC	IAF	SDA	RW	FAR	PED	PRC	TOT
10	0	0	30	0	20	10	0	10	20	100

Maint code: T08 = Shop/Service Buildings

Station rank: 3   Dist rank: [ ]   Reg rank: 999   Nat rank: 23
                                                      DOI rank: 1000

RO support needs: ☒ Engineering ☒ Contracting ☐ Force Account ☐ Hold

Project notes:

Updated 12/31/97

RMIS - Maintenance Management System (MMS)
Record View

Station: Fort Niobrara NWR   HQ: Fort Niobrara NWR

Main ecosys: Platte/Kansas Rivers

Org code: 64520   State: NE   Cong dist: NE03

Project no.: 97004   Project no. subelement: A (97004-a)

Prop desc: Storage building   Prop #: 7

Project title: Replace 100+ year old, rodent occupied storage building

Project desc: Construct a new rodent-resistant storage building. The current storage building was constructed as a hay shed by the army pre-1900; it and its contents are currently closed to use due to Hantavirus, histoplasmosis and rabies concerns; it is deteriorated, rodent and bat occupied.   A new building is needed to protect Government materials and property from theft, vandalism, weather and rodents.

Measures: Number of buildings: 1   Square feet: 2860

Cost estimate: $298   Engineering cost included in cost est: $44

Cost est date: 1999   Cost est method: Cost Estimating Guide   FY group: 2005

Backlog: $298   FY completed: FY obligations: 50

Cumulative obligations: 50

Fund source: R = Resource Management   Percent complete: 0%

Other possible fund source:
- o TEA21 (Refuge Roads) o Fire o Contaminants
- o TEA21 (Other) o Quarters o Supplemental
- o Title V o RecFee o Other

Fix type: o Repair/rehab ⊚ Replace o Remove   Condition assessment: Poor

Emphasis:	CHS	CRP	CM	OI	TOT	Type:	DM	CI	TOT	Safety? ☒	C
	50	0	50	0	100		100	0	100		

Outcomes:	ES	WF	OMB	HEC	IAF	SDA	RW	FAR	PED	PRC	TOT
	10	0	0	30	0	20	10	0	20	10	100

Maint code: 106 = Storage Buildings

Station rank: 4   Dist rank: Reg rank: 108   Nat rank: 526

DOI rank: 700

RO support needs: ☒ Engineering ☒ Contracting ☐ Force Account ☐ Hold

Project notes:

The building to be replaced is a historic structure and will likely need to be retained and preserved in some form - see project phase B.

Updated 12/31/97

RMIS - Maintenance Management System (MMS)
Record View

Station: Fort Niobrara NWR   HQ: Fort Niobrara NWR

Main ecosys: Platte/Kansas Rivers

Org code: 64520   State: NE   Cong dist: NE03

Project no.: 97004   Project no. subelement: B   (97004-b)

Prop desc: Storage building   Prop #: 7

Project title: Rehab and preserve 100+ year old historic military hay shed

Project desc: Rehab historic cavalry hay shed by installing rodent and bat barriers; relocate bat colony; clean and decontaminate the army pre-1900; it and its contents are currently closed to use due to Hantavirus, histoplasmosis and rabies concerns; it is deteriorated, rodent and bat occupied.

Measures: Number of buildings: 1   2860

Cost estimate: $240   Engineering cost included in cost est: $42

Cost est date: 1999   Cost est method: Cost Estimating Guide   FY group: 2003

Backlog: $240   FY completed: FY obligations: $0

Cumulative obligations: $0

Fund source: R = Resource Management   Percent complete: 0%

Other possible fund source:
- o TEA21 (Refuge Roads) o Fire   o Contaminants
- o TEA21 (Other)   o Quarters   o Supplemental
- o Title V   o RecFee   o Other

Pix type: ⊙ Repair/rehab o Replace o Remove   Condition assessment: Poor

Emphasis:

CHS	CRP	CM	OI	TOT	Type:	DM	CI	TOT	Safety? ☒	I
0	0	0	100	100		100	0	100		

Outcomes:

ES	WF	OMB	HEC	IAF	SDA	RW	FAR	PED	PRC	TOT
0	0	0	20	0	40	0	0	40	0	100

Maint code: 106 = Storage Buildings

Station rank: 5   Dist rank: 999   Reg rank: 999   Nat rank:

DOI rank: 300

RO support needs: ☒ Engineering ☒ Contracting ☐ Force Account ☐ Hold

Project notes:

The building to be replaced is a historic structure and will likely need to be retained and preserved in some form - see project phase B.

Updated 5/9/99

RMIS - Maintenance Management System (MMS)
Record View

Station: Fort Niobrara NWR   HQ: Fort Niobrara NWR

Main ecosys: Platte/Kansas Rivers

Org code: 64520   State: NE   Cong dist: NE03

Project no.: 97002   Project no. subelement: C (97002-c)

Prop desc: Horse barn   Prop #: 6

Project title: Rehab roof and roof ventilation on Ft. Niobrara NWR horse barn.

Project desc: Rehab roof and loft ventilation on horse barn by leveling sagging rafters, repairing underlayment, and installing low maintenance metal roof on Ft. Niobrara horse barn. The existing roof leaks; the project will protect the building, stored hay, saddles, horses, etc, used to handle Bison, elk, and to conduct Service operations in the Ft. Niobrara Wilderness Area.

Measures: Number of buildings: 1

Cost estimate: $35   Engineering cost included in cost est: $5

Cost est date: 1999   Cost est method: Cost Estimating Guide   FY group: 2004

Backlog: $35   FY completed: FY obligations: $0

Cumulative obligations: $0

Fund source: R = Resource Management   Percent complete: 0%

Other possible fund source:
o TEA21 (Refuge Roads) o Fire o Contaminants
o TEA21 (Other) o Quarters o Supplemental
o Title V o RecFee o Other

Fix type: ⊙ Repair/rehab o Replace o Remove   Condition assessment: Poor

Emphasis:	CHS	CRP	CM	OI	TOT	Type:	DM	CI	TOT	Safety? ☒	Y
	0	0	0	100	100		100	0	100		

Outcomes:	ES	WP	OMB	REC	IAF	SDA	RW	PAR	PED	PRC	TOT
	10	0	0	0	0	30	30	0	0	30	100

Maint code: IOB = Shop/Service Buildings

Station rank: 6   Dist rank: 999   Reg rank: 999   Nat rank:

DOI rank: 300

RO support needs: ☒ Engineering ☒ Contracting o Force Account o Hold

Project notes:

Multiple buildings in the Ft. Niobrara Headquarters are identified as needing roofs; all are in close proximity; several are subject to historical / cultural resource considerations. All should be evaluated and reroofed in similar manner with similar materials to insure compatible appearance.

Updated 5/9/99

RMIS - Maintenance Management System (MMS)
Record View

Station: Fort Niobrara NWR   HQ: Fort Niobrara NWR

Main ecosys: Platte/Kansas Rivers

Org code: 64520   State: NE   Cong dist: NE0?

Project no.: 91027   Project no. subelement:

Prop desc: Office/visitor center   Prop #: 101

Project title: Rehab office, archival and storage space: Ft. Niobrara Office

Project desc: Rehab office, archival, storage space in Ft. Niobrara NWR Office / Visitor Center by removing counters, etc and dividing large lab and meeting room to provide needed office and records storage space; rewire electrical accordingly. This project would permit better use of space as office and administrative space to facilitate operations on 90,000 + acres of Service owned lands, easements, etc.

Measures: Number of buildings: 1

Cost estimate: 5225   Engineering cost included in cost est: $40

Cost est date: 1999   Cost est method: Cost Estimating Guide   FY group: 2004

Backlog: 5225   FY completed: FY obligations: $0

Cumulative obligations: $0

Fund source: R - Resource Management   Percent complete: 0%

Other possible fund source:
- ○ TEA21 (Refuge Roads) ○ Fire   ○ Contaminants
- ○ TEA21 (Other)   ○ Quarters ○ Supplemental
- ○ Title V   ○ RecFee   ○ Other

Fix type: ⊙ Repair/rehab ○ Replace ○ Remove   Condition assessment: Good

Emphasis:

CHS	CRP	CM	OI	TOT
0	0	50	50	100

Type:

DM	CI	TOT
0	100	100

Safety? ⊠ I

Outcomes:

ES	WF	OMB	HEC	IAF	SDA	RW	FAR	PED	PRC	TOT
10	10	10	20	0	10	10	10	10	10	100

Maint code: 101 = Office Buildings

Station rank: 7   Dist rank: Reg rank: 999   Nat rank:

DOI rank: 350

RO support needs: ⊠ Engineering ⊠ Contracting ☐ Force Account ☐ Hold

Project notes:

Project will require Asbestos mitigation and some structural modification.

Updated 12/17/97

RMIS - Maintenance Management System (MMS)
Record View

Station: Fort Niobrara NWR   HQ: Fort Niobrara NWR

Main ecosys: Platte/Kansas Rivers

Org code: 64520   State: NE   Cong dist: NE03

Project no.: 990809   Project no. subelement: [ ]

Prop desc: Excavator, Cat 120B   Prop #: 617937

Project title: Rehab boom and hydraulics on 1992 Caterpillar Excavator

Project desc: Rehab hydraulic valves to allow operation so "thumb" to be installed in retrofit of boom on Cat Excavator. The excavator is used extensively for tree removal along dikes, bridges, etc, throughout the Complex and easements. Retrofit will allow safer and more efficient use of the machine in critical facility maintenance and rehab projects.

Measures: Number of vehicles: 1

Cost estimate: $15   Engineering cost included in cost est: [ ]

Cost est date: 1999   Cost est method: Historical/Manager   FY group: 2005

Backlog: $15   FY completed: [ ]   Estimate   FY obligations: $0

                                    Cumulative obligations: $0

Fund source: R = Resource Management   Percent complete: 0%

Other possible fund source:
○ TEA21 (Refuge Roads)   ○ Fire   ○ Contaminants
○ TEA21 (Other)   ○ Quarters   ○ Supplemental
○ Title V   ○ RecFee   ○ Other

Fix type: ⊙ Repair/rehab ○ Replace ○ Remove   Condition assessment: Good

Emphasis:
CHS	CRP	CM	OI	TOT		Type:	DM	CI	TOT		Safety? ☒	T
0	0	0	100	100			100	0	100			

Outcomes:
ES	WF	OMB	HEC	IAF	SDA	RW	FAR	PED	PRC	TOT
10	20	20	0	0	20	10	0	0	20	100

Maint code: 780 = Agr/Const/Industrial Vehicles

Station rank: 8   Dist rank: 999   Reg rank: 999   Nat rank: [ ]

                                                        DOI rank: 300

RO support needs: ☐ Engineering ☒ Contracting ☐ Force Account ☐ Hold

Project notes:

Updated 5/9/99

RMIS - Maintenance Management System (MMS)
Record View

Station: Fort Niobrara NWR   HQ: Fort Niobrara NWR

Main ecosys: Platte/Kansas Rivers

Org code: 64520   State: NE   Cong dist: NE03

Project no.: 87023   Project no. subelement: A (87023-a)

Prop desc: Garage/machine shed   Prop #: 109

Project title: Rehab substandard wiring, lighting, in Machine Storage Building

Project desc: Rehab substandard wiring in equipment storage bays with adequate circuits, lighting, and outlets. current electrical service to storage portion of the building will not support cold weather engine heaters on equipment during winter; lighting is not adequate for use. Implementation will result in safe, functional utilization of the building for year-round equipment and vehicle storage.

Measures: Number of buildings: 1

Cost estimate: $12   Engineering cost included in cost est: $2

Cost est date: 1999   Cost est method: Cost Estimating Guide   FY group: 2005

Backlog: $10   FY completed: FY obligations: $0

Cumulative obligations: $2

Fund source: R = Resource Management   Percent complete: 17%

Other possible fund source:
- ☐ TEA21 (Refuge Roads)
- ☐ TEA21 (Other)
- ☐ Title V
- ☐ Fire
- ☐ Quarters
- ☐ RecFee
- ☐ Contaminants
- ☐ Supplemental
- ☐ Other

Fix type: ⦿ Repair/rehab ○ Replace ○ Remove   Condition assessment: Poor

Emphasis:

CHS	CRP	CM	OI	TOT	Type:	DM	CI	TOT	Safety? ☒	I
0	0	50	50	100		100	0	100		

Outcomes:

ES	WF	OMB	HEC	IAF	SDA	RW	FAR	PED	PRC	TOT
10	0	0	30	0	30	10	0	10	10	100

Maint code: 106 = Storage Buildings

Station rank: 9   Dist rank: Reg rank: 999   Nat rank:

DOI rank: 350

RO support needs: ☒ Engineering ☒ Contracting ☒ Force Account ☐ Hold

Project notes:

Updated 12/17/97

RMIS - Maintenance Management System (MMS)
Record View

Station: Fort Niobrara NWR   HQ: Fort Niobrara NWR

Main ecosys: Platte/Kansas Rivers

Org code: 64520   State: NE   Cong dist: NE03

Project no.: 87023   Project no. subelement: C (87023-c)

Prop desc: Garage/machine shed   Prop #: 109

Project title: Rehab approach apron in front of shop / vehicle storage building.

Project desc: Rehab apron/approach to garage by removing deteriorated material and replacing reinforced concrete. Virtually all vehicle and equipment repairs and inside storage is in this building; the area in front of he building is often rutted and muddy, the apron made up of broken asphalt and gravel. Completion of this project will facilitate all weather access to the building with all vehicles and equipment.

Measures: Number of buildings: 1

Cost estimate: $160   Engineering cost included in cost est: $24

Cost est date: 1999   Cost est method: Cost Estimating Guide   FY group: 2005

Backlog: $160   FY completed: FY obligations: $0

Cumulative obligations: $0

Fund source: R = Resource Management   Percent complete: 0%

Other possible fund source:
○ TEA21 (Refuge Roads)   ○ Fire   ○ Contaminants
○ TEA21 (Other)   ○ Quarters   ○ Supplemental
○ Title V   ○ RecFee   ○ Other

Fix type: ⦿ Repair/rehab ○ Replace ○ Remove   Condition assessment: Poor

Emphasis:

CHS	CRP	CM	OI	TOT	Type:	DM	CI	TOT	Safety? ○
0	0	0	100	100		100	0	100	

Outcomes:

ES	WF	OMB	HEC	IAF	SDA	RW	PAR	PED	PRC	TOT
10	0	0	20	0	30	10	0	10	20	100

Maint code: 106 = Storage Buildings

Station rank: 10   Dist rank: Reg rank: 999   Nat rank:

DOI rank: 300

RO support needs: ☒ Engineering ☒ Contracting ☒ Force Account ☐ Hold

Project notes:

Updated 12/17/97

Appendix E.
Compatibility
Determinations

Station Name: Fort Niobrara National Wildlife Refuge

Date Established: 1912

Establishing and Acquisition Authorities:
Executive Order 1461 on January 11, 1912,
Executive Order 1642, on November 14, 1912
Executive Order 3256, on March 31, 1920
Executive Order 7301, on February 21, 1936

Purposes for which the Refuge was established:
The Refuge was originally established on January 11, 1912, from the public domain as a "preserve and breeding ground for native birds," and was expanded by Executive Order on November 14, 1912, setting aside additional lands as the Fort Niobrara Game Preserve for the preservation of bison and elk herds representative of those that once roamed the Great Plains. Executive Orders in 1920 and 1936 were for various purposes including roost sites for sharp-tailed grouse and prairie chickens, migratory bird food sites, and pronghorn antelope management.

Furthermore, the Wilderness Act of 1964 calls for designated wilderness areas within a National Wildlife Refuge to receive equal consideration in management decisions and become a supplemental purpose of the Refuge. Section 4. (a) of this Act reads: *"The purposes of this Act are hereby declared to be within and supplemental to the purposes for which national forests and units of the national park and national wildlife refuge systems are established and administered."* Thus, the purpose of the designated wilderness area within this Refuge is to be supplemental and not subservient to the other purposes of the Refuge.

Refuge Goals and Objectives
P Habitat Management Goal: Preserve, restore, and enhance the unique diversity of upland and riparian plant communities and associated water resources representative of the physiographic regions described as Sandhills Prairie, Mixed Prairie, Rocky Mountain Coniferous Forest, Eastern Deciduous Forest, and Northern Boreal Forest within the Northern Great Plains to ensure their rarity, richness, and representativeness is sustainable into the future.

Grasslands Objective: Maintain the approximate 14,264 acres of Sandhill Prairie and Mixed Prairie vegetation communities in early through late successional stages to meet nesting, brooding, feeding and/or protective cover requirements of various grassland dependent birds, fenced animals, and other wildlife. Species composition on a minimum of 90 percent of the grasslands will be middle-to-late successional stage and consist of 75-85 percent grasses, 5-10 percent grass-like plants, 5-10 percent forbs, and 5 percent shrubs (dominant species as described by Kaul and Rolfsmeier 1993, Schneider *et al.* 1996, USDA Soil Conservation Service 1983). Vegetation structure will exist in a range of heights and densities with complete visual obstruction to an average height of six inches in the fall on a minimum of 50 percent of the grassland acreage (Prose 1985; Prose 1987). A minimum of 50 percent of the grasslands will not have planned burning or grazing during the native bird breeding season (April 15 - July 15).

Ponderosa Pine Savanna/Woodland Objective: Manage the approximate 3,022 acres of Rocky Mountain Coniferous Forest community to provide nesting, brooding, feeding and/or protective cover requirements of various native birds, fenced animals, and other wildlife. Approximately 85 percent of the acreage will be maintained as savanna and consist of 70 percent grasses, 10 percent grass-like plants, 5 percent forbs, 5 percent shrubs, and 10 percent trees with the remaining acreage managed as a woodland/forest. Species composition to manage for will be based on descriptions by Kaul and Rolfsmeier 1993, Schneider *et al.* 1996, USDA Soil Conservation Service 1983. A minimum of 50 percent of this community type will not have planned grazing or burning during the native bird breeding season (April 15 - July 15).

Riparian Eastern Deciduous/Northern Boreal Forest

Objective: Maintain and preserve the approximate 1,296 acres of Eastern Deciduous Forest/Northern Boreal Forest riparian community to provide nesting, brooding, feeding and/or protective cover requirements of various native birds and other wildlife. Species composition to manage for will be based on descriptions by Kaul and Rolfsmeier 1993 and Schneider *et al.* 1996. Habitat diversity will be enhanced by managing for a mix of trees (size and age classes with a minimum of 10 percent mature trees) and well-developed shrub and herbaceous layers. Strips of woodlands (150 acres) in habitat units utilized by fenced animals will be protected to the extent necessary to ensure regeneration. A minimum of 50 percent of this community type will not have planned grazing or burning during the native bird breeding season (April 15 - July 15).

Niobrara River and Associated Wetlands Objectives:

Restore and maintain the approximate 375 acres of the Niobrara River and associated wetlands with emphasis on maintaining streambed quality, stream bank stability, water flow, water temperature, and quality. Use existing data on the Niobrara River water flow, quality (sediment, nitrate, pollutants) and water temperature as minimum baseline levels and repeat at five year intervals. Ensure vegetation adjacent to the River and streams are adequate to minimize erosion, dissipate water energy, and trap sediments.

Exotic and Invading Species Objective:
Prevent additional exotic plant species from becoming established and reduce the occurrence, frequency, and stand density of existing invading and exotic vegetation. Target level of combined total of invading and exotic plant species is less than 5 percent of species composition. Invading and exotic plant species to manage include leafy spurge, purple loosestrife, Canada thistle, Kentucky bluegrass, smooth brome, downy brome, sweet clover, reed canary grass, eastern red cedar, Russian olive, and phragmites.

p Wildlife Goals:
Preserve, restore, and enhance the ecological diversity and abundance of migratory and resident wildlife with emphasis on native birds.

Maintain representative breeding herds of nationally significant animals under reasonably natural conditions.

Prairie Grouse Objective: Maintain a five-year average density of one prairie grouse lek/1.4 square mile with an annual target of 100 sharp-tailed grouse and 65 prairie chicken breeding males in the grasslands (approximately 12,271 acres) south and east of the Niobrara River (USFWS, unpublished Refuge data).

Native Birds Objective: Maintain or increase breeding and migration use on Fort Niobrara by Species of Management Concern, U.S. Fish and Wildlife Service, Region 6, including northern harrier, ferruginous hawk, upland sandpiper, long-billed curlew, burrowing owl, short-eared owl, red-headed woodpecker, loggerhead shrike, dickcissel, lark bunting, grasshopper sparrow, chestnut-collared longspur, eastern meadowlark, and other habitat sensitive migratory birds such as western meadowlark, bobolink, clay-colored sparrow, belted kingfisher, willow flycatcher, and yellow-breasted chat. Monitor and document migration use by peregrine falcons as it occurs. Use existing data as minimum baseline levels and implement monitoring procedures that provide an index to overall species richness/diversity and document population trends of selected species over a five- year period.

Bison and Elk Objective: Preserve and maintain breeding populations of bison and elk with age and sex composition approximating historic herds. Implement management actions that maintain or increase levels of genetic variability to assure viable, sustainable populations according to accepted standards of conservation biology (Berger 1996, Berger and Cunningham 1994).

Rocky Mountain Bighorn Sheep Objective:
Reintroduce, if feasible and in accordance with the State's future Bighorn Sheep Management Plan, Rocky Mountain bighorn sheep to the Refuge to restore an indigenous species into its historic range.

Prairie Dog Objective: Allow the expansion of the existing black-tailed prairie dog town in the Refuge to a manageable size to enhance Refuge biological diversity.

Other Indigenous Wildlife Objective: Ensure the diversity and abundance of other indigenous mammals, reptiles, amphibians, fish, and invertebrates continues. Use existing data as minimum baseline levels and monitor periodically to document population trends. (Bogan, 1995)

P Threatened and Endangered Species Goal:
Contribute to the preservation and restoration of threatened and endangered flora and fauna that occur or have historically occurred in the area of Fort Niobrara NWR.

Blowout Penstemon Objective: Evaluate the Refuge for blowout penstemon habitat. If suitable habitat exists, establish plants in at least two sites

Bald Eagle Objective: Maintain a minimum of 10 percent of the woodlands within the Niobrara River corridor in mature or old-growth timber with an open and discontinuous canopy to provide undisturbed roosting habitat for wintering populations of bald eagles. Monitor and document eagle use on the Refuge and mortality in the area.

Whooping Crane, Piping Plover, and Least Tern Objective: Maintain the shallow braided River habitat above Cornell Dam for use by whooping cranes, piping plovers, and least terns during migration. Keep use areas free from human disturbance. Monitor and document migration use by whooping cranes, piping plover, and least terns as it occurs.

American Burying Beetle Objective: Determine if American burying beetles inhabit the Refuge. Implement appropriate management strategies if a population exists.

P Interpretation and Recreation Goal:
Provide the public with quality opportunities to learn about and enjoy the ecological diversity, wildlands, wildlife, and history of the Refuge in a largely natural setting and in a manner compatible with the purposes for which the Refuge was established.

Interpretation, Wildlife Observation and Photography, and Environmental Education Objectives: Provide visitors with quality interpretation, environmental education, wildlife observation, and photography opportunities.

Ensure a safe, quality River-floating experience on the Wild and Scenic Niobrara River that follows the standards of the National Wild and Scenic Rivers Act, National Wildlife Refuge System, and maintains the integrity of the Fort Niobrara Wilderness Area.

Protect and interpret Refuge cultural and paleontological sites.

Fishing Objective: Provide opportunities for warm water fishing in the Niobrara River and Minnichaduza Creek.

Hunting Objective: Offer ethically sound, limited and strictly controlled hunting opportunities for elk and, if reintroduced, bighorn sheep to facilitate removal of herd excess.

P Ecosystem Goal:
Promote partnerships to preserve, restore, and enhance a diverse, healthy, and productive ecosystem of which the Fort Niobrara and Valentine NWR's are part.

Ecosystem Objectives/Strategies for the Fort Niobrara/Valentine NWR Complex: Support the National Park Service and Niobrara River Council to meet desired future conditions of the Niobrara Scenic River.

Support the Sandhills Management Plan through Partners for Wildlife Program to enhance wildlife habitat on private lands.

Support use of Refuges as research areas for relevant natural resource studies. Conduct applied research on management of threatened and endangered plant and animal populations.

Develop an effective outreach program that results in two wildlife habitat/public use projects completed annually with nongovernmental organizations.

Develop greater cooperation with State and local governments that result in completion of at least two projects annually. Projects are to benefit area wildlife resources or enhance public use opportunities such as fish rearing in Refuge ponds.

Use this Plan to help in marketing Refuge needs through grant writing and networking with other entities.

Support the National Scenic River; coordinate and cooperate as appropriate with River management partners including the National Park Service, Natural Resource Districts, etc., to meet desired future conditions of the Niobrara Scenic River and related resources.

Other Applicable Laws, Regulations, and Policies:
Please refer to Appendix G. Compliance Requirements.

Description of Proposed Use
Wildlife Observation, Wildlife Photography, Interpretation and Environmental Education

Based on general observations and data collected in the visitor center and on the River, an estimated 100,000 people visit the Refuge annually for wildlife/wildland observation, photography, interpretation/education, picnicking, hiking, and floating on the Niobrara River. The majority of visits to the Refuge utilize the River or the auto tour route and Fort Falls nature trail. The 15-stop self-guiding auto tour route is located in the exhibition habitat unit and provides information on the prairie dog town, bison, elk, Texas longhorns, and other prairie inhabitants.

The Fort Falls nature trail is approximately one mile long and educates the hiker through a brochure describing the different vegetation communities and associated wildlife found in this unique, biologically diverse area.

The visitor center, with a variety of 20+-year-old displays interpreting the history of the military fort, area wildlife and habitat, and Refuge management, is open Monday through Friday year-round and on weekends Memorial Day to Labor Day with use recorded at approximately 6,000 visits.

Other interpretive facilities include a kiosk at the canoe launch with education panels titled "Niobrara Valley," "Welcome to Fort Niobrara," "Canoeing the Niobrara River"; the observation deck above Fort Falls includes education panels titled "Prairie Oasis," "Fort Falls," "Sand, Rock & Water"; and an interpretive panel to be located in the exhibition habitat unit providing information on elk and prairie dogs.

The Bur Oak Picnic area is located along the Niobrara River at the Refuge entrance. Tables and rest rooms are used mainly by people visiting the Refuge for wildlife observation.

The main portion of the Fort Niobrara Wilderness Area included in the habitat unit north of the Niobrara River and used as winter pasture for the main bison herd is also open to the public for wildlife observation and photography, accessible by foot, horseback, or cross country skiing. No accurate count of visitors has been made; however, estimates are less than 200 per year.

Interpretation and environmental education services are provided when staff are available and include talks or guided tours for school groups (elementary through college level), scouts, 4-H clubs, and special projects. The public is invited to observe fall roundups and auctions of bison and longhorns, participate in Migratory Bird Day activities, and other Refuge programs.

News releases on Refuge events are written and provided to area television, radio, and newspaper outlets. The Fort Niobrara/Valentine NWR Complex also hosts special events including the Nebraska Federal Junior Duck Stamp Contest, annual Kids Fishing Day, annual steel shot clinic, and nature fest.

The Comprehensive Conservation Plan (CCP) proposes continuing with the uses described and adding the following to improve interpretation and access for visitors:

P   The Service will seek funds to construct and staff a new environmental education/visitor center to improve environmental education and interpretation of wildlife, cultural, and paleontological resources on the Refuge. A Site Plan, being developed, will include a concept design for the new center and suggestions for improving the existing visitor center until such time as a new center is constructed. Interim projects to complete include updating exhibits and broadening themes to include wildlife and their habitats; unusual ecological diversity; cultural and paleontological resources; and management. The Service will also investigate the possibility of a shared environmental education/visitor center with the Nebraska Game and Parks Commission, National Park Service, Forest Service, The Nature Conservancy, Valentine Chamber of Commerce, and others.

P   Provide a wilderness access point. Use will be limited to three groups at one time with a maximum group size of five horses or ten people. An outfitter, selected by lottery, would be allowed to guide a maximum of one group per day and would be required to pay a fee and/or percent of gross receipts to the Refuge.

P   Construct a trail to a scenic overlook of the Niobrara Canyon and provide appropriate interpretation.

P   Establish a concessionaire contract to view and interpret the bison and elk herds during the summer tourist season.

P   Continue to improve the main auto tour route by resurfacing with gravel and closing/revegetating the numerous side trails.

P   Expand the display habitat unit and provide a more natural and aesthetic setting by removing and/or relocating fence.

P   Staff and expand the hours of operation of the visitor/environmental education center.

P   Update Refuge brochures to new Service standards.

P   Develop a Refuge specific environmental education curricula for teachers to use independently.

Anticipated Impacts on Service Lands, Waters, or Interests:

Some disturbance to wildlife, both birds and mammals, will occur in areas of the Refuge frequented by visitors. In the past, visitation for these uses has been concentrated at the Office/Visitor Center area, exhibition pasture unit and on the River corridor. Use of the main unit in the Wilderness Area has been limited. It is anticipated that all uses will increase, particularly if better access and interpretation are offered. Monitoring of activities and their impacts, and regulation of the number and frequency of visits will maintain use at an acceptable level.

Construction of interpretive facilities, a new headquarters, and improved roads will result in the loss of a small amount of habitat for wildlife. The removal of some existing fence and improved roads may increase both the amount of traffic and vehicle speeds and result in increased wildlife mortality. Of particular concern is the occurrence of accidents involving the bison and elk herds. Due to the size of these animals, these accidents could result in serious injury to both wildlife and visitors.

Determination: Wildlife Observation, Wildlife Photography, Interpretation and Environmental Education are compatible.

The following stipulations are required to ensure compatibility:

P   Monitor use, regulate access, maintain necessary facilities to prevent erosion in high public use areas.
P   Monitor levels of use and effects on wildlife and habitat, especially in critical areas such as Wilderness Area.
P   Implement additional educational and interpretive programs.
P   Horseback and other Refuge tours will follow designated routes, schedules, and group size guidelines.
P   Road or trail construction will focus on existing roads and trails.
P   Speed limits on roads will be restricted to 25 mph.

Justification: Based upon the biological impacts presented above and in the Environmental Assessment, it is determined that wildlife observation, wildlife photography, interpretation, and environmental education within the Fort Niobrara National Wildlife Refuge will not materially interfere with or detract from the purposes for which this Refuge was established.

Although wildlife observation and other human activities have been shown to disturb wildlife, the stipulations presented above and in the Comprehensive Conservation Plan are sufficient to reduce impacts to a minimal level. One of the goals of the National Wildlife Refuge System is to provide opportunities for the public to develop an understanding and appreciation for wildlife. The four priority public uses identified in the National Wildlife Refuge System Improvement Act of 1997 will help meet that goal at the proposed Fort Niobrara National Wildlife Refuge, with only minimal conflicts with the wildlife conservation mission of the Refuge System.

Description of Proposed Use: Recreational Fishing

The Niobrara River, downstream of the Cornell Dam, and the Minnichaduza Creek are open to public sport fishing in accordance to Nebraska Game and Parks Commission established rules and regulations, with the exception of being closed to the taking of frogs, turtles, and minnows. Angler opportunities are limited with most fishing occurring immediately below Cornell Dam. Primary access is by foot, via a trail from the Refuge parking area off Nebraska Highway 12. Limited fishing also occurs throughout the remainder of the River downstream, with access generally by canoe. No motorboats are allowed. Fishing is primarily for catfish and occasionally trout. Fishing opportunities in the Niobrara River are limited and do not attract many visitors to the Refuge for this purpose.

A Kids Fishing Day is held annually in September and includes trout, catfish, and bluegill fishing in a NG&PC stocked pond located on the Refuge. The day's events include fish identification and casting contests, as well as, the opportunity to clean, cook, and eat fish. The event is cosponsored by the Nebraska Game and Parks Commission and is hosted with the assistance of the Fort Niobrara Natural History Association, volunteers, and Refuge staff.

The Comprehensive Conservation Plan (CCP) proposes continuing with the uses as described above.

Anticipated Impacts on Service Lands, Waters, or Interests:

A limited acreage of potential wildlife habitat (estimated at less than two acres) would be lost to access roads, parking lot, new trails and River bank trampling by people fishing below Cornell Dam. Virtually all fishing downstream from the Dam is from canoe with no impact on habitat.

Fishing and other human activities cause disturbance to wildlife, both birds and mammals.

Determination: Fishing is compatible.

The following stipulations are required to ensure compatibility:

P   Parking lot, road, trail, and related access facilities will be maintained as necessary to prevent erosion.
P   Public access for fishing immediately below Cornell Dam will be restricted to the number of people supported by size of the parking area.
P   Taking of frogs, turtles, and minnows will not be allowed as part of public fishing.
P   No additional streams, ponds or areas of the Niobrara River on the Refuge will be open to fishing.
P   Motorboats will not be allowed.

Justification: Based upon the biological impacts presented above, it is determined that recreational fishing within the Fort Niobrara National Wildlife Refuge will not materially interfere with or detract from the purposes for which this Refuge was established.

One of the goals of the National Wildlife Refuge System is to provide opportunities for public fishing, and it is identified as a priority use in the National Wildlife Refuge System Improvement Act of 1997. Fishing meets part of the goal for interpretation and recreation with only minor conflicts with the wildlife conservation mission of the Refuge System.

Description of Proposed Use: Hunting

Fort Niobrara National Wildlife Refuge has never been open to hunting. However, the Comprehensive Conservation Plan (CCP) proposes to, as appropriate, offer limited, strictly controlled hunting opportunities for elk and, if reintroduced, bighorn sheep to facilitate removal of herd excess.

If and when hunting becomes feasible and appropriate, a Hunting Plan will be developed and implemented to assure a safe, ethical, quality opportunity.

Anticipated Impacts on Service Lands, Waters, or Interests:

Hunters both disturb non-target species and harvest target species. Those species proposed to be hunted on Fort Niobrara NWR are elk and bighorn sheep. Hunting will take place only when and if populations provide an identified harvestable surplus. Hunting will be strictly limited and will involve very few hunters, under regulated conditions, resulting in minimal disturbance to non- target wildlife.

Determination: Hunting is compatible.

The following stipulations are required to ensure compatibility:

P   Hunting will be implemented only if determined appropriate based on herd size and a harvestable surplus.
P   Hunting will be evaluated to provide an ethical, quality hunt. Special attention will be given to fair chase.
P   Hunt will be coordinated with the Nebraska Game and Parks Commission in an effort to meet objectives of both the Fish and Wildlife Service and the State of Nebraska.
P   Monitor these uses to assure they do not interfere with and are compatible with other wildlife-dependent recreational activities.

Justification: Based upon the biological impacts presented above and in the Environmental Assessment contained in the CCP, it is determined that hunting on the Fort Niobrara National Wildlife Refuge will not materially interfere with or detract from the purposes for which this Refuge was established.

The State of Nebraska has established a bighorn sheep herd in western Nebraska and has recently implemented a limited hunting program. Free-ranging herds of elk are in other areas of Nebraska, now also managed under a limited hunt. It is appropriate for the Service to participate in planning and implementing a complementing program for both species at Fort Niobrara.

Description of Proposed Use: River Recreation

Local commercial outfitters provide tubes, canoes, shuttle services, transportation, beverages and/or food for an estimated 95 percent of River users. A large share of canoeing and tubing takes place during the summer on weekends, particularly Saturdays. Canoers can take either a day trip or an overnight trip. Tubers generally take only half day or day trips. The Refuge portion of trips runs from the canoe launch site to the east Refuge boundary and takes from 1.5 to 3 hours to complete. In 1998, 18,658 people canoed and 8,658 tubed down the River through the Refuge. This use is concentrated on summer weekends, especially Saturdays. On a busy summer Saturday, one vessel launches every 16 seconds. For some, a trip down the River is a social event with a party atmosphere. Most other days of the week and times of year, the River is not crowded.

The Refuge provides a canoe launch area with six ramps. Eleven launch areas are designated for outfitters, and approximately 65 cars can park in the lot. Outfitters are required to shuttle their customers to the launch in buses on weekends during the summer. No camping or alcohol consumption is allowed on the Refuge. Landing areas for hiking are provided at Fort Falls and the Niobrara Wilderness Area near Buffalo Bridge. Canoers and tubers also stop on sandbars to sunbathe and rest. The portion of the Niobrara River from the Refuge's west boundary to the canoe launch area is seldom used by canoers or tubers because of the numerous sandbars and shallow water.

Outfitters are required to purchase a Special Use Permit for operating a commercial business on the Refuge. The cost of the Special Use Permit is a nominal administrative fee of $5.00. In addition, outfitters are required to purchase a $25 annual permit for each vessel launched on the Refuge. Individuals may purchase an annual permit for $25 or a daily permit for $2.00 per vessel. Permit revenues are used to defray operating costs of the River recreation program, which include law enforcement, maintenance, interpretation, facilities, trash disposal, rest room/outhouse pumping, information, administration, and supplies.

The majority of River recreation users begin their trip at the Refuge canoe launch site and travel to take out points and campgrounds downstream from the Refuge. Take out points are owned and/or managed by private individuals, outfitters, the Middle Niobrara Natural Resources District, the Nebraska Game and Parks Commission, and The Nature Conservancy.

The Niobrara River, including the portion on the Refuge, is part of the Wild and Scenic River System. The Niobrara River downstream of the launch area to the Refuge boundary is part of the National Wilderness Preservation System.

Anticipated Impacts on Service Lands, Waters, or Interests:

Presently, little disturbance to vegetation exists along the river. Most visitors do not get out of their canoe or off their tube except on sandbars. Two developed sites, Fort Falls Trail and the Niobrara Wilderness Access, are only lightly used and the only vegetation disturbed is on the foot path.

Visitor use results in disturbance to wildlife on the Refuge. Research on birds has shown that boat traffic, including canoes, can cause lower productivity, reduce use of habitat, and reduce use of refuges. Observations by Refuge staff are that birds roosting or feeding in the River are the most susceptible to disturbance and include herons, ducks, and shorebirds. Only small numbers, probably less than 10 from each group, of these birds use the part of the River most frequented by canoers and tubers. The portion of the River above the Cornell Dam is used more by these groups of birds and is an area only lightly used by visitors. Disturbance to birds using the riparian areas adjacent to the River may also occur.

Disturbance to soil is, at present, minor. In a few locations, people are climbing the River bluffs and steep banks, which hastens the erosion of these areas.

Presently, little impact on federally listed threatened and endangered species (peregrine falcon, bald eagle, least tern, and whooping crane) exists primarily because the majority of recreational use is confined to June, July, and August. With the exception of the State listed river otter, threatened and endangered species documented on the Refuge are present in spring, winter, and fall. If use expands into these seasons, however, potential for disturbance would exist.

Presently, opportunities exist for visitors to use and enjoy the wilderness area and experience solitude. Visitors to the Refuge during the off-season or on weekdays in the summer do not see large numbers of other visitors. As recreational use of the River increases, opportunities for solitude in these off-peak periods will decrease or be eliminated.

Determination: River recreation is compatible.

The following stipulations are required to ensure compatibility:

P   A River Recreation Plan will be prepared within the next two years to determine the number of visitors permitted to use the River for floating. This Plan will determine carrying capacity based upon the requirements of the Wilderness Act, the National Wildlife Refuge Improvement Act, the Wild and Scenic Rivers Act, and the effects of visitation on wildlife, vegetation, soils, and visitor experience.

P   Biological studies will be conducted to determine the impact of River floaters on Refuge wildlife, vegetation, and soils.

P   During the development of the River Recreation Plan, no additional permits for outfitting on the Refuge will be issued and River use will be capped at 1998 levels.

P   River recreation will not be developed in that part of River above Cornell Dam.

P   Permits will be required for groups such as Scouts, church, and educational institutions and limited to one group with a maximum of 30 people per day.

P   Bans on possession of alcohol, high volume radios (normally known as boom boxes), or any device whatsoever capable of shooting or directing a projectile or liquid at another person to include, but not limited to, water balloons, high pressure water guns (normally known as water cannons), paint ball guns, potato guns, and sling shots will be implemented. No more than five tubes will be allowed to be tied together.

Justification: Based upon the impacts presented, it is determined that River recreation within the Fort Niobrara National Wildlife Refuge will not materially interfere with or detract from the purposes for which this Refuge was established.

Although wildlife observation and other human activities have been shown to disturb wildlife and habitat, the stipulations presented above may result in only minimal impacts. The River Recreation Plan, to be prepared, will measure these impacts and adjust visitation to meet the compatibility standards of the National Wildlife Refuge System. People using the River come to observe wildlife and wildlands. Wildlife observation is one of the priority uses listed in the National Wildlife Improvement Act and is one of the goals of the National Wildlife Refuge System.

NEPA Compliance:

Categorical Exclusion _____
Environmental Assessment __X__
Environmental Impact Statement _____
FONSI _____

Signatures:

Project Leader: _____ Date: 9/30/99
Royce R. Huber
Fort Niobrara - Valentine NWR Complex

Concurrence:

_____ Date: 9/30/99
Refuge Supervisor

_____ Date: 5/2/00
Assistant Regional Director, Refuges and Wildlife

Appendix F.
List of Animal and Plant Species at Fort Niobrara NWR

Birds (* = Species known to nest on the Refuge)

Grebes
Pied-billed Grebe	*Podilymbus podiceps*
Horned Grebe	*Podiceps auritus*
Eared Grebe	*Podiceps nigricollis*
Western Grebe	*Aechmophorus occidentalis*
Clark's Grebe	*Aechmophorus clarkii*

Pelicans
American White Pelican	*Pelecanus erythrorhynchos*

Cormorants
Double-crested Cormorant	*Phalacrocorax auritus*

Bitterns, Herons
American Bittern	*Botaurus lentiginosus*
Great Blue Heron	*Ardea herodias*
Cattle Egret	*Bubulcus ibis*
Green Heron	*Butorides virescens*
Black-crowned Night-Heron	*Nycticorax nycticorax*

Vultures
Turkey Vulture	*Cathartes aura*

Geese
Greater White-fronted Goose	*Anser albifrons*
Snow Goose	*Chen caerulescens*
Canada Goose*	*Branta canadensis*

Swans
Trumpeter Swan	*Cygnus buccinator*

Ducks
Wood Duck*	*Aix sponsa*
Gadwall*	*Anas strepera*
American Wigeon	*Anas americana*
Mallard*	*Anas platyrhynchos*
Blue-winged Teal*	*Anas discors*
Cinnamon Teal	*Anas cyanoptera*
Northern Shoveler*	*Anas clypeata*
Northern Pintail*	*Anas acuta*
Green-winged Teal	*Anas crecca*
Canvasback	*Aythya valisineria*
Redhead*	*Aythya americana*
Ring-necked Duck	*Aythya collaris*
Lesser Scaup	*Aythya affinis*
Bufflehead	*Bucephala albeola*
Common Goldeneye	*Bucephala clangula*
Hooded Merganser	*Lophodytes cucullatus*
Common Merganser	*Mergus merganser*
Red-breasted Merganser	*Mergus serrator*
Ruddy Duck	*Oxyura jamaicensis*

Hawks, Kites, Eagles
Osprey	*Pandion haliaetus*
Bald Eagle	*Haliaeetus leucocephalus*
Northern Harrier	*Circus cyaneus*
Sharp-shined Hawk	*Accipiter striatus*
Cooper's Hawk	*Accipiter cooperii*
Northern Goshawk	*Accipiter gentilis*
Red-shouldered Hawk	*Buteo lineatus*
Broad-winged Hawk	*Buteo platypterus*
Swainson's Hawk*	*Buteo swainsoni*
Red-tailed Hawk*	*Buteo jamaicensis*
Ferruginous Hawk	*Buteo regalis*
Rough-legged Hawk	*Buteo lagopus*
Golden Eagle	*Aquila chrysaetos*

Falcons
American Kestrel*	*Falco sparverius*
Merlin	*Falco columbarius*
Peregrine Falcon	*Falco peregrinus*
Prairie Falcon	*Falco mexicanus*

Gallinaceous Birds
Gray Partridge	*Perdix perdix*
Ring-necked Pheasant*	*Phasianus colchicus*
Ruffed Grouse	*Bonasa umbellus*
Sharp-tailed Grouse*	*Tympanuchus phasianellus*
Greater Prairie-Chicken*	*Tympanuchus cupido*
Wild Turkey*	*Meleagris gallopavo*
Northern Bobwhite*	*Colinus virginianus*

Rails
Virginia Rail	*Rallus limicola*
Sora	*Porzana carolina*
American Coot	*Fulica americana*

Cranes
Sandhill Crane	*Grus canadensis*
Whooping Crane	*Grus americana*

Plovers
Semipalmated Plover	*Charadrius semipalmatus*
Piping Plover	*Charadrius melodus*
Killdeer*	*Charadrius vociferus*

Stilt, Avocet
American Avocet	*Recurvirostra american*

Sandpipers

Greater Yellowlegs	*Tringa melanoleuca*
Lesser Yellowlegs	*Tringa flavipes*
Solitary Sandpiper	*Tringa solitaria*
Willet	*Catoptrophorus semipalmatus*
Spotted Sandpiper	*Actitis macularia*
Upland Sandpiper*	*Bartramia longicauda*
Long-billed Curlew*	*Numenius americanus*
Marbled Godwit	*Limosa fedoa*
Western Sandpiper	*Calidris mauri*
Least Sandpiper	*Calidris minutilla*
White-rumped Sandpiper	*Calidris fuscicollis*
Baird's Sandpiper	*Calidris bairdii*
Pectoral Sandpiper	*Calidris melanotos*
Dunlin	*Calidris alphina*
Long-billed Dowitcher	*Limnodromus scolopaceus*
Common Snipe	*Gallinago gallinago*

Phalaropes

Wilson's Phalarope	*Phalaropus tricolor*

Gulls

Franklin's Gull	*Larus pipixcan*
Ring-billed Gull	*Larus delawarensis*
California Gull	*Larus californicus*

Terns

Common Tern	*Sterna hirundo*
Forster's Tern	*Sterna forsteri*
Black Tern	*Chlidonias niger*

Pigeons, Doves, Parakeet

Mourning Dove*	*Zenaida macroura*

Cuckoos

Black-billed Cuckoo*	*Coccyzus erythropthalmus*
Yellow-billed Cuckoo	*Coccyzus americanus*

Owls

Eastern Screech Owl*	*Otus asio*
Great Horned Owl*	*Bubo virginianus*
Snowy Owl	*Nyctea scandiaca*
Burrowing Owl*	*Athene cunicularia*
Long-eared Owl	*Asio otus*
Short-eared Owl	*Asio flammeus*

Goatsuckers

Common Nighthawk*	*Chordeiles minor*
Common Poorwill	*Phalaenoptilus nuttallii*

Swifts

Chimney Swift	*Chaetura pelagica*

Hummingbirds

Ruby-throated Hummingbird	*Archilochus colubris*

Kingfisher

Belted Kingfisher*	*Ceryle alcyon*

Woodpeckers

Red-headed Woodpecker*	*Melanerpes erythrocephalus*
Downy Woodpecker*	*Picoides pubescens*
Hairy Woodpecker*	*Picoides villosus*
Northern Flicker*	*Colaptes auratus*

Flycatchers

Olive-sided Flycatcher	*Contopus cooperi*
Western Wood-Pewee*	*Contopus sordidulus*
Eastern Wood-Pewee	*Contopus virens*
Alder Flycatcher	*Empidonax alnorum*
Willow Flycatcher	*Empidonax traillii*
Eastern Phoebe*	*Sayornis phoebe*
Say's Phoebe*	*Sayornis saya*
Great Crested Flycatcher*	*Myiarchus crinitus*
Western Kingbird*	*Tyrannus verticalis*
Eastern Kingbird*	*Tyrannus tyrannus*
Scissor-tailed Flycatcher	*Tyrannus forficatus*

Shrikes

Loggerhead Shrike	*Lanius ludovicianus*
Northern Shrike	*Lanius excubitor*

Vireo

Bell's Vireo*	*Vireo bellii*
Warbling Vireo*	*Vireo gilvus*
Red-eyed Vireo*	*Vireo olivaceus*

Jays, Magpies, Crows, Ravens

Steller's Jay	*Cyanocitta stelleri*
Blue Jay*	*Cyanocitta cristata*
Clark's Nutcracker	*Nucifraga columbiana*
Black-billed Magpie*	*Pica pica*
American Crow*	*Corvus brachyrhynchos*

Lark

Horned Lark*	*Eremophila alpestris*

Swallows

Purple Martin	*Progne subis*
Tree Swallow*	*Tachycineta bicolor*
Northern Rough-winged Swallow*	
	Stelgidopteryx serripennis
Bank Swallow	*Riparia riparia*
Cliff Swallow*	*Petrochelidon pyrrhonota*
Barn Swallow*	*Hirundo rustica*

Chickadees, Titmice, Verdin, Bushtit

Black-capped Chickadee*	*Poecile atricapillus*

Nuthatches

Red-breasted Nuthatch	*Sitta canadensis*
White-breasted Nuthatch*	*Sitta carolinensis*

Creeper

Brown Creeper	*Certhia americana*

Wrens, Dipper

Rock Wren*	*Salpinctes obsoletus*
House Wren*	*Troglodytes aedon*
Sedge Wren	*Cistothorus platensis*
Marsh Wren	*Cistothorus palustris*

Kinglets

Ruby-crowned Kinglet	*Regulus calendula*

Thrushes, Bluebirds
Eastern Bluebird*	*Sialia sialis*
Mountain Bluebird	*Sialia currucoides*
Townsend's Solitaire	*Myadestes townsendl*
Gray-cheeked Thrush	*Catharus minimus*
Swainson's Thrush	*Catharus ustulatus*
Wood Thrush	*Hylocichla mustelina*
American Robin*	*Turdus migratorius*

Thrashers
Gray Catbird*	*Dumetella carolinensis*
Northern Mockingbird*	*Mimus polyglottos*
Brown Thrasher*	*Toxostoma rufum*

Starling
European Starling*	*Sturnus vulgaris*

Pipits
American (Water) Pipit	*Anthus rubescens*

Waxwings
Bohemian Waxwing	*Bombycilla garrulus*
Cedar Waxwing	*Bombycilla cedrorum*

Warblers
Golden-winged Warbler	*Vermivora chrysoptera*
Tennessee Warbler	*Vermivora peregrina*
Orange-crowned Warbler	*Vermivora celata*
Yellow Warbler*	*Dendrocia petechia*
Chestnut-sided Warbler	*Dendroica pensylvanica*
Yellow-rumped Warbler	*Dendrocia coronata*
Blackburnian Warbler	*Dendrocia fusca*
Palm Warbler	*Dendrocia palmarum*
Blackpoll Warbler	*Dendrocia striata*
Black-and-white Warbler*	*Mniotilta varia*
American Redstart*	*Setophaga ruticilla*
Prothonotary Warbler	*Protonotaria citrea*
Ovenbird*	*Seiurus aurocapillus*
Connecticut Warbler	*Oporornis agilis*
Common Yellowthroat*	*Geothlypis trichas*
Wilson's Warbler	*Wilsonia pusilla*
Yellow-breasted Chat*	*Icteria virens*

Tanagers
Scarlet Tanager*	*Piranga olivacea*
Western Tanager	*Piranga ludoviciana*

Towhee, Sparrows
Eastern Towhee*	*Pipilo erythrophthalmus*
American Tree Sparrow	*Spizella arborea*
Chipping Sparrow*	*Spizella passerina*
Clay-colored Sparrow	*Spizella pallida*
Field Sparrow*	*Spizella pusilla*
Vesper Sparrow*	*Pooecetes gramineus*
Lark Sparrow*	*Chondestes grammacus*
Lark Bunting	*Calamospiza melanocorys*
Savannah Sparrow*	*Passerculus sandwichensis*
Grasshopper Sparrow*	*Ammodramus savannarum*
Baird's Sparrow	*Ammodramus bairdii*
Fox Sparrow	*Passerella iliaca*
Song Sparrow	*Melospiza melodia*
Lincoln's Sparrow	*Melospiza lincolnii*
White-throated Sparrow	*Zonotrichia albicollis*
Harris' Sparrow	*Zonotrichia querula*
White-crowned Sparrow	*Zonotrichia leucophrys*
Dark-eyed Junco	*Junco hyemalis*
McCown's Longspur	*Calcarius mccownii*
Lapland Longspur	*Calcarius lapponicus*
Chestnut-collared Longspur	*Calcarius ornatus*

Grosbeaks, Buntings
Northern Cardinal	*Cardinalis cardinalis*
Rose-breasted Grosbeak	*Pheucticus ludovicianus*
Black-headed Grosbeak*	*Pheucticus melanocephalus*
Blue Grosbeak*	*Guiraca caerulea*
Lazuli Bunting	*Passerina amoena*
Indigo Bunting	*Passerina cyanea*
Dickcissel	*Spiza americana*

Blackbirds, Orioles
Bobolink	*Dolichonyx oryzivorus*
Red-winged Blackbird*	*Agelaius phoeniceus*
Eastern Meadowlark*	*Sturnella magna*
Western Meadowlark*	*Sturnella neglecta*
Yellow-headed Blackbird	*Xanthocephalus xanthocephalus*
Rusty Blackbird	*Euphagus carolinus*
Brewer's Blackbird*	*Euphagus cyanocephalus*
Common Grackle*	*Quiscalus quiscula*
Brown-headed Cowbird*	*Molothrus ater*
Orchard Oriole*	*Icterus spurius*
Baltimore Oriole*	*Icterus galbula*

Finches
House Finch	*Carpodacus mexicanus*
Red Crossbill	*Loxia curvirostra*
Common Redpoll	*Carduelis flammea*
Pine Siskin*	*Carduelis pinus*
American Goldfinch	*Carduelis tristis*
Evening Grosbeak	*Coccothraustes vespertinus*

Old World Sparrow
House Sparrow*	*Passer domesticus*

Mammals

Virginia Opossum	*Didelphis virginiana*
Masked Shrew	*Sorex cinereus*
Northern Short-tailed Shrew	*Blarina brevicauda*
Least Shrew	*Cryptotis parva*
Eastern Mole	*Scalopus aquaticus*
Eastern Red Bat	*Lasiurus borealis*
Silver-haired Bat	*Lasionycteris noctivagans*
Big Brown Bat	*Eptesicus fuscus*
Desert Cottontail	*Sylvilagus audubonii*
Eastern Cottontail	*Sylvilagus floridanus*
Black-tailed Jackrabbit	*Lepus californicus*
White-tailed Jackrabbit	*Lepus townsendii*
Spotted Ground Squirrel	*Spermophilus spilosoma*
Thirteen-lined Ground Squirrel	
	Spermophilus tridecemlineatus
Black-tailed Prairie Dog	*Cynomys ludovicianus*
Eastern Fox Squirrel	*Sciurus niger*
Plains Pocket Gopher	*Geomys bursarius*
Olive-backed Pocket Mouse	*Perognathus fasciatus*
Plains Pocket Mouse	*Perognathus flavescens*
Hispid Pocket Mouse	*Chaetodipus hispidus*
Ord's Kangaroo Rat	*Dipodomys ordii*
Beaver	*Castor canadensis*
Western Harvest Mouse	*Reithrodontomys megalotis*
Plains Harvest Mouse	*Reithrodontomys montanus*
White-footed Mouse	*Peromysus leucopus*
Deer Mouse	*Peromyscus maniculatus*
Northern Grasshopper Mouse	*Onychomys leucogaster*
Eastern Woodrat	*Neotoma floridana*
House Mouse	*Mus musculus*
Prairie Vole	*Microtus ochrogaster*
Meadow Vole	*Microtus pennsylvanicus*
Common Muskrat	*Ondatra zibethicus*
Southern Bog Lemming	*Synaptomys cooperi*
Meadow Jumping Mouse	*Zapus hudsonius*
Common Porcupine	*Erethizon dorsatum*
Coyote	*Canis latrans*
Common Raccoon	*Procyon lotor*
Long-tailed Weasel	*Mustela frenata*
Least Weasel	*Mustela nivalis*
Mink	*Mustela vison*
American Badger	*Taxidea taxus*
Eastern Spotted Skunk	*Spilogale putorius*
Striped Skunk	*Mephitis mephitis*
Northern River Otter	*Lutra canadensis*
Bobcat	*Lynx rufus*
Elk	*Cervus elaphus*
Mule Deer	*Odocoileus hemionus*
White-tailed Deer	*Odocoileus virginianus*
Pronghorn	*Antilocapra americana*
American Bison	*Bison bison*
Texas Longhorn	*Bos indicus*

Amphibians and Reptiles

Tiger Salamander	*Ambystoma tigrinum*
Woodhouse's Toad	*Bufo woodhousii*
Plains Spadefoot	*Spea bombifrons*
Blanchard's Cricket Frog	*Acris crepitans*
Western Chorus Frog	*Pseudacris triseriata*
Bullfrog	*Rana catesbeiana*
Northern Leopard Frog	*Rana pipiens*
Western Spiny Softshell	*Apalone spinifera*
Common Snapping Turtle	*Chelydra serpentina*
Painted Turtle	*Chrysemys picta*
Blanding's Turtle	*Emydoidea blandingii*
Yellow Mud Turtle	*Kinosternon flavescens*
Ornate Box Turtle	*Terrapene ornata*
Prairie Racerunner	*Cnemidophorus sexlineatus*
Lesser Earless Lizard	*Holbrookia maculata*
Northern Prairie Lizard	*Sceloporus undulatus*
Eastern Yellow-bellied Racer	*Coluber constrictor*
Eastern Hognose Snake	*Heterodon platyrhinos*
Pale milk Snake	*Lampropeltis triangulum*
Northern Water Snake	*Nerodia sipedon*
Bullsnake	*Pituophis catenifer*
Plains Garter Snake	*Thamnophis radix*
Red-sided Garter Snake	*Thamnophis sirtalis*
Prairie Rattlesnake	*Crotalus viridis*

Plants

VASCULAR CRYPTOGRAMS (Pteridophytes)

Selaginellaceae Spikemoss Family
rock spikemoss — *Selaginella rupestris*

Equisetaceae Horsetail Family
field horsetail — *Equisetum arvense*
intermediate horsetail — *Equisetum ferrissii*
common scouring rush — *Equisetum hyemale*
smooth scouring rush — *Equisetum laevigatum*

Ophioglossaceae Adder's-tongue Family
grape fern — *Botrychium matricariifolium*
rattlesnake fern — *Botrychium virginianum*
adders tongue — *Ophioglossum vulgatum var. pseudopodum*

Polypodiaceae True Fern Family
bladder/fragile fern — *Cystopteris fragilis*
wood fern — *Dryopteris carthusiana*
shield/spinulose wood fern — *Dryopteris spinulosa*
sensitive fern — *Onoclea sensibilis*
marsh fern — *Thelypteris palustris*
Oregon woodsia — *Woodsia oregana*

Marsileaceae Pepperwort Family
western water clover — *Marsilea vestita*

Division PINOPHYTA (Gymnosperms)

Cupressaceae Cypress Family
creeping juniper — *Juniperus horizontalis*
eastern red cedar — *Juniperus virginiana*

Pinaceae Pine Family
blue spruce — *Picea pungens*
ponderosa pine — *Pinus ponderosa*

Division MAGNOLIOPHYTA (Flowering Plants)
Class MAGNOLIOPSIDA (Dicots)

Aceraceae Maple Family
box elder — *Acer negundo var. interius*

Amaranthaceae Pigweed Family
sandhills pigweed — *Amaranthus arenicola*
prostrate pigweed — *Amaranthus graecizans*
rough pigweed — *Amaranthus retroflexus*
field snake cotton — *Froelichia floridana var. campestris*
slender snake cotton — *Froelichia gracilis*

Anacardiaceae Cashew Family
fragrant sumac — *Rhus aromatica var. serotina*
fragrant sumac — *Rhus aromatica var. trilobata*
smooth sumac — *Rhus glabra*
poison ivy — *Toxicodendron rydbergii*

Apiaceae Parsley Family
water parsnip — *Berula erecta var. incisum*
bulbous water hemlock — *Cicuta bulbifera*
common water hemlock — *Cicuta maculata*
poison hemlock — *Conium maculatum*
cow parsnip — *Heracleum sphondylium ssp. montanum*
wild parsley — *Lomatium orientale*
sweet cicely — *Osmorhiza claytonii*
anise root — *Osmorhiza longistylis var. longistylis*
black snakeroot — *Sanicula canadensis*
water parsnip — *Sium suave*

Apocynaceae Dogbane Family
spreading dogbane — *Apocynum androsaemifolium*

Araliaceae Ginseng Family
wild sarsaparilla — *Aralia nudicaulus*

Asclepiadaceae Milkweed Family
sand milkweed — *Asclepias arenaria*
swamp milkweed — *Asclepias incarnata incarnata*
wooly milkweed — *Asclepias lanuginosa*
plains milkweed — *Asclepias pumila*
narrow-leafed milkweed — *Asclepias stenophylla*
whorled milkweed — *Asclepias verticillata*
green milkweed — *Asclepias viridiflora*

Asteraceae Sunflower Family
yarrow — *Achillea millefolium ssp. lanulosa*
false dandelion — *Agoseris glauca*
common/short ragweed — *Ambrosia artemisiifolia*
western ragweed — *Ambrosia psilostachya*
giant ragweed — *Ambrosia trifida*
field pussy toes — *Antennaria neglecta*
pussy toes — *Antennaria parvifolia*
common burdock — *Arctium minus*
biennial wormwood — *Artemisia biennis*
western sagewort — *Artemisia campestris caudata*
sand sagebrush — *Artemisia filifolia*
fringed sagewort — *Artemisia frigida*
white sage — *Artemisia ludoviciana*
white aster — *Aster ericoides*
smooth blue aster — *Aster laevis*
New England aster — *Aster novae-angliae*
aromatic aster — *Aster oblongifolius*
willowleaf aster — *Aster praealtus var. nebraskensis*
swamp aster — *Aster puniceus*
panicled aster — *Aster simplex*
nodding beggar-ticks — *Bidens cernua*
tickseed sunflower — *Bidens coronata*
beggar-ticks — *Bidens frondosa*
golden aster — *Chrysopsis stenophylla*
tall/roadside thistle — *Cirsium altissimum*
Platte thistle — *Cirsium canescens*
horse-weed — *Conyza canadensis*
spreading fleabane — *Conyza ramossima*
hawks beard — *Crepis runcinata runcinata*
fetid marigold — *Dyssodia papposa*
purple coneflower — *Echinacea angustifolia var. angustifolia*
annual fleabane — *Erigeron annuus*
western fleabane — *Erigeron bellidiastrum var. bellidiastrum*
Philadelphia fleabane — *Erigeron philadelphicus*
daisy fleabane — *Erigeron strigosus var. strigosus*

joe-pye weed	*Eupatorium maculatum* var. *bruneri*
boneset	*Eupatorium perfoliatum*
vicid euthamia	*Euthamia gymnospermoides*
Indian blanket flower	*Gaillardia pulchella*
curly-top gumweed	*Grindelia squarrosa* var. *squarrosa*
snakeweed	*Gutierrezia sarothrae*
cutleaf ironplant	*Haplopappus spinulosus*
sneeze weed	*Helenium autumnale*
common sunflower	*Helianthus annuus*
sawtooth sunflower	*Helianthus grosseseratus*
maximilian sunflower	*Helianthus maximilianii*
Nutall's sunflower	*Helianthus nuttallii nuttallii*
sunflower sp.	*Helianthus nuttallii rydbergii*
rigid sunflower	*Helianthus rigidus subrhomboideus*
Jerusalem-artichoke	*Helianthus tuberosus*
ox-eye/false sunflower	*Heliopsis helianthoides* var. *scabra*
fineleaf hymenopappus	*Hymenopappus filifolius*
woolly white hymenopappus	*Hymenopappus tenuifolius*
false boneset	*Kuhnia eupatorioides* var. *corymbulosa*
wild lettuce	*Lactuca canadensis*
blue lettuce	*Lactuca oblongifolia*
blazing stars	*Liatris aspera*
scaly gayfeather	*Liatris glabrata*
dotted gayfeather	*Liatris punctata*
gayfeather sp.	*Liatris squarrosa* var. *glabrata*
skeleton weed	*Lygodesmia juncea*
beaked skeleton plant	*Lygodesmia rostrata*
wavyleaf agoseris	*Microseris cuspidata*
	Pectis angustifolia
prairie coneflower	*Ratibida columnifera*
blackeyed-susan	*Rudbeckia hirta*
ragwort	*Senecio integerrimus*
prairie ragwort	*Senecio plattensis*
riddell ragwort	*Senecio riddellii*
groundsel sp.	*Senecio tridenticulatus*
skeleton weed sp.	*Shinnersoseris rostrata*
Canada goldenrod	*Solidago canadensis* var. *gilvocanescens*
Canada goldenrod	*Solidago canadensis* var. *scabra*
late goldenrod	*Solidago gigantea*
late goldenrod	*Solidago gigantea* var. *serotina*
grassleaf goldenrod	*Solidago graminifolia* var. *media*
prairie goldenrod	*Solidago missouriensis*
ashy goldenrod	*Solidago mollis*
gray goldenrod	*Solidago nemoralis*
rigid goldenrod	*Solidago rigida*
showy-wand goldenrod	*Solidago speciosa*
common tansy	*Tanacetum vulgare*
common dandelion	*Taraxacum officinale*
greenthread	*Thelesperma filifolium*
Easter daisy	*Townsendia exscapa*
goats beard	*Tragopogon dubias*
ironweed	*Vernonia fasciculata* var. *fasciculata*
cocklebur	*Xanthium strumarium*

Balsaminaceae Touch-me-not Family

spotted touch-me-not	*Impatiens biflora*
spotted touch-me-not	*Impatiens capensis*

Betulaceae Birch Family

paper birch	*Betula papyrifera*
hazelnut	*Corylus americana*
hop-hornbeam/ironwood	*Ostrya virginiana*

Boraginaceae Borage Family

borage sp.	*Cryptantha minima*
American stickseed	*Hackelia deflexa*
Virginia stickseed	*Hackelia virginiana*
beggars lice/stickseed	*Lappula redowskii*
puccoon	*Lithospermum carolinense*
puccoon sp.	*Lithospermum incisum*
forget-me-not	*Myosotis laxa*
false gromwell	*Onosmodium molle*

Brassicaceae Mustard Family

rock-cress	*Arabis hirsuta* var. *pycnocarpa*
small seeded false flax	*Camelina microcarpa*
shepard's purse	*Capsella bursa-pastoris*
spring cress	*Cardamine bulbosa*
blue mustard	*Chorispora tenella*
tansy mustard	*Descurainia pinnata*
herb-sophia	*Descurainia sophia*
white whittlewort	*Draba reptans*
western wallflower	*Erysium asperum*
wormseed wallflower	*Erysium cheiranthoides*
small flower wallflower	*Erysium inconspicuum*
dame's rocket	*Hesperis matronalis*
peppergrass	*Lepidium densiflorum*
bladder pod	*Lesquerella ludoviciana*
water cress	*Nasturtium officinale*
marsh cress	*Rorippa palustris*
tumbling mustard	*Sisymbrium altissimum*
tall hedge mustard	*Sisymbrium loeselii*
field pennycress	*Thlaspi arvense*

Cactacea Cactus Family

nipple cactus	*Mammillaria vivipara*
prickly pear	*Opuntia compressa*
little prickly pear	*Opuntia fragilis*

Campanulacceae Bellflower Family

tall bellflower	*Campanula americana*
marsh bellflower	*Campanula aparinoides*
harebell	*Campanula rotundiflora*
blue cardinal flower	*Lobelia siphilitica*
palespike lobelia	*Lobelia spicata*
Venus' looking glass	*Triodanis perfoliata*

Cannabaceae Hemp Family

hemp/marijuana	*Cannabis sativa*

Capparaceae Caper Family

Rocky Mountain bee plant	*Cleome serrulata*
cristatella	*Cristatella jamesii*
clammy weed	*Polanisia dodecandra*

Caprifoliaceae Honeysuckle Family

limber/wild honeysuckle	*Lonicera dioica* var. *glaucescens*
common elderberry	*Sambucus canadensis*
snowberry	*Symphoricarpos albus*
western snowberry	*Symphoricarpos occidentalis*

Caryophyllaceae Pink Family

grove sandwort	*Arenaria lateriflora*
mouse-ear chickweed	*Cerastium brachypodium*
white cockle	*Lychnis alba*
sleepy catchfly	*Silene antirrhina*
white champion catchfly	*Silene pratensis*
chickweed/starwort	*Stellaria longifolia*

Celastraceae Staff Tree Family

bittersweet	*Celastrus scandens*
hornwort/coontail	*Ceratophyllum demersum*

Chenopodiaceae Goosefoot Family

lamb's quarters	*Chenopodium album*
maple leaf goosefoot	*Chenopodium hybridum*
Standley goosefoot	*Chenopodium standleyanum*
hyssoleaf tickseed	*Corispermum hyssopifolium*
bugseed	*Corispermum nitidum*
winged pigweed	*Cycloloma atriplicifolium*
summer-cypress	*Kochia scoparia*

Cistaceae Rockrose Family

frostweed	*Helianthemum bicknelii*
pinweed	*Lechea stricta*

Clusiaceae St. John's Wort Family

St. John's wort	*Hypercum majus*

Convolvulaceae Morning Glory Family

field bindweed	*Convolvulus arvensis*
Nuttal's evolvulus	*Evolvulus nuttallianus*
bush morning glory	*Ipomea leptophylla*

Cornaceae Dogwood Family

red osier	*Cornus stolonifera*

Crassulaceae Stonecrop Family

ditch stone-crop	*Penthorum sedoides*

Cucurbitaceae Cucumber Family

balsam apple/wild cucumber	*Echinocystis lobata*

Cuscutaceae Dodder Family

dodder	*Cuscuta coryli*

Elaeaganaceae Oleaster Family

Russian olive	*Elaeagnus angustifolia*
buffalo-berry	*Shepherdia argentea*

Elatinaceae Waterwort Family

waterwort	*Elatine triandra*

Euphorbiaceae Spurge Family

three-seeded mercury	*Acalypha virginica*
skunkweed	*Croton texensis*
six-angled spurge	*Euphorbia hexagona*
Missouri spurge	*Euphorbia missurica*
leafy spurge	*Euphorbia pseudovirgata*
round leaved spurge	*Euphorbia serpens*

Fabaceae Bean Family

leadplant	*Amorpha canescens*
false indigo	*Amorpha fruticosa*
hogpeanut	*Amphicarpaea bracteata*
groundnut	*Apios americana*
Canada milk-vetch	*Astragalus canadensis*
painted milk-vetch	*Astragalus ceramicus*
ground/prairie plum	*Astragalus crassicarpus*
lotus milk-vetch	*Astragalus lotiflorus*
golden prairie clover	*Dalea aurea*
white prairie clover	*Dalea candida* var. *oligophylla*
nine-anther prairie clover	*Dalea enneandra*
purple prairie clover	*Dalea purpurea* var. *purpurea*
silky prairie clover	*Dalea villosa*
Canada tickclover	*Desmodium canadense*
tick-trefoil	*Desmodium glutinosum*
wild licorice	*Glycyrrhiza lepidota* var. *lepidota*
vetching/wild peas	*Lathyrus polymorphus*
round-head lespedeza	*Lespedeza capitata*
prairie trefoil	*Lotus purshianus*
black medick	*Medicago lupulina*
alfalfa	*Medicago sativa sativa*
white sweet clover	*Melilotus alba*
yellow sweet clover	*Melilotus officinalis*
purple locoweed	*Oxytropis lambertii* var. *lambertii*
white prairie clover	*Petalostemon occidentale*
silver leaf scurf pea	*Psoralea argophylla*
tall-bread scurf pea	*Psoralea cuspidata*
palm-leaved scurf pea	*Psoralea digitata*
prairie turnip	*Psoralea esculenta*
little breadroot	*Psoralea hypogaea* var. *hypogaea*
lemon scurf pea	*Psoralea lanceolata*
wild bean	*Strophostyles leiosperma*
alsike clover	*Trifolium hybridum elegans*
red clover	*Trifolium pratense*
white clover	*Trifolium repens*
vetch	*Vicia villosa* var. *villosa*

Fagaceae Oak Family

bur oak	*Quercus macrocarpa*

Fumariaceae Fumitory Family

corydalis	*Corydalis aurea* var. *occidentalis*

Gentianaceae Gentian Family

closed gentian	*Gentiana andrewsii*

Geraniaceae Geranium Family

crane's bill	*Geranium carolinianum*

Grossulariaceae Currant Family

wild black currant	*Ribes americanum*
gooseberry	*Ribes missouriense*
golden current	*Ribes odoratum*
northern gooseberry	*Ribes oxycanthoides*

Hydrophyllaceae Waterleaf Family

waterpod	*Ellisia nyctelea*

Juglandaceae Walnut Family

black walnut	*Juglans nigra*

Lamiaceae Mint Family

dragonhead	*Dracocephalum parviflorum*
ground ivy	*Glecoma hederacea*
false penny-royal	*Hedeoma hispida*
American bugleweed	*Lycopus americanus*
rough bugleweed	*Lycopus asper*
field mint	*Mentha arvensis*
wild bergamonts	*Monarda fistulosa* var. *fistulosa*
wild bergamonts	*Monarda fistulosa* var. *menthaefolia*
lemon mint	*Monarda pectinata*
catnip	*Nepeta cataria*
selfheal	*Prunella vulgaris*
mountain mint	*Pycnanthemum virginianum*
sage	*Salvia pitcheri*
Rocky Mountain sage	*Salvia reflexa*
marsh skullcap	*Scutellaria galericulata*
blue skullcap	*Scutellaria lateriflora*
small skullcap	*Scutellaria parvula* var. *leonardi*
wood sage	*Teucrium canadense* var. *occidentale*

Lentibulariaceae Bladderwort Family

bladderwort	*Utricularia vulgaris*

Linaceae Flax Family

flax	*Linum rigidum* var. *compactum*
flax	*Linum rigidum* var. *rigidum*

Loasaceae Stickleaf Family

bractless mentzelia	*Mentzelia nuda*
sand lily/ten petal mentzelia	*Mentzelia decapetala*

Lythraceae Loosestrife Family

toothcup	*Ammannia robusta*
loosestrife	*Lythrum alatum* var. *alatum*
winged loosestrife	*Lythrum dacotanum*
purple loosestrife	*Lythrum salicaria*

Malvaceae Mallow Family

common mallow	*Malva neglecta*
common mallow	*Malva rotundiflora*
scarlet mallow	*Sphaeralcea coccinea*

Mimosaceae Mimosa Family

prairie mimosa	*Desmanthus illinoensis*
sensitive briar	*Schrankia nuttalli*

Molluginaceae Carpetweed Family

carpet-weed	*Mollugo verticillata*

Monotropaceae Indian Pipe Family

pine-drops	*Pterospora andromedea*

Moraceae Mulberry Family

white mulberry	*Morus alba*

Nyctaginaceae Four-O'Clock Family

hairy four-o'clock	*Mirabilis hirsuta*
narrow leaf four-o'clock	*Mirabilis linearis*
wild four-o'clock	*Mirabilis nyctaginea*

Nymphaeaceae Waterlily Family

fragrant white waterlily	*Nymphaea odorata*

Oleacae Olive Family

green ash	*Fraxinus pennsylvanica* var. *pennsylvanica*
common lilac	*Syringa vulgaris*

Onagraceae Evening Primrose Family

plains yellow primrose	*Calylophus serrualtus*
enchanter's nightshade	*Circaea lutetiana* ssp. *canadensis*
willow-herb sp.	*Epilobium adenocaulon*
willow herb sp.	*Epilobium ciliatum*
purple-leaved willow herb	*Epilobium coloratum*
narrow-leaved willow herb	*Epilobium leptophyllum*
scarlet gaura/butterfly weed	*Gaura coccinea*
velvety gaura	*Gaura parviflora*
marsh seedbox	*Ludwigia palustris*
manyseed seedbox	*Ludwigia polycarpa*
prairie primrose	*Oenothera albicaulis*
evening primrose	*Oenothera biennis*
cut-leaved evening primrose	*Oenothera laciniata*
white stemmed evening primrose	*Oenothera nuttallii*
four point evening primrose	*Oenothera rhombipetala*

Orobanchaceae Broomrape Family

broomrape	*Orobanche fasciculata*

Oxalidaceae Wood Sorrel Family

gray-green wood sorrel	*Oxalis dillenii*
yellow wood sorrel	*Oxalis stricta*

Papaveraceae Poppy Family

prickly poppy	*Argemine polyanthemos*

Pedaliaceae Unicorn-Plant Family

unicorn plant	*Proboscidea louisianica*

Plantaginaceae Plantain Family

common plantain	*Plantago major*
buckhorn	*Plantago patagonica* var. *patagonica*

Polemoniaceae Polemonium Family

collomia	*Collomia linearis*
whiteflower gilia	*Ipomopsis longiflora*
moss phlox	*Phlox andicola*

Polygalaceae Milkwort Family

white milkwort	*Polygala alba*
whorled milkwort	*Polygala verticillata*

Polygonaceae Buckwheat Family

annual wild buckwheat	*Eriogonum annuum*
knotweed	*Polygonum achoreum*
water smartweed	*Polygonum amphibium* var. *stipulaceum*
common knotweed	*Polygonum arenastrum*
black bindweed	*Polygonum convolvulus*
erect knotweed	*Polygonum erectum*
nodding willow weed	*Polygonum lapathifolium*
lady's thumb	*Polygonum persicaria*
smartweed	*Polygonum punctatum*
false buckwheat	*Polygonum scandens*
slender knotweed	*Polygonum tenue*
water/pale dock	*Rumex altissimus*
sour/curly dock	*Rumex crispus*
golden dock	*Rumex maritimus* var. *fueginus*
dock sp.	*Rumex stenophyllus*
sour greens/wild begonia	*Rumex venosus*

Portulacaceae Purslane Family
fameflower/rock pink   *Talinum calycinum*
prairie fameflower   *Talinum parviflorum*

Primulaceae Primrose Family
western rock jasmine   *Androsace occidentalis*
chaffweed   *Centunculus minimus*
fringed loosestrife   *Lysimachia ciliata*
tufted loosestrife   *Lysimachia thyrsiflora*

Ranunculaceae Buttercup Family
Carolina anemone   *Anemone carolinana*
candle anemone   *Anemone cylindrica*
pasque flower   *Anemone patens*
wild columbine   *Aquilegia canadensis*
western virgins bower/western clematis
                                Clematis ligusticifolia
virgins bower   *Clematis virginiana*
prairie larkspur   *Delphinium carolinianum*
prairie larkspur   *Delphinium virescens*
small flowered buttercup /early wood buttercup
                                Ranunculus abortivus
seaside crowfoot/shore buttercup
                                Ranunculus cymbalaria
white water crowfoot   *Ranunculus longirostris*
cursed crowfoot   *Ranunculus scleratus* var. *scleratus*
white water crowfoot   *Ranunculus subrigidus*
meadow rue   *Thalictrum dasycarpum*

Rhamnaceae Buckthorn Family
New Jersey tea   *Ceanothus herbaceus* var. *pubescens*
lance-leaved buckthorn   *Rhamnus lanceolata*
                                var. *glabratus*

Rosaceae Rose Family
hooked agrimony   *Agrimonia gryposepala*
Saskatoon service-berry   *Amelanchier alnifolia*
woodland strawberry   *Fragaria vesca* var. *americana*
yellow avens   *Geum aleppicum*
white avens   *Geum canadense*
apple   *Malus sylvestris*
ninebark   *Physocarpus opulifolius*
tall cinquefoil   *Potentilla arguta*
Norwegian cinquefoil   *Potentilla norvegica*
cinquefoil   *Potentilla pensylvanica*
brook cinquefoil   *Potentilla rivalis*
wild plum   *Prunus americana*
western sandcherry   *Prunus besseyi*
sand/dwarf cherry   *Prunus pumila*
chokecherry   *Prunus virginiana*
wild prairie rose   *Rosa arkansana*
western wild rose   *Rosa woodsii*
black raspberry   *Rubus occidentalis*

Rubiaceae Madder Family
cleavers   *Galium aparine*
catchweed bedstraw   *Galium circaezans*
sweet-scented bedstraw   *Galium triflorum*

Rutaceae Citrus Family
prickly ash   *Zanthoxylum americanum*

Salicaceae Willow Family
white/silver poplar   *Populus alba*
cottonwood   *Populus deltoides*
cottonwood   *Populus sargentii*
quaking aspen   *Populus tremuloides*
peach-leaved-willow   *Salix amygdaloides*
sandbar/coyote willow   *Salix exigua* ssp. *interior*
heart-leaved willow   *Salix rigida* var. *rigida*

Santalaceae Sandalwood Family
bastard toadflax   *Comandra umbellata*

Saxifragaceae Saxifrage Family
alumroot   *Heuchera richardsonii*

Scrophulariaceae Figwort Family
gerardia sp.   *Agalinis aspera*
gerardia sp.   *Agalinis tenuifolia*
water hyssop   *Bacopa rotundifolia*
downy paintbrush   *Castilleja sessiliflora*
false pimpernel   *Lindernia dubia*
roundleaf monkey-flower   *Mimulus glabratus*
                                var. *fremontii*
Alleghany monkey-flower   *Mimulus ringens*
white beardtongue   *Penstemon albidus*
narrow beardtongue   *Penstemon angustifolius*
                                var. *angustifolius*
slender beardtongue   *Penstemon gracilis* var. *gracilis*
large beardtongue   *Penstemon grandiflorus*
figwort   *Scrophularia lanceolata*
common mullein   *Verbascum thapsus*
brooklime/speedwell   *Veronica americana*
waterspeedwell   *Veronica anagallis-aquatica*
purslane speedwell   *Veronica peregrina* var. *xalapenis*

Solanaceae Potato or Nightshade Family
matrimony vine   *Lycium halimifolium*
clammy ground cherry   *Physalis heterophylla*
Virginia ground cherry   *Physalis virginiana*
black nightshade   *Solanum americanum*
black nightshade   *Solanum ptycanthum*
buffalo bur; Kansas thistle   *Solanum rostratum*
cut-leaved nightshade   *Solanum triflorum*

Tiliaceae Linden Family
linden/basswood   *Tilia americana*

Ulmaceae Elm Family
hackberry   *Celtis occidentalis*
American elm   *Ulmus americana*
red elm   *Ulmus rubra*

Urticaceae Nettle Family
false nettle   *Boehmeria cylindrica*
woodnettle   *Laportea canadensis*
pellitory   *Parietaria pensylvanica*
clearweed   *Pilea pumila*
stinging nettle   *Urtica dioica* ssp. *gracilis*

Verbenaceae Vervain Family
lopseed   *Phryma leptostachya*
prostrate vervain   *Verbena bracteata*
blue vervain   *Verbena hastata*
hoary vervain   *Verbena stricta*
white/needle leaved vervain   *Verbena urticifolia*

Violaceae Violet Family
Canada/tall white violet *Viola canadensis* var. *rugulosa*
northern bog violet *Viola nephrophylla*
meadow/blue prairie violet *Viola pratincola*

Vitaceae Grape Family
Virginia creeper *Parthenocissis quinquefolia*
woodbine/thicket creeper *Parthenocissis vitacea*
riverbank grape *Vitis riparia*

Zygophyllaceae Caltrop Family
puncture vine/goathead *Tribulus terrestris*

Class LILIOPSIDA (Monocots)
Agavaceae Agave Family
soapweed/yucca *Yucca glauca*

Alismataceae Water Plantain Family
water plantain *Alisma subcordatum*
arrowhead *Sagittaria engelmannia* var. *brevirostrata*
duck-patato/arrowhead *Sagittaria latifolia*

Commelinaceae Spiderwort Family
erect dayflower *Commelina erecta* var. *augustifolia*
spiderwort *Tradescantia occidentalis*

Cyperaceae Sedge Family
sedge *Carex aurea*
sedge *Carex blanda*
sedge *Carex brevior*
sedge *Carex comosa*
sedge *Carex diandra*
sedge *Carex eburnea*
sedge *Carex eleocharis*
sedge *Carex filifolia*
sedge *Carex granularis*
sedge *Carex heliophila*
sedge *Carex hystricina*
sedge *Carex interior*
sedge *Carex lanuginosa*
sedge *Carex meadii*
sedge *Carex nebraskensis*
sedge *Carex peckii*
sedge *Carex praegracilis*
sedge *Carex saximontana*
sedge *Carex scoparia*
sedge *Carex sprengelli*
sedge *Carex stipata*
sedge *Carex stricta*
sedge *Carex tetanica*
sedge *Carex vulpinoidea*
umbrella sedge *Cyperus acuminatus*
umbrella sedge *Cyperus aristatus*
umbrella sedge *Cyperus diandrus*
umbrella sedge *Cyperus erythrorhizos*
umbrella sedge *Cyperus odoratus*
umbrella sedge *Cyperus rivularis*
umbrella sedge *Cyperus schweinitzii*
umbrella sedge *Cyperus strigosus*
spikerush *Eleocharis acicularis*
spikerush *Eleocharis erythropoda*
spikerush *Eleocharis obtusa*
  Fimbristylis puberula
bulrush sp. *Scirpus acutus*
bulrush sp. *Scirpus americanus*

bulrush sp. *Scirpus atrovirens*
bulrush sp. *Scirpus pallidus*
bulrush sp. *Scirpus validus*

Hydrocharitaceae Frog's-bit Family
water weed *Elodea nuttallii*

Iridaceae Iris Family
blue-eyed grass *Sisyrinchium montanum*

Juncaceae Rush Family
rush *Juncus alpinus*
rush *Juncus balticus*
rush *Juncus brachyphyllus*
rush *Juncus bufonius*
rush *Juncus dudleyi*
rush *Juncus longistylis*
rush *Juncus marginatus*
rush *Juncus nodosus*
rush *Juncus torreyi*

Juncaginaceae Arrowgrass Family
arrowgrass *Triglochin maritima*
arrowgrass *Triglochin palustris*

Lemnaceae Duckweed Family
duckweed *Lemna minor*
star duckweed *Lemna trisulca*
greater duckweed *Spirodela polyrrhiza*

Liliaceae Lily Family
onion *Allium perdulce*
wild asparagus *Asparagus officinales*
stargrass *Hypoxis hirsuta*
solomon's seal *Polygonatum biflorum*
false solomon's seal/spikenard *Smilacina stellata*

Smilaceae Catbrier Family
carrion-flower *Smilax herbacea* var. *lasioneuron*

Orchidaceae Orchid Family
northern green orchis *Habenaria hyperborea*
twayblade *Liparis loeselii*
ladies-tresses *Spiranthes cernua*

Poaceae Grass Family
X *Agrohordeum macounii*
slender wheatgrass *Agropyron caninum*
crested wheatgrass *Agropyron cristatum*
western wheatgrass *Agropyron smithii*
redtop sp. *Agrostis alba*
ticklegrass *Agrostis scabra*
redtop *Agrostis stolonifera*
short-awn foxtail *Alopecurus aequalis*
big bluestem *Andropogon gerardi*
sand bluestem *Andropogon hallii*
little bluestem *Andropogon scoparius*
three-awn sp. *Aristida basiramea*
three-awn sp. *Aristida longiseta*
Fendler three-awn *Aristida purpurea* var. *longiseta*
sideoats grama *Bouteloua curtipendula*
blue grama *Bouteloua gracilis*
hairy grama *Bouteloua hirsuta*
earleaf brome *Bromus altissimus*
fringed brome *Bromus ciliatus*

smooth brome	*Bromus inermis*
Japanese brome	*Bromus japonicus*
brome sp.	*Bromus latiglumis*
downy brome/cheatgrass	*Bromus tectorum*
buffalo grass	*Buchloe dactyloides*
bluejoint reedgrass	*Calamagrostis canadensis*
reedgrass sp	*Calamagrostis inexpansa*
northern reedgrass	*Calamagrostis stricta*
prairie sandreed	*Calamovilfa longifolia*
brookgrass	*Catabrosa aquatica*
sandbur	*Cenchrus longispinus*
woodreed	*Cinna arundinacea*
orchard grass	*Dactylis glomerata*
small prairie grass	*Dichanthelium acuminatum*
Scribner dicanthelium	*Dichanthelium oligosanthes*
wilcox dichanthelium	*Dichanthelium wilcoxianum*
hairy crabgrass	*Digitaria sanguinalis*
smallflower barnyard grass	*Echinochloa muricata* var. *microstachya*
Canada wild rye	*Elymus canadensis*
hairy wild rye	*Elymus villosus*
Virginia wild rye	*Elymus virginicus*
stinkgrass	*Eragrostis cilianensis*
teal lovegrass	*Eragrostis hypnoides*
Carolina lovegrass	*Eragrostis pectinacea*
purple lovegrass	*Eragrostis spectabilis*
sand lovegrass	*Eragrostis trichodes*
nodding fescue	*Festuca obtusa*
six-weeks fescue/blue bunchgrass	*Festuca octoflora*
American/tall manna grass	*Glyceria grandis*
fowl mannagrass	*Glyceria striata*
foxtail barley	*Hordeum jubatum*
little barley	*Hordeum pusillum*
junegrass	*Koeleria pyrimidata*
rice cutgrass	*Leersia oryzoides*
whitegrass	*Leersia virginica*
scratchgrass	*Muhlenbergia asperifolia*
plains muhly	*Muhlenbergia cuspidata*
pullup muhly	*Muhlenbergia filiformis*
common/wirestem muhly	*Muhlenbergia mexicana*
sand muhly	*Muhlenbergia pungens*
marsh muhly	*Muhlenbergia racemosa*
false buffalo grass	*Munroa squarrosa*
little seed ricegrass	*Oryzopsis micrantha*
common witchgrass	*Panicum capillare*
fall panicum	*Panicum dichotomiflorum*
switchgrass	*Panicum virgatum*
sand paspalum	*Paspalum setaceum* var. *stramineum*
timothy	*Phleum pratense*
Canada bluegrass	*Poa compressa*
Kentucky bluegrass	*Poa pratensis*
woodland bluegrass	*Poa sylvestris*
rabbitfoot grass	*Polypogon monspleliensis*
blowout grass	*Redfieldia flexuosa*
tumblegrass	*Schedonnardus paniculatus*
rye	*Secale cereale*
yellow foxtail	*Setaria glauca*
green foxtail	*Setaria viridis*
Indian grass	*Sorghastrum nutans*
prairie cordgrass/slough grass	*Spartina pectinata*
wedgegrass	*Sphenopholis obtusata*
sand dropseed	*Sporobolus cryptandrus*
needle-and-thread	*Stipa comata*
porcupine-grass	*Stipa spartea*

green needlegrass	*Stipa viridula*
sandgrass	*Triplasis purpurea*

Potamogetonaceae Pondweed Family

longleaf pondweed	*Potamogeton nodosus*

Sparganiaceae Bur-reed Family

bur-reed	*Sparganium eurycarpum*

Typhaceae Cat-tail Family

broad-leaved cattail	*Typha latifolia*

Zannichelliaceae Horned Pondweed Family

horned pondweed	*Zannichellia palustris*

Appendix G. Compliance Requirements

Many procedural and substantive requirements of Federal and applicable State and local laws and regulations affect Refuge establishment, management, and development. This appendix identifies the key permits, approvals, and consultations needed to implement the strategies.

In undertaking the proposed action, the Service would comply with the following Federal laws, Executive orders, and legislative acts:

In undertaking the proposed action, the following Executive Orders and legislative acts have been or will be acted upon.

American Indian Religious Freedom Act of 1978: Directs agencies to consult with native traditional religious leaders to determine appropriate policy changes necessary to protect and preserve Native American religious cultural rights and practices.

Americans With Disabilities Act of 1992: Prohibits discrimination in public accommodations and services.

Antiquities Act of 1906: Authorizes the scientific investigation of antiquities on Federal land and provides penalties for unauthorized removal of objects taken or collected without a permit.

Archaeological and Historic Preservation Act of 1974: Directs the preservation of historic and archaeological data in Federal construction projects.

Archaeological Resources Protection Act of 1979, as amended: Protects materials of archaeological interest from unauthorized removal or destruction and requires Federal managers to develop plans and schedules to locate archaeological resources.

Architectural Barriers Act of 1968: Requires federally owned, leased, or funded buildings and facilities to be accessible to persons with disabilities.

Bald and Golden Eagle Protection Act of 1940, as amended: Calls for the protection of these raptorial species on and off Federal Lands.

Clean Air Act of 1977, as amended: The primary objective of this Act is to establish Federal standards for various pollutants from both stationary and mobile sources and to provide for the regulation of polluting emissions via state implementation plants. In addition, and of special interest for National Wildlife Refuges, some amendments are designed to prevent significant deterioration in certain areas where air quality exceeds national standards, and to provide for improved air quality in areas which do not meet Federal standards ("non-attainment" areas). Federal facilities are required to comply with air quality standards to the same extent as nongovernmental entities (42 U.S.C. 7418). Part C of the 1977 amendments stipulates requirements to prevent significant deterioration of air quality and, in particular, to preserve air quality in national parks, national wilderness areas, national monuments, and national seashores (42 U.S.C. 7470).

Clean Water Act of 1977: Requires consultation with the Corps of Engineers (404 permits) for wetland modifications.

Emergency Wetlands Resources Act of 1986: The purpose of the Act is "To promote the conservation of migratory waterfowl and to offset or prevent the serious loss of wetlands by the acquisition of wetlands and other essential habitat, and for other purposes."

Endangered Species Act of 1973, as amended: Requires all Federal agencies to carry out programs for the conservation of endangered and threatened species. An Intra-Service Section 7 consultation was conducted prior to implementation of this CCP (attached to this CCP as an appendix). No significant impact is expected from the implementation of this Plan.

Executive Order 11644, Use of Off-Road Vehicles on Public Lands

Executive Order No. 11593, Protection and Enhancement of the Cultural Environment (1971). If the Service proposes any development activities that would affect the archaeological or historical sites, the Service will consult with Federal and State Historic Preservation Officers to comply with Section 106 of the National Historic Preservation Act of 1966, as amended.

Executive Order No. 11988, Floodplain Management. Each Federal agency shall provide leadership and take action to reduce the risk of flood loss and minimize the impact of floods on human safety, and preserve the natural and beneficial values served by the floodplains. No structures or other barriers that could either be damaged by or significantly influenced the movement of flood waters are planned for construction by the Service in the project area. This Plan supports the preservation and enhancement of the natural and beneficial values of floodplains.

Executive Order No. 11990, Protection of Wetlands. The proposal will help conserve the natural and beneficial values of the wetland habitat. The Service will undertake no activity that would be detrimental to the continuance of the vital wetlands.

Executive Order No. 12372, Intergovernmental Review of Federal Programs. The State of Nebraska and counties encompassing the Refuge were sent copies of the Draft Comprehensive Conservation Plan and Environmental Assessment for distribution to State and County agencies and departments. Coordination and consultation is ongoing with local and State governments, Tribes, Congressional representatives, and other Federal agencies.

Executive Order No. 12898, Environmental Justice in Minority Populations and Low-income Populations. This environmental justice analysis concluded that the socioeconomic, cultural, physical, and biological effects of the preferred alternative (the CCP) does not predict any outcomes that would cause disproportionately high and adverse human health impacts in any population, nor would they result in disproportionally high or adverse impact to low-income or minority populations, nor would create a greater burden on low-income households.

Executive Order 12996 Management and General Public Use of the National Wildlife Refuge System (1996): Defines the mission, purpose, and priority public uses of the National Wildlife Refuge System. It also presents four principles to guide management of the System. Through the development of this Comprehensive Conservation Plan, the Service has completed compatibility determinations for existing wildlife-dependent recreational activities that will be allowed to continue.

Executive Order 13007 Indian Sacred Sites (1996): Directs Federal land management agencies to accommodate access to and ceremonial use of Indian sacred sites by Indian religious practitioners, avoid adversely affecting the physical integrity of such sacred sites, and where appropriate, maintain the confidentiality of sacred sites.

Executive Order 13084, Consultation and Coordination with Indian Tribal Governments

Federal Noxious Weed Act of 1990: Requires the use of integrated management systems to control or contain undesirable plant species; and an interdisciplinary approach with the cooperation of other Federal and State agencies.

Fish and Wildlife Act of 1956: Established a comprehensive national fish and wildlife policy and broadened the authority for acquisition and development of refuges.

Fish and Wildlife Coordination Act of 1958: Allows the Fish and Wildlife Service to enter into agreements with private landowners for wildlife management purposes.

Land and Water Conservation Fund Act of 1965: Uses the receipts from the sale of surplus Federal land, outer continental shelf oil and gas sales, and other sources for land acquisition under several authorities.

Migratory Bird Conservation Act of 1929: Establishes procedures for acquisition by purchase, rental, or gift of areas approved by the Migratory Bird Conservation Commission.

Migratory Bird Hunting and Conservation Stamp Act (1934): Authorized the opening of part of a refuge to waterfowl hunting.

Migratory Bird Treaty Act of 1918: Designates the protection of migratory birds as a Federal responsibility. This Act enables the setting of seasons, and other regulations including the closing of areas, Federal or non-Federal, to the hunting of migratory birds.

National Environmental Policy Act of 1969 (40 CFR 1500): Requires all Federal agencies to examine the impacts upon the environment that their actions might have, to incorporate the best available environmental information, and the use of public participation in the planning and implementation of all actions. All Federal agencies must integrate NEPA with other planning requirements, and prepare appropriate NEPA documentation to facilitate sound environmental decision making. NEPA requires the disclosure of the environmental impacts of any major Federal action that affects in a significant way the quality of the human environment. The process, from its inception, to prepare this Plan complied with all of NEPA requirements.

National Historic Preservation Act of 1966, as amended: Establishes as policy that the Federal Government is to provide leadership in the preservation of the nation's prehistoric and historic resources. This Plan is in compliance with this law as the 1897 "hay barn" National Historic Building will not be affected by the implementation of the goals and objectives of this CCP.

National Trails System Act of 1968, as amended: Deals with the establishment of National Recreational Trails by the Secretaries of Interior or Agriculture on land wholly or partly within their jurisdiction, with the consent of the involved State(s), and other land managing agencies, if any. National Scenic and National Historic Trails may only be designated by an Act of Congress. The proposal contained in this Plan will not impact the 5 miles of Congressionally designated National Recreational Trail System trails that currently exist within the Refuge.

National Trails Act of 1982: Designated a portion of the Niobrara River through Fort Niobrara NWR a National Canoe Trail.

National Wildlife Refuge System Administration Act of 1966 as amended by the National Wildlife Refuge System Improvement Act of 1997, 16 U.S.C. 668dd-668ee. (Refuge Administration Act): Defines the National Wildlife Refuge System and authorizes the Secretary to permit any use of a refuge provided such use is compatible with the major purposes for which the refuge was established. The Refuge Improvement Act clearly defines a unifying mission for the Refuge System; establishes the legitimacy and appropriateness of the six priority public uses (hunting, fishing, wildlife observation and photography, or environmental education and interpretation); establishes a formal process for determining compatibility; established the responsibilities of the Secretary of Interior for managing and protecting the System; and requires the preparation and implementation of a Comprehensive Conservation Plan for each refuge by the year 2012. This Act amended portions of the Refuge Recreation Act and National Wildlife Refuge System Administration Act of 1966. This Plan is in compliance with the National Wildlife Refuge System Act of 1966, as amended.

Native American Graves Protection and Repatriation Act of 1990: Requires Federal agencies and museums to inventory, determine ownership of, and repatriate cultural items under their control or possession. No known Native American cultural items are known to exist or are in possession of the Refuge.

Refuge Recreation Act of 1962, as amended: Allows the use of refuges for recreation when such uses are compatible with the refuge's primary purposes and when sufficient funds are available to manage the uses. This Plan is in compliance with the Refuge Recreation Act.

Refuge Revenue Sharing Act of 1935, as amended (16 U.S.C. 715s): provides for payments to counties in lieu of taxes, using revenues derived from the sale of products from refuges. Public Law 88-523 (1964) revised this Act and required that all revenues received from refuge products, such as animals, timber and minerals, or from leases or other privileges, be deposited in a special Treasury account and net receipts distributed to counties for public schools and roads. Payments to counties were established as: 1) on acquired land, the greatest amount calculated on the basis of 75 cents per acre, three-fourths of one percent of the appraised value, or 25 percent of the net receipts produced from the land; and 2) on land withdrawn from the public domain, 25 percent of net receipts and basic payments under Public Law 94-565 (31 U.S.C. 1601-1607, 90 Stat. 2662), payment in lieu of taxes on public lands. The current and proposed management of this Refuge under this Plan is in compliance with this Act.

Rehabilitation Act of 1973: Requires programmatic accessibility in addition to physical accessibility for all facilities and programs funded by the Federal government to ensure that anybody can participate in any program.

Secretarial Order 3127 (602 DM 2) Contaminants and Hazardous Waste Determination. No contaminants or hazardous waste are know to exist on the Refuge and none will be created.

Wild and Scenic Rivers Act of 1968 (16 U.S.C 1271-1287: This Public Law (90-542, as amended) states that: "It is hereby declared to be the policy of the United States that certain selected rivers of the Nation which, with their immediate environments, possess outstandingly remarkable scenic, recreational, geologic, fish and wildlife, historic, cultural, or other similar values, shall be preserved in free-flowing condition, and that they and their immediate environments shall be protected for the benefit and enjoyment of present and future generations. The Congress declares that the established national policy of dam and other construction at appropriate sections of the rivers of the United States needs to be complemented by a policy that would preserve other selected rivers or sections thereof in their free-flowing condition to protect the water quality of such rivers and to fulfill other vital national conservation purposes."

A 76 mile stretch of the Niobrara River including the River through Ft. Niobrara NWR was designated Scenic by Public Law 102-50 in 1991.

Wilderness Act of 1964 (Public Law 88-577 [16 U.S.C. 1131-1136]): defines wilderness as follows: "A wilderness, in contrast with those areas where man and his works dominate the landscape, is hereby recognized as an area where the earth and its community of life are untrammeled by man, where man himself is a visitor who does not remain. An area of wilderness is further defined to mean in this Act an area of undeveloped Federal land retaining its primeval character and influence, without permanent improvements or human habitation, which is protected and managed so as to preserve its natural conditions and which (1) generally appears to have been affected primarily by the forces of nature, with the imprint of man's work substantially unnoticeable; (2) has outstanding opportunities for solitude or a primitive and unconfined type of recreation; (3) has at least five thousand acres of land or is of sufficient size as to make practicable its preservation and use in an unimpaired condition; and (4) may also contain ecological, geological, or other features of scientific, educational, scenic, or historical value."

The 4,635 acre Fort Niobrara Wilderness Area was established by Public Law 94-557 on October 19, 1976, as cited in Section 1.n of this Act.

Appendix H. NEPA Documentation

Finding of No Significant Impact and Decision Notice

Four management alternatives for Fort Niobrara National Wildlife Refuge were assessed as to their effectiveness in achieving the stated purpose of the Refuge and their impact on the human environment. Two alternatives, maximization of economic uses and placing the Refuge in custodial status, were briefly considered but discarded because they violate the National Wildlife Refuge System Improvement Act of 1997 and do not meet the mission and goals of Fort Niobrara and the National Wildlife Refuge System.

Based on the analysis in the Environmental Assessment, I have selected the Modified Historical (Preferred) Alternative, with slight modifications from its draft form, to be implemented on the Refuge.

The Preferred Alternative was selected because it is most responsive to the purposes for which the Refuge was established by Congress and is preferable to other alternatives considered in light of physical, biological, economic and social factors.

I find that the proposed action will not have a significant impact on the human environment in accordance with Section 102 of the National Environmental Policy Act and in accordance with the Service's Administrative Manual (30 AM.9B (2) (d)) and concluded that it is not necessary nor warranted to prepare an Environmental Impact Statement in order to proceed with the implementation of this Plan.

My rationale for this finding is as follows:

- The Modified Historical Alternative would not have detrimental impacts on threatened or endangered species or adversely modify their habitats.

- The Modified Historical Alternative would not adversely affect or cause damage, loss or destruction of any archaeological and / or historical resources within the Refuge.

- The Modified Historical Alternative would have long-term positive effects on public use and recreation, habitat and wildlife management, water management, fishing, and environmental education and interpretation through a balanced approach to management of all programs with benefits to both wildlife and people.

- The Modified Historical Alternative would have no negative impact on wildlife or wildlife habitats. Modifications to current public use and habitat programs are likely to reduce wildlife and wildlife habitat disturbance that will ultimately have positive consequences to Federal trust resources.

- There will be no impact on minority and low-income populations or communities.

_____   9/30/99
Regional Director, Region 6   Date
Fish and Wildlife Service
Denver, Colorado

Summary of the Environmental Assessment

Purpose of and Need for Action (Management of the Refuge)

Fort Niobrara NWR, located in north-central Nebraska is a unique and ecologically important component of the National Wildlife Refuge System. This Refuge was established in 1912 to provide habitat and preserve breeding grounds for native birds. Later that year, an Executive Order was issued enlarging the Refuge and its mission to encompass the preservation of bison and elk herds representative of those that once roamed the Great Plains.

However, some uses presently occurring in the Refuge were recently evaluated for compatibility with the purpose of the Refuge. It is necessary to take action to modify or eliminate all activities on the Refuge that are found to be incompatible with its purposes.

The Service recognized the need for strategic planning for all the components of its System and in September 1996, Executive Order 12996 was enacted which gave the System guidance on issues of compatibility and public uses of its land. Later on Congress passed the National Wildlife Refuge System Improvement Act in October 1997, which, for the first time in the System's history, required that Comprehensive Conservation Plans be prepared for all refuges within 15 years.

The comprehensive conservation planning effort is intended to help this Refuge to meet the changing needs of wildlife species and the public. The planning effort provided the opportunity to meet with Refuge neighbors, and customers, and other agencies to ensure that this Plan was relevant and truly addressed natural resource issues and public interests.

Fort Niobrara National Wildlife Refuge Vision Statement

Fort Niobrara NWR will strive to preserve, restore, and enhance the exceptional diversity of native flora and fauna and significant historic resources of the Niobrara River Valley and Sandhills of Nebraska for the benefit of present and future generations of Americans.

Fort Niobrara NWR habitat management goals will seek to maintain a healthy Refuge environment that will provide opportunities for visitors to enjoy wildlife-dependent uses of the Refuge in a natural setting. Interpreting a unique assemblage of habitats, wildlife, and the Refuge's historical heritage, as well as improving facilities will enhance the visitor's experience while protecting the cultural integrity of the area. To meet these challenges, the Service will seek partnerships with other agencies, interest groups, landowners, and local communities. These efforts will result in greater protection of wildlife, fish, and plant resources throughout north-central Nebraska.

Alternatives and Impacts

Four management alternatives were analyzed in the Environmental Assessment for this Plan. Of these four, the Modified Historical (with some modifications from its draft form) is the preferred one because, in light of physical, biological, economic and social factors, it is most responsive to the purposes for which the Refuge was established. The three other alternatives were as follows:

Alternative A.
Current Management (No Action):

Continuing current management activities and public use

P Maintain winter population levels of 350 bison, 70 elk, and 250 Texas longhorns to receive primary consideration in management.

P Accomplish native bird management actions to the extent possible.

P Continue limited flexibility in habitat management programs with approximately 96 percent of the Refuge grazed annually.

P Maintain approximately 50 miles of interior fence and 50 miles of boundary fence to control timing of grazing and access/movement of bison, elk, and longhorn cattle.

P Manage less than 3 percent of Refuge through prescribed burning yearly to control cedars.

P Control exotic and invading plants with beneficial insects, grazing, and herbicides.

P Effect minimal management of Niobrara River, numerous streams, and associated riparian habitat.

P Maintain black-tailed prairie dog colony at 20 acres, not allowing it to expand.

P Effect limited biological monitoring of Refuge plant communities and animal populations.

P Effect minimal protection and interpretation of cultural and paleontological resources.

P Maintain current public use opportunities, including fishing, wildlife/wildland observation, photography, interpretation/education, picnicking, and hiking.

P Continue current level of 11 river-floating outfitters and no restriction on number of launches per outfitter.

P Continue cooperative agreements and partnerships in place.

Consequences of Implementing the Current Management (No Action) Alternative

On Natural Resources: Continuation of current management would result in bison, elk, and Texas longhorn herds receiving primary consideration in management. Maintaining the bison herd at 350 animals would allow the genetic integrity and variability of the herd to be maintained without introductions. Periodic introductions to the elk herd and longhorn exchanges between Wichita Mountains and Fort Niobrara NWRs would continue to be accomplished for genetic and health management purposes.

Little flexibility would continue in habitat management with emphasis placed on maintaining various habitats in their current condition and meeting the needs of the fenced animals. Bison, elk, and Texas longhorns will continue to consume and/or remove by trampling an estimated 8,400 AUMs of forage a year which is approximately 40 percent of total plant production, leaving approximately 60 percent of the vegetation for plant vigor and use by other wildlife (Waller *et al.* 1986, USDA Natural Resources Conservation Service 1996). Texas longhorns, exhibition herds, and government horses will be supplemented during the winter as conditions warrant with approximately 600 tons of prairie hay harvested from Valentine NWR.

Most of Fort Niobrara NWR's habitat management objectives would not be met due to numbers of bison, elk, and longhorns maintained on the Refuge. Refuge habitats rested one or more years would only total 4 percent of the acreage, approximately 30 percent of the Refuge would not be disturbed (no planned grazing or burning) during the native bird breeding season which is less than the desired level, and prescribed burning would have limited opportunity for use in invigorating native plants or control of cedar invasion.

Limited management efforts would be directed toward the Refuge's enabling legislative purpose of native birds. Numbers of birds (species and individuals) would probably remain unchanged because management actions necessary to improve habitat conditions for some of the native bird populations would not be possible. For example, prairie grouse populations would be present but at below optimal levels because residual grassland vegetation on many areas of the Refuge would not meet minimum habitat requirements. Various wildlife species associated with prairie dog habitat would remain at their current minimum population levels because the prairie dog town would be held to its current size of approximately 20 acres. Possible impacts of current management on the various vegetation communities, native bird populations, and other wildlife species would not be known because no additional biological monitoring would be accomplished. Woodland management would be limited and not adequately address concerns that some of the unique forest types are not regenerating, cedars are becoming dominant, and some woodlands are lacking in understory.

On Cultural and Paleontological Resources: Cultural and paleontological resources would have no additional protection or interpretation under current management. The historic barn, which currently houses the summer bat colony, would continue to deteriorate. The present level of interpretation provided by the existing visitor center would continue. No existing funds are available to improve interpretation of cultural and paleontological resources.

On Public Use: River floating under the current management alternative would continue with the number of outfitters maintained at 11 and no restriction on the number of launches per outfitter. This alternative, however, does not provide adequate measures to control growth, alleviate the crowding situation, nor does it protect the wilderness character and experience of this River section which ultimately could result in River floating through the Refuge being determined incompatible and shut down.

Other public use activities which include wildlife/wildland observation, environmental education/interpretation, and fishing will continue but not be improved or expanded.

On Socio-Economic Conditions: This alternative has the least initial consequences to the local area economy. Maintenance of bison herds and longhorn herds and their subsequent sale of excess animals would continue to contribute to Cherry County Revenue Sharing receipts.

The lack of controls on River use on the Refuge initially do not curtail the current growth occurring in the tourism industry of Cherry County. Ultimately, however, this increased growth, if not responsibly managed, could result in enough deterioration of wilderness quality on the Refuge, to force a closure of this use. Should that occur, serious economic consequences could occur for a number of businesses in the Valentine area.

This alternative maintains the other existing public uses. Revenues derived from out-of-town visitors to view animal herds in the exhibition habitat unit or use other facilities on the Refuge would remain unchanged.

Staffing and funding levels for the Refuge under this alternative would also remain unchanged. Expansion of staffs and increased efforts to expand the Refuge infrastructure under other alternatives being considered would not occur with this alternative. The multiplier effect of these changes through the economy would therefore also not occur.

Alternative B.
Historical:

Manage Refuge habitats and wildlife to replicate pre-settlement conditions

P   Maintain bison and elk herds at current management levels.

P   Reintroduce Rocky Mountain bighorn sheep to the Refuge, and allow its population to grow to 50 animals.

P   Texas longhorns would no longer be managed on the Refuge.

P   Expand big game fence to enclose nearly the entire Refuge.

P   Remove much of the interior fence to allow more natural grazing patterns.

P   Increase prescribed burns to simulate historic fire intervals (Leenhouts 1995).

P   Remove Cornell Dam and all tributary impoundments returning these areas to a natural state.

P   Establish a second site for prairie dogs and allow it to expand to approximately 380 acres.

P   Continue control of exotic/invading plants with beneficial insects, prescribed burns, and herbicides.

P   Increase monitoring of the various habitats and wildlife populations.

P   Increase management of cultural and paleontological resources.

P   Continue current management opportunities for wildlife/wildland observation, photography, picnicking, hiking and fishing.

P   Construct new visitor center to increase environmental education/interpretation.

P   Periodic, limited, and strictly controlled bison, elk, and bighorn sheep public hunting opportunities to assist with population management.

P   Reduce River floating by continuing the current restriction on number of outfitters and restricting the number of launches by all users to 1993 levels.

P   Continue existing cooperative agreements and partnerships (except fish rearing in impounded tributaries as they would no longer be impounded). Seek additional partnerships.

Consequences of Implementing the Historical Alternative

On Natural Resources: This alternative would attempt to replicate historic ecological conditions to the extent possible on the Refuge. Bison and elk herds would be maintained at their current levels and the genetic integrity of the herds kept intact. Bighorn sheep would be reintroduced to the Refuge. Texas longhorns would no longer be managed on this Refuge. Removal of interior fence will enable bison and elk to establish more natural and historic distribution or habitat use patterns. Although highly mobile, bison show a strong preference for certain areas (influenced by plant growth stage, vegetation type and species, topography) during different seasons and have varying impacts. It is expected that bison will spend less time in the hills and more time on the more level and open areas. Fire, water, and salt will be used to distribute some of the use. Native prairie plant composition, height and density will be affected both positively and negatively by differing amounts and degrees of large ungulate grazing, fire, and rest. Large ungulate herds will consume and/or remove by trampling an estimated 5,610 AUMs of forage a year which is approximately 27 percent of total plant production, leaving approximately 73 percent of the vegetation for plant vigor and use by other wildlife (Waller *et al.* 1986, USDA Natural Resources Conservation Service 1996). At this level, forage consumption will be about 33 percent less than the current management regime which should result in increased standing vegetation (height and density) which should favor prairie grouse. Prairie dog acreage will increase providing additional habitat for various birds (i.e., burrowing owl, a species of management concern), mammals, reptiles, and insect species. Fire, a historic ecological force, will be used in various prescriptions to distribute bison grazing, invigorate grasslands, reduce cedar presence, and encourage regeneration of native tree species. Management efforts in the various woodland communities may have short-term negative effects on some species of native birds; however, the long-term effects will be positive after the tree, shrub, and herbaceous layers become more diverse and sustainable. The federally listed blowout penstemon would be established in suitable habitat which would enhance biological diversity. The Niobrara River would return to a more natural condition by removing Cornell Dam and tributary impoundments within the Refuge. This would allow increased flows into the River and upstream fish migrations would no longer be stopped. Braided sandy river habitat upstream of Cornell Dam would decrease, which would negatively affect the federally listed whooping crane, interior least tern, and piping plover migratory use. Overall, this alternative would result in a more natural mosaic of habitat conditions favoring most native bird species and thus allow the enabling purpose of the Refuge to be achieved.

On Cultural and Paleontological Resources:

Management efforts towards cultural and paleontological resources under this alternative would increase with completion of a cultural resource survey and development of a management plan.

This alternative seeks to protect the historic barn from further degradation by supplying alternative bat habitat and preventing bats from re-entering the barn. Interpretation and education would also increase from current management.

On Public Use: The historic alternative returns the Niobrara River to a more natural condition by removing Cornell Dam. This would increase the length of the River on the Refuge that is suitable for canoeing and tubing.

This alternative would result in a reduction of River use to 1993 levels which would be approximately 74 percent of the current level. User fees initiated in 1998 would continue and be adjusted as necessary to assist with funding of law enforcement and maintenance of River recreation.

This alternative would seek to construct a new environmental education/visitor center which would allow increased interpretation of Refuge cultural, paleontological and natural resource programs. It would improve Refuge efforts to educate both school age groups and the general public about wildlife and the natural resources which exist in the Nebraska Sandhills.

This alternative would initiate a limited Refuge hunting program for large animals including bison, elk, deer, and bighorn sheep. The hunts would be primarily used to assist in control of excess animals, not to replace roundups and existing strategies for surplus animal removal.

On Socio-Economic Conditions: This alternative would reduce the amount of revenue sharing funds distributed to Cherry County as a result of a loss of annual longhorn cattle sales. Using 1997 levels as an example, it is estimated that the surplus longhorn cattle auction generated approximately $40,000 in Refuge receipts. Cherry County receives a percentage of these proceeds under the Refuge Revenue Sharing Act.

The use of prescribed fire may cause concern for local residents over the consequences of a prescribed burn that escapes containment and becomes a wildfire that burns off the Refuge onto adjacent private land. The Refuge fire program will continue to minimize the risk of escapes by adhering to Service policy which requires that a Prescribed Burn Plan be approved before any prescribed burning takes place. The Burn Plan addresses the potential for escape and specifies the personnel and equipment needed, weather requirements, contingency plans, and many other aspects of the burn to ensure it stays within prescription. Additional personnel and equipment that are necessary to conduct prescribed burns will benefit the community by being available to assist local rural fire departments in the suppression of lightning and human caused wildfires that occur in the local area.

This alternative would reduce the number of people allowed to use the River through the Refuge. It is difficult to determine an actual economic impact from this reduction, because response of the public may be extremely varied. Some of the people that no longer use the River because of human congestion may return. Some of those denied use on the Refuge portion of the River may just put in further downstream or upstream, perhaps causing some additional costs to outfitters, but not a significant reduction in overall profits. Other more significant impacts would occur with those that simply canceled their trips to go elsewhere. The Refuge recognizes this cost and as a result is working with other agencies to provide other facilities for River use outside of the Refuge. This is important so that trip cancellations and opportunities to use the Scenic Niobrara River are present and viable for all concerned.

This alternative would increase Refuge expenditures on infrastructure. Infrastructure investment of this type would provide opportunity for local contractors to complete projects and thus add to the local economy.

Alternative C.
Intensive Wildlife Management:

Intensify and diversify management of Refuge habitats and wildlife

P   Native birds would receive greater management emphasis.

P   Manage approximately 225 bison, 50 elk, and 125 longhorns on the Refuge.

P   Periodic use of Texas longhorns as a grazing tool on the Refuge.

P   Reintroduce bighorn sheep and allow to expand to 50 animals.

P   Establish second site for prairie dogs and allow to expand to approximately 380 acres.

P   Retain boundary and interior fences in current configuration and habitat units managed under a deferred grazing rotation (reduced herd levels would increase management options).

P   Increase prescribed fire and use to control cedars, invigorate native prairie, and encourage regeneration of woodlands.

P   Increase use of fenced animals and rest as management tools.

P   Maintain Cornell Dam and all functional tributary impoundments and restore breached impoundments based on their value to native birds and fishes.

P   Increase control of exotic/invading plants with prescribed burns, grazing, beneficial insects and herbicides.

P   Expand endangered and threatened species management.

P   Increase monitoring of various habitats and wildlife populations.

P   Increase protection and interpretation of cultural and paleontological resources.

P   Expand wildland/wildlife observation, environmental education/interpretation, hiking, and horseback riding opportunities.

P   Construct a new environmental education/visitor center.

P   Periodic, limited, and strictly controlled elk and bighorn sheep public hunting opportunities to assist with population management.

P   Decrease River floating through the Refuge after the Service determines acceptable peak use levels and management strategies that fairly distribute reduced floating opportunities among outfitters and the general public. During the interim, River use would be capped at 1998 levels and current restrictions on number of outfitters continued.

P   Continue current cooperative agreements and partnerships and seek additional ones for bison management and possible acquisition of nondevelopment easements around the Refuge.

Consequences of Implementing the Intensive Wildlife Management Alternative

On Natural Resources: Management under this alternative would be very intense but would enable native bird needs to be considered in habitat management decisions as well as continue to provide habitat for bison, elk, and Texas longhorns. Fenced animal numbers would be reduced with the bison herd maintained at 225, elk at 50, and longhorns at 125. Bighorn sheep would be reintroduced to the Refuge. Maintaining lower herd numbers would require periodic introductions to meet genetic and health management needs of the fenced animals. Longhorn management would require increased cooperation with and management assistance from Wichita Mountains Wildlife Refuge. Habitat units would be managed similar to the current management program with herds moved under a deferred grazing rotation. Large ungulate herds will consume and/or remove by trampling an estimated 5,115 AUMs of forage a year which is approximately 24 percent of total plant production, leaving approximately 76 percent of the vegetation for plant vigor and use by other wildlife (Waller *et al.* 1986, USDA Natural Resources Conservation Service 1996). At this level, most habitat objectives should be met because forage consumption will be about 39 percent less than current management, acreage rested for at least one year would increase to 10 percent, and at least 50 percent of the Refuge would be rested during the native bird breeding season. An estimated 250 tons of prairie hay from Valentine NWR would be required for supplemental feeding of longhorns during the winter.

Prescribed fire would be used on at least 500 acres a year to reduce cedar invasion, renovate native prairie, and encourage regeneration of native tree species. It is expected that changes in grassland management will result in an increase in mid- and tallgrass abundance which will favor prairie grouse populations and other grassland birds.

Species diversity will be enhanced by allowing the black-tailed prairie dog colony to an estimated 400-acre size and by establishing endangered blowout penstemon.

Management efforts in the various woodland communities may have short-term negative effects on some species of native birds; however, the long-term effects will be positive after the tree, shrub, and herbaceous layers become more diverse and sustainable.

Biological monitoring efforts will increase providing better data to document habitat condition, wildlife populations, and evaluate management.

If the longhorns are used by the Valentine NWR habitat program described in Intensive Wildlife Management Alternative of the Valentine NWR CCP, habitat management flexibility on this Refuge would increase; however, costs (labor, equipment, facility maintenance) would increase.

On Cultural and Paleontological Resources:

Management of cultural and paleontological resources will increase under this alternative. A Cultural and Paleontological Resource Management Plan will be developed and include a Refuge-wide cultural resource survey and paleontological resource inventory strategies. It will also include increased interpretation, education, and protection of cultural and paleontological resources of the Refuge.

This alternative seeks to protect the historic barn from further degradation by supplying alternative bat habitat and preventing bats from reentering the barn.

On Public Use:

This alternative will initially stabilize River canoeing and tubing use by allowing only the existing 11 outfitters to launch on the Refuge and capping use on weekends during the summer at 1998 levels. The alternative provides for a research/monitoring period of two years to determine River carrying capacities that will preserve wildlife use and wilderness character and values of solitude. It is expected that these final levels will be lower than use today. Ultimately, this alternative will reduce this use on the Refuge. The phased approach will allow River outfitters and recreationists time to adjust to the anticipated change. The Service will work with other entities to develop other take-in and take-out locations off Refuge to more equitably distribute use throughout the Scenic River corridor.

This alternative would seek to construct a new environmental education/visitor center which would allow increased interpretation of Refuge cultural, paleontological and natural resource programs. It would improve Refuge efforts to educate both school age groups and the general public about wildlife and the natural resources which exist in the Nebraska Sandhills.

This alternative would add an access point for hiking and horseback riding in the Wilderness Area, provide for one concessionaire to take people to view large animal herds, and provide a trail to a scenic Niobrara Canyon overlook on the Refuge.

This alternative would initiate a limited Refuge hunting program for elk, deer, and bighorn sheep. The hunts would be primarily used to assist in control of excess animals, not to replace roundups and existing strategies for excess animal removal.

On Socio-Economic Conditions:

This alternative would have a small negative effect on Refuge Revenue Sharing to Cherry County. By reducing herd sizes of bison and longhorns, smaller numbers of excess animals would be sold, thus reducing Refuge receipts, and eventually County revenues. It is difficult to predict precise levels of reduction. The longhorn herd will be primarily a cow-calf herd with very small numbers of bulls and steers, so potential production and eventual animal turnover will be only slightly less than currently exists. Bison numbers will be reduced, and fewer bison will be at sales from this herd.

This alternative will have a phased in effect on River use and economic activity associated with that use. Initially, placing a ceiling on Refuge use will not cause reductions in business or tourism activity; it will maintain current levels. Growth of this use over 1998 levels will transfer into other areas of the River. This will expand opportunities for some businesses and landowners. Eventually, Refuge use will decrease. The phased in approach is being made because the Refuge is aware that this will cause loss of tourism and business activity associated with the Refuge. By delaying the reduction, River outfitters and area businesses are given the opportunity to adjust their businesses. Looking long-term, the stabilization of this use on the Refuge to acceptable levels will add security and stability to River outfitters. Without this, the specter of River use becoming incompatible on the Refuge is possible. If this occurred, it could result in a complete shutdown of River use on the Refuge.

This alternative would increase Refuge expenditures on infrastructure. Investment of this type would provide opportunity for local contractors to complete projects and thus add to the local economy. This alternative does not reduce the current work effort required by existing Refuge activities and adds a significant number of new work activities. To address that need, additional staff will be needed. Salary increases for Refuge staff add to the overall local economy.

The provision for a concessionaire to provide tours of the main bison herd would have a slight increase on Refuge receipts, and provide a local entrepreneur the opportunity to start a new business.

The use of prescribed fire may cause concern for local residents over the consequences of a prescribed burn that escapes containment and becomes a wildfire that burns off the Refuge onto adjacent private land. The Refuge fire program will continue to minimize the risk of escapes by adhering to Service policy which requires that a Prescribed Burn Plan be approved before any prescribed burning takes place. The Burn Plan addresses the potential for escape and specifies the personnel and equipment needed, weather requirements, contingency plans, and many other aspects of the burn to ensure it stays within prescription. Additional personnel and equipment that is necessary to conduct prescribed burns will benefit the community by being available to assist local rural fire departments in the suppression of lightning and human caused wildfires that occur in the local area.

Preferred (Modified Historical) Alternative

The selection of this alternative was based on an analysis of its environmental consequences, the requirement to manage for the Refuge's enabling legislated purpose of native birds, bison and elk, and the desire to implement a more natural/historic management regime

P   Maintain bison herd at current population size and elk herd at 70-100.

P   Rocky Mountain bighorn sheep could be reintroduced into the Refuge and allowed to expand to 50 animals if the Service determines that this action complies with the State's Bighorn Sheep Management Plan requirements.

P   Texas longhorns would no longer be managed on the Refuge.

P   Expand big game boundary fence to enclose nearly the entire Refuge and, where possible and feasible for habitat management goals, remove interior fence to manage grazing patterns.

P   Implement management actions to improve health and sustainability of the various habitats and meet needs of various native bird populations and herds of bison, elk, and, if reintroduced, bighorn sheep.

P   Increase and use prescribed fire to control cedars, invigorate native prairie, encourage regeneration of woodlands, and distribute bison and elk grazing.

P   Maintain current condition of Niobrara River, tributaries, and associated riparian habitats while studying effects on these habitats by recreational River users.

P   Continue control of invading and exotic plant species with beneficial insects, prescribed burning, and herbicides.

P   Allow the expansion of the existing prairie dog colony to a manageable size.

P   Accomplish sufficient biological monitoring to document diversity, population trends, health, and genetics.

P   Increase protection and interpretation of cultural and paleontological resources.

P   Expand opportunities for wildland/wildlife observation, environmental education/interpretation, hiking, and horseback riding.

P   Seek funds to construct a new environmental education/visitor center and improve interpretive displays during the interim period.

P   Periodic, limited, and strictly controlled elk and, if reintroduced and ethically sound, bighorn sheep public hunting opportunities to assist with herd management.

P   Continue current fishing opportunities.

P   Reduce River floating through the Refuge after the Service determines acceptable peak use levels and management strategies that fairly distribute reduced floating opportunities among outfitters and general public, and ensures compliance with statutes of the Wild and Scenic River and Wilderness Acts. In the interim, cap River use at 1998 levels and continue current restrictions on number of outfitters.

P   Continue current cooperative agreements and partnerships and seek additional ones such as big game management, new environmental education/visitor center, and possible acquisition of nondevelopment easements around the Refuge.

Consequences of Implementing the Modified Historical (Preferred) Alternative

On Natural Resources: The preferred alternative is a more natural, ecological approach to management of the Refuge's natural resources. Herds of bison and elk will continue to be managed at current populations.

Bighorn sheep might be reintroduced to the Refuge if, after deliberations with Nebraska's Game and Parks Commission, the Service finds this reintroduction to be feasible and in accordance with the State's future Bighorn Sheep Management Plan. Management strategies that maintain these animals as wild species to the extent possible will be employed. Animal introductions will be accomplished in accordance with recommendations from geneticists and population ecologists for genetic and health management purposes.

Texas longhorns will no longer be managed on the Refuge. As a consequence, more rest will be allowed on grasslands which will in turn favor development of adequate habitats for migratory and resident bird species.

Some interior fence will be removed enabling bison and elk to establish more natural and historic distribution or habitat use patterns. Although highly mobile, bison show a strong preference for certain areas (influenced by plant growth stage, vegetation type and species, as well as topography) during different seasons and have varying impacts. It is expected that bison will spend less time in the hills and more time on the more level and open areas. However, the Refuge will manage the movements and grazing patterns of bison with fencing as well as prescribed fire, salt supplementation, and water management.

Fire, a historic ecological force, will be used in various prescriptions to distribute bison grazing, invigorate grasslands, reduce cedar presence, and encourage regeneration of native tree species. Native prairie plant composition, height, and density will be affected both positively and negatively by differing amounts and degrees of large ungulate grazing, fire, and rest. Large ungulate herds will consume and/or remove by trampling an estimated 3,400 - 5,000 AUMs of forage a year which is approximately 16 to 28 percent of the total plant production, leaving approximately 72 to 84 percent of the vegetation for plant vigor and use by other wildlife (Waller *et al.* 1986, Natural Resources Conservation Service 1996). At these levels, forage consumption will be about 40 to 58 percent less than the current management regime which will increase management flexibility and result in increased standing vegetation (height and density) in the grasslands which will favor prairie grouse and other grassland birds.

Species diversity will increase with the establishment of the endangered blowout penstemon and an increase in prairie dog acreage. Prairie dogs and the burrow systems they create can provide important habitat for burrowing owls (a species of management concern), other birds, mammals, reptiles, and insects.

Prescribed burns in the various woody habitats may have short-term negative effects on native birds; however, the resulting regeneration and regrowth of the understory will be positive in the long-term.

Biological monitoring will be increased providing additional information on various vegetation communities and associated wildlife which will improve management strategies. This management should result in a more natural mosaic of sustainable habitats that meet the needs of native and migratory birds, mammals, and other wildlife.

On Cultural and Paleontological Resources:
Management and subsequent protection of cultural and paleontological resources under this alternative will increase from the current management regime. Completion of a Refuge-wide cultural resource survey will meet legislated requirements and provide more comprehensive information to develop necessary protection/preservation strategies outlined in a cultural resource management plan. Cooperative agreements/ partnerships will be sought for completion of a paleontological survey. Interpretation and education will increase with the development of new interpretive displays utilizing information and specimens collected from previous work and new surveys. Future use of the historic barn will be determined with appropriate renovation measures completed after the bat colony is relocated.

On Public Use: This alternative will initially stabilize River canoeing and tubing use by allowing only the existing 11 outfitters to launch on the Refuge and capping use on weekends during the summer at 1998 levels. Two years of research/monitoring will be completed to determine River carrying capacities that will preserve wildlife habitat, wilderness character and values of solitude. It is expected that these final levels will be lower than use today. Ultimately, this alternative will reduce River use on the Refuge. The phased-in approach will allow River outfitters and recreationists time to adjust to the anticipated change. The Service will work with other entities to develop other take-in and take-out locations off Refuge to more equitably distribute use throughout the scenic River corridor.

Fishing opportunities will remain the same with fishing allowed on the Niobrara River and Minnichaduza Creek. Special youth fishing days will continue.

Hunting opportunities may be added to the public use program. Ethically sound, limited and strictly controlled elk and bighorn sheep (if introduced) hunts will be conducted periodically to remove surplus animals. It is expected that a high demand will exist for these limited opportunities.

Wildlife/wildland observation opportunities will be increased under this alternative with the establishment of an access point for hiking and horseback riding in the wilderness area and construction of a trail to a scenic overlook of the Niobrara Canyon. Also, this alternative enables a concessionaire to provide guided tours of the main herd of bison during the summer months.

Efforts to educate visitors (i.e., school groups, general public) would increase with implementation of this alternative through construction of a new environmental education/visitor center, and development of new displays, leaflets, and an outdoor education curriculum.

On Socio-Economic Conditions: This alternative will temporarily reduce Refuge revenue sharing to Cherry County. However, BLM payments to the County will make up for the difference and no net loss of income should occur (see explanation under Planning Issues section of the Plan). Under the existing formula in use, Cherry County would receive a portion of these receipts in revenue sharing.

This alternative will have a phased in effect on River use and economic activity associated with that use. Initially, placing a ceiling on Refuge use will not cause reductions in business or tourism activity; it will maintain current levels. Growth of this use over 1998 levels will transfer into other areas of the River. This will expand opportunities for some businesses and landowners. Eventually, Refuge use will decrease. The phased in approach is being made because the Refuge is aware that this will cause loss of tourism and business activity associated with the Refuge. By delaying the reduction, River outfitters and area businesses are given the opportunity to adjust their businesses. Looking long-term, the stabilization of this use on the Refuge to acceptable levels will add security and stability to River outfitters. Without this, the specter of River use becoming incompatible on the Refuge is possible. If this occurred, it could result in a complete shutdown of River use on the Refuge.

This alternative would increase Refuge expenditures on infrastructure. Infrastructure investment of these types would provide opportunity for local contractors to complete projects and thus add to the local economy.

This alternative does not reduce the current work effort required by existing Refuge activities and adds a significant number of new work activities. To address that need, the Refuge Complex will have to add staff. Salary increases for Refuge staff add to the overall local economy.

This alternative would have a positive effect through provision for a concessionaire to provide tours to the main herds. This will provide a local entrepreneur the opportunity to start a new business.

The Fort Niobrara/Valentine NWR Complex has long been an important contributor to the economy, recreation, and social atmosphere of Cherry County. Choices made by this alternative recognize that relationship, and the future Refuge activities and programs will continue to contribute in a positive way to the area and its people.

The use of prescribed fire may cause concern for local residents over the consequences of a prescribed burn that escapes containment and becomes a wildfire that burns off the refuge onto adjacent private land. The Refuge fire program will continue to minimize the risk of escapes by adhering to Service policy which requires that a Prescribed Burn Plan be approved before any prescribed burning takes place. The Burn Plan addresses the potential for escape and specifies the personnel and equipment needed, weather requirements, contingency plans, and many other aspects of the burn to ensure it stays within prescription. Additional personnel and equipment that is necessary to conduct prescribed burns will benefit the community by being available to assist local rural fire departments in the suppression of lightning and human caused wildfires that occur in the local area.

Appendix I. Summary of Public Involvement/Comments and Consultation/ Coordination

The National Environmental Policy Act requires all Federal agencies to examine the impacts upon the environment that their actions might have, to incorporate the best available environmental information, and the use of public participation in the planning and implementation of all actions. All public participation involved in the planning process that ultimately led to the development of this Plan was led and complied with the requirements of NEPA and sound stewardship of our Nation's natural resources.

Key steps in the development of this Plan, in its present form included: (1) preplanning; (2) identifying issues and developing a vision; (3) gathering information; (4) analyzing resource relationships; (5) developing alternatives and assessing environmental effects; (6) identifying a preferred alternative; (7) publishing the Draft Plan and soliciting public comments on the Draft Plan; (8) reviewing comments and effecting necessary and appropriate changes to the Draft CCP; and, (9) preparing this final Plan for approval by the Region 6 Regional Director, and finally (10) implementing the Plan.

In January, 1997 at a meeting at Fort Niobrara NWR, a core team was formed to prepare this Plan by following the Service's planning process and ensuring NEPA procedures for public involvement were followed. A review team was set up to provide guidance and direction to the core planning team. Public involvement began when a working group was organized to provide interchange of information between Service personnel, outside agencies, and interested stakeholders of the Refuge.

On March 20, 1997, in an effort by the Service to disseminate information and involve the public, an open house scoping session was held in the Cherry County Hall meeting room, Valentine, Nebraska. The open house provided participants an opportunity to learn about the Refuge's purposes, mission and goals, and issues currently facing management. People attending were provided the chance to speak with Service representatives and to share their comments.

On October 28, 1997, a meeting was held with Refuge permittees that are actively involved with canoeing and tubing on the Niobrara River through the Fort Niobrara NWR to discuss the issues of common interest on the future uses of this River. The Service scheduled this and other meetings to let people know what the Service was doing to manage the wildlife and habitats of the Refuge and to elicit their input on topics of interest to them.

The Draft CCP/EA was the first opportunity that these groups and the public had to review the entire planning effort and the Draft Plan. The Draft Plan was released on the last week of April 1999 and distributed in the first week of May 1999. A 60-day comment period was provided in which the Service requested information, comments, concerns, suggestions, and complaints from the public regarding the Draft CCP/EA. Because of the tremendous amount of public interest in this Plan, the Service extended the comment period for 45 more days, for a total of 105 days of public comment period. With this extension, the public comment period did not close until August 19, 1999.

The voluminous amount of comment letters and electronic mail communications were reviewed and summarized by category and subject. The summary of these comments was presented to the Service's core team and the regional directorate to help them in the preparation of the final Plan. Appropriate modifications were made to the Draft CCP/EA in accordance with scientifically based new information provided by the public during the comment period. The present Plan contains the changes made by the Service in accordance to the recommendations of the directorate and Service biologists and managers.

Public comments were received orally at meetings, scoping sessions, open house forums, via e-mail messages and in writing, both before and during the public comment period phase of the comprehensive conservation planning process. The following issues, concerns, and comments are a compilation and summary of the concerns expressed by the public.

For further information on Public Involvement and Issues, please see the Plan's section on Planning Process.

Appendix J.
Mailing List

Federal Officials

P U.S. Senator Bob Kerry
Doug Durry, Jr. Leg. Ass't, Omaha, NE
P U.S. Senator Charles Hagel
Doug Lamude, Leg. Ass't., Omaha, NE
P U.S. Representative Bill Barrett
Mark Whitacre, Leg. Director, Grand Island, NE
Greg Beam, Bill Barrett's Office

Federal Agencies

P USDA/APHIS, Dr. Kathleen Akin, Lincoln, NE
P USDA/Forest Service, Gregg Schenbeck
P USDA/Forest Service, Don Carpenter
P USDA/Natural Resource Conservation Service
P US EPA, Denver, CO
P USDI/Fish and Wildlife Service, Denver, CO;
Albuquerque, NM; Portland, OR; Anchorage, AK;
Fort Snelling, MN; Atlanta, GA; Hadley, MA;
Washington, D.C.
P USDI/Fish and Wildlife Service, Lacreek NWR,
Martin, SD; National Bison Range, Moiese, MT;
Witchita Mountains NWR, Indiahoma, OK; Crescent
Lake NWR, Scottsbluff, NE; Rainwater Basin
NWR, Kearney, NE; Benton Lake NWR, Black
Eagle, MT; Ecological Services, Grand Island, NE
P USDI/ NPS, Niobrara/Missouri Natl. Scenic River,
Paul Hedren
P USGS/BRD, Rick Schroeder, Fort Collins, CO
P USGS/National Wildlife Health Center, Dr. Thomas
Raffe, Bozeman, MT

State Officials

P Governor Mike Johanns, Lincoln, NE
P Senator Jim Jones, Lincoln, NE

State Agencies

P Department of Agriculture, Chadron, NE
P Middle Niobrara NRD, Robert F. Hilske
P NE Game and Parks Commissino, Rex Amack
P NE Game and Parks Commission, Bill Vodehnal
P NE Game and Parks Commission, Joel Klammer
P NE Game and Parks, Valentine Fish Hatchery
P Smith Falls State Park, Sparks, NE
P State Historic Preservation Officer, Lincoln, NE

City/County/Local Governments

P Melvin Christensen, Cherry County
P Dean Jacobs, Valentine Chamber of Commerce
P Rick Medena, City Manager-Valentine
P Valentine City Council
P Brown County Commissioners
P Keya Paha County Commissioners
P Cherry County Commissioners
P Valentine Niobrara Council

Libraries

P Valentine Public Library
P Ainsworth Public Library

Organizations

P Audubon Society, Dave Sands
P Audubon Society, Gretchen Muller, Washington, D.C.
P Central Mountain and Plains Section of the
Wildlife Society:
    Jeff Nichols, Ogallala, NE
    Dr. Pat Reece, Scottsbluff, NE
    Tom Rider, Lander, WY
    Dr. Terry Riley, Aberdeen, SD
P Cherry County Pheasants Forever, Valentine, NE
P Cooperative Alliance for Refuge Enhancement
(CARE), Washington, D.C.
P Defenders of Wildlife, Washington, D.C.
P Fort Niobrara Natural History Association,
Valentine, NE
P Great Plains Buffalo Association
P Intertribal Bison Cooperative, Tony Willman
P Midcontinent Eco. Science Center, Fritz Knopf
P National Bison Association
P National Rifle Association, Fairfax, VA
P National Wildlife Refuge Association, Washington, D.C.
P National Wildlife Refuge Association, Colorado
Springs, CO
P The Nature Conservancy, Al Steuter
P Nebraska Branch for Holistic Management
P Nebraska Cattleman, Troy Bredenkamp
P Nebraska Chapter of the American Fisheries
Society, Lincoln, NE
P Nebraska Chapter TWS, Carl Wolfe
P Nebraska State Buffalo Assoc, Dave Hutchinson
P Nebraska State Buffalo Assoc, Larry Mason
P Nebraska Wildlife Federation, Lincoln, NE
P Niobrara Canoe Outfitters Assoc., Roy Breuklander
P Niobrara Council:
    Nola Moosman, Recreation Rep, Valentine, NE
    Dwight Sawle, Forestry Rep, Springview, NE
    Brad Arrowsmith, Keya Paha, Bassett, NE
    Harlin Welch, Brown County, Ainsworth, NE
    Paul L. Hedren, National Park Service, O'Neill, NE
    Tom Higgins, Newport, NE
    Warren Arganbright, Valentine, NE
    Jim Van Winkle, Cherry County Commissioner,
      Valentine, NE
    Bill Mulligan, Middle Niobrara NRD, Valentine, NE
    Jim Harlin, Rock County, Bassett, NE
    Betty Palmer, Keya Paha County Commissioner,
      Springview, NE
    Lloyd Alderman, Rock County Commissioner,
      Newport, NE
    Larry Voecks, Nebraska Game and Parks,
      Norfolk, NE
    Betty Hermsmeyer, Brown County Commissioner,
      Ainsworth, NE
P Rocky Mountain Elk Foundation, Pratt, KS
P Sandhills Task Force, Kearney, NE
P Southern Missouri Ascertainment, Puxico, MO
P Texas Longhorn Breeders Assoc, Tim Miller
P Texas Longhorn Trails, Carolyn Hunter
P Wilderness Society, Washington, D.C.
P Wilderness Watch, Missoula, MT

Newspapers/Radio

P   Ainsworth Star-Journal, Ainsworth, NE
P   Associated Press, Omaha, NE
P   The Chadron Record, Chadron, NE
P   Grand Island Daily Independent, Grand Island, NE
P   Journal-Star Printing, Lincoln, NE
P   The Kearney Daily Hub, Kearney, NE
P   KVSH Radio, Valentine, NE
P   Lincoln Star, Lincoln, NE
P   The Midland News, Valentine, NE
P   Nebraska Public Radio, Lincoln, NE
P   The Norfolk Daily News, Norfolk, NE
P   North Platte Telegraph, North Platte, NE
P   Omaha-World Herald, Omaha, NE
P   The Outdoorsmen, Hartington, NE
P   Rock County Leader, Bassett, NE
P   Springview Herald, Springview, NE
P   United Press International, Omaha, NE

Universities/Colleges

P   Dr. Tom Bragg, Department of Biology, UNO
P   Dr. James Derr, Dept. of Veterinary Pathobiology, Texas A&M
P   Ken Higgins, SD Coop Unit, SDSU, Brookings
P   Mark Morgan, KSU, Dept of Horticulture, Forestry, & Recreation, Manhattan, KS
P   Dr. James Shaw, Dept. of Zoology, Oklahoma State University
P   Dr. Curtis Strobeck, Dept. of Biological Sciences, University of Alberta
P   Dr. James Stubbendieck, Dept. of Agronomy, University of NE
P   Dr. Joe Templeton, Dept. of Veterinary Pathobiology, Texas A&M

Individuals

Adamson, Mark
Allen, Dave
Badura, Laurel
Ballard, Doug
Ballard, Richard and Jeri
Bancroft, Cal
Barnard, Dick
Barragy, T.J.
Bartling, Steve
Bennett, Dennis
Bennett, Shane
Birger, Dick
Birger, N.H.
Blome, George
Bredthauer, Marty
Breuklander, Steve
Brown, Greg
Bullock, Ronald
Burge, Mike
Burge, Russell
Carter, Wayne
Christiansen, Lou
Churchill, Dean
Cloutier, Terry
Colburn, Dean
Cole, Pat
Connor, Keith and Sally
Cook, Georgia
Cornelius, Bob
Coyle, Joseph F.
Crawford, Mary
Custard, Rick
Damrow, Roger
Davenport, John
Davis, Debbie
Davis, John
DeOrnellas, George
Ducey, Jim
Ellis, Bob
Equhoff, Richard
Fields, Robert
Fishell, Ralph
Fitch, Ken
Frick, Carl
Gallino, Orville
Gass, Bob
Geddie, John
Geib, Sandy
Geiger, Steve
Getusan, Bob
Gillespie, Jerry
Gordon, Troy
Grabher, Bob
Graff, Martin
Graham, Doug
Graham, Twyla

Graves, Leroy
Grooms, Jerry
Gudden, Andrew
Gudgel, Duane
Gunnty, Kent
Gustafson, Bob
Hanna, Jeff
Hanson, John
Hartman, Darrel
Heathershaw, Pat
Hellmund, Paul Cawood
Henry, Dale
Hickerson, Hal
Higgins, Tom
Hoehne, Paul
Hollenbeck, Rex
Hollopeter, Willard
Hunsaker, Josh
Hunter, Carolyn
Huscher, Nora
Hutchinson, Dave
Ingle, Kay
Isom, Stephen
Jackson, Bob
Jarvi, Guy
Jeffers, Dick
Johnson, Dale
Jones, Doug
Kasselder, Charles
Keenan, Mike
Kerr, Steve
Kramer, Kaye
Kuck, Lance
Kuhre, Beryl
Kutilek, William R.
Lee, Jim
Leeper, Rick
Lintz, Tom
Long, Larry
Lord, Elver
Lorenzen, Robin
Maginnis, Berdine
Maginnis, Monty
Marlott, Kenneth
Mathey, Kevin
Mason, Larry
Mattson, Dr. Neil
May, Maynard
McPeak, Janet
Mecure, Randy
Mecure, Rich
Metschke, Corey
Millard, Scott
Miller, Randy
Muller, Gretchen
Muller, Roxann
Murphy, John
Nagorski, Rod
Nelson, Leonard
Nichols, Meachelle
Nielsen, Einar
O'Kief, Mike
Olsen, Dr. Steven
Olson, Ole
Parks, Rueben

Penlerick, LeRoy
Perrett, Brian
Peters, Bill
Peterson, Chad
Peterson, Georgia
Peterson, Kent
Peterson, Sheila
Pierce, Roger
Price, Dave
Reimann, K.F.
Riley, Terry
Robart, Kevin
Robbins, Jr., Dick
Roberts, Jerome
Rogers, Ron
Rokita, Thomas J.
Rosfeld, Otto
Roth, Robin
Rupe, John
Rutten, Ben
Ryschon, Jerry
Salyer, Jim
Scheffler, Delbert
Schneider, Julie
Schroeder, Mr. & Mrs. Don
Searle, Charles
Segar, John
Sharp, Wayne
Sherwood, Greg
Simmons, Carl
Simmons, Jean
Smiley, Jay
Smith, Neil
Sokol, Dick
Soper, Don
Sovereign, Ron
Stack, Taylor & Linda
Sterry, Rich
Stoeger, Doug
Stokes, Alan
Streeter, Bob
Stroup, William
Stump, Dr. Bill
Suhr, Jenny
Tegtmeier, Jim
Terhaar, Dennis
Thortall, Vic
Tibbs, Raymond
Toman, Tom
Torgerson
Turner, Bill
Turner, Lawrence
VanDerPloegh, Marvin
Vineyard, Brian
Vosicky, George
Vyain, Dave
Walkling, Al
Waln, Bill
Walton, Judy
Wescott, Mike
Witthuhn, John
Young, Cork and Mary
Young, Loren
Young, Mike

Appendix K.
List of Preparers

This document is a compilation of efforts by several Service people. The Core Planning Team consisted of Jon Kauffeld (Regional Office Refuge Planner) who was later replaced by Bernardo Garza (Regional Office Refuge Planner), Kathy McPeak (Wildlife Biologist), Mark Lindvall (Refuge Operations Specialist), Jim Sellers (Refuge Operations Specialist), Jim Kelton (Fire Management Officer), Len McDaniel (Wildlife Biologist), and Doug Staller (Regional Public Use Specialist) and was responsible for gathering and preparing information.

Royce Huber (Refuge Manager), Wayne King (Regional Wildlife Biologist), Bob Nagel (Refuge Supervisor), Larry Shanks (Refuge Supervisor), and Carol Taylor (Regional Office Planning Supervisor) provided guidance and assisted with review and editing.

Rhoda Lewis (Regional Archaeologist), Stephanie Jones (Regional Nongame Bird Biologist), and Cheryl Willis (Water Resource Specialist) provided technical expertise. Jaymee Fojtik (GIS Coordinator) prepared the various maps.

Barb Shupe (Regional Writer/Editor) compiled the document and completed all desktop publishing aspects of the document.

Appendix L.
Intra-Service Section 7
Consultation

INTRA-SERVICE SECTION 7 BIOLOGICAL EVALUATION FORM

Originating Persons:	Royce Huber
	José Bernardo Garza
Telephone Numbers:	(402) 376-3789
	(303) 236-8145 x 672
Date:	September 28, 1999

I. Region: 6

II. Service Activity (Program):   Refuges & Wildlife, Fort Niobrara National Wildlife Refuge

III. Pertinent Species and Habitat:

A. Listed species and/or their critical habitat within the action area:

bald eagle, *Haliaeetus leucocephalus* (listed threatened)

whooping crane, *Grus americana* (listed endangered)

piping plover, *Charadrius melodus* (listed threatened)

least tern, *Sterna antillarum* (listed endangered)

American burying beetle, *Nicrophorus americanus* (listed endangered)

blowout penstemon, *Penstemon haydenii* (listed endangered)

There is no federally designated critical habitat on the action area (Fort Niobrara NWR)

B. Proposed species and/or proposed critical habitat within the action area: None

C. Candidate species within the action area:

swift fox, *Vulpes velox*

D. Include species/habitat occurrence on a map: see attachment

IV Geographic area or station name and action:

Station: Fort Niobrara National Wildlife Refuge (Sandhills region in north-central Nebraska)
Action: Issuance and Implementation of the Comprehensive Conservation Plan for Fort
Niobrara NWR

V Location (map attached):

C. Ecoregion Number and Name: Fort Niobrara NWR is located within the Service's Region 6, Mountain-Prairie Region, and specifically in the Platte/Kansas Rivers Ecosystem

D. County and State: Cherry County, Nebraska

E. Section, township, and range:

Fort Niobrara NWR includes parts or all of Sections 5, 6, 7 & 8, Township 33 North, Range 26 West; Sections 1, 2, 3, 4, 11 & 12, Township 33 North, Range 26 West; Sections 7, 8, 17, 18, 19, 20, 29, 30, 31 & 32, Township 34 North, Range 26 West; and Sections 12, 13, 14, 22, 23, 24, 25, 26, 27, 33, 34, 35 & 36, Township 34 North, Range 27 West.

F. Distance & direction to nearest town: Fort Niobrara NWR is 5 miles east of Valentine, NE

G. Species/habitat occurrence:

bald eagle:	migrates through the Refuge and some roost in mature trees along the riparian corridor of the Niobrara River that runs through the Refuge; average wintering eagles go from five to seven, with a high of fifteen eagles
whooping crane:	rare visitor to the Refuge but has been documented on the shallow braided Niobrara River habitat above Cornell Dam within Refuge boundaries during spring and/or fall migrations
piping plover:	rare visitor to the Refuge but has been documented on the shallow braided Niobrara River habitat above Cornell Dam within Refuge boundaries during spring and/or fall migrations
least tern:	rare visitor to the Refuge but has been documented on the shallow braided Niobrara River habitat above Cornell Dam within Refuge boundaries during spring and/or fall migrations
American burying beetle:	the refuge is within the historical range of this listed species but no specimen of this beetle has ever been documented on lands currently occupied by the Refuge
blowout penstemon:	the refuge is within the historical range of this listed species but no specimen of this plant has ever been documented on lands currently occupied by the Refuge
swift fox:	the refuge is within the historical range of this candidate species but no specimen of this mammal has ever been documented on lands currently occupied by the Refuge

VI Description of proposed action

The proposed action is the development and implementation of a Comprehensive Conservation Plan for Fort Niobrara NWR. Implementation of this Plan comprises implementation of all actions and activities to achieve the stated goals contained in the Plan that will ultimately lead to the fulfilment of the purposes for which Congress established Fort Niobrara NWR.

VII Determination of effects:

A. Explanation of effects of the action on species and critical habitats in items III. A, B & C

bald eagle: the proposed action will have a beneficial effect on this threatened species as the eagle's wintering habitat along the Niobrara River will be protected and the step-down management plans to be prepared by the Refuge will ensure protection from harassment from Refuge visitors

whooping crane: this species is a rare visitor to the Refuge during migration. The Plan calls for preservation of Cornell dam, which creates the habitat conducive to this species. Thus, implementation of the Plan will have a beneficial effect on the habitats utilized by this species and, hence, on this endangered species

piping plover: this species is a rare visitor to the Refuge during migration. The Plan calls for preservation of Cornell dam, which creates the habitat conducive to this species. Thus, implementation of the Plan will have a beneficial effect on the habitats utilized by this species and, hence, on this endangered species

least tern: this species is a rare visitor to the Refuge during migration. The Plan calls for preservation of Cornell dam, which creates the habitat conducive to this species. Thus, implementation of the Plan will have a beneficial effect on the habitats utilized by this species and, hence, on this endangered species

American burying beetle: while the Refuge is within the historical range of this endangered insect no specimen of this species has ever been found on the Refuge. The Plan calls for surveys to determine if the species is present at the Refuge, and if so, the Plan further calls for implementation of appropriate management strategies that would conserve beetle populations in the Refuge. Thus, implementation of this Plan will have a beneficial effect on this endangered insect species

blowout penstemon: while the Refuge is within the historical range of this endangered plant no specimen of this species has ever been found on the Refuge. The Plan calls for surveys to determine if the Refuge contains adequate habitats for this species, and if so, the Plan further calls for introduction and protection of this listed species in at least two sites in the Refuge. Thus, implementation of this Plan will have a beneficial effect on this endangered plant species

swift fox: while the Refuge is within the historical range of this candidate species no specimen of this mammal has ever been documented on lands currently occupied by the Refuge. Nevertheless, none of the actions proposed in the Plan will adversely impact the species or its habitats on the Refuge. The Refuge will participate in actions to determine the species' presence or absence should the species be listed under the Endangered Species Act

There is no federally designated critical habitat on the action area (Fort Niobrara NWR) and the Plan does not find a need to propose designating critical habitat within the Refuge

A. Explanation of actions to be implemented to reduce adverse effects: Not Applicable

VIII Effect determination and response requested: [* = optional]

A. Listed species/designated critical habitat:

Determination   Response requested

no effect/no adverse modification   _JParker_ *Concurrence
(species: bald eagle, whooping crane, piping plover, least tern
            American burying beetle, blowout penstemon)

may affect, but is not likely to adversely affect   _____ Concurrence
species/adversely modify critical habitat
(species: NONE)

may affect, and is likely to adversely affect species   _____ Formal Consultation
/adversely modify critical habitat
(species: NONE)

B. Proposed species/proposed critical habitat:

Determination   Response requested

no effect on proposed species/no adverse   _Parker_ *Concurrence
modification of proposed critical habitat
(species: NONE)

Is likely to jeopardize proposed species/
adversely modify proposed critical habitat
(species: NONE)

Conference _____

C. Candidate Species:

Determination

Response requested

no effect (species: swift fox)

_____✓_____ *Concurrence

is likely to jeopardize candidate species
(species: NONE)

Conference _____

_____
Royce Huber, Refuge Manager,
Fort Niobrara/Valentine Refuge Complex

9/28/99
Date

IX Reviewing ESO Evaluation:

A. Concurrence _____✓_____   Nonconcurrence_____

B. Formal Consultation required: ____

C. Conference required: ____

D. Informal conference required: ____

E. Remarks:

_____
Steve Anschutz
Nebraska Field Supervisor, U.S. Fish & Wildlife Service

9/28/99
Date